H-utopia

Humanist Philosophies for a Sustainable Future

P. W. Thurston

Independently Published
ISBN: 979-8-7081-0898-2

Paperback edition published in the UK in 2021

In memory of my daughter, Romana. I know you would have changed this world for the better, had you stayed in it.

Preface

Several years have passed since I began my ambitious study into all aspects of human history, human nature, and human potential. Applying the wisdom attained from failed historic attempts at describing utopia, in this essay, I re-define the meaning of the word, whilst envisioning a better future based on humanist and realistic ideals. H-utopia is a legacy built on the foundations of positive changes that consider all parts of human society equally.

If the events of 2020 have taught us anything, it is that nothing is sacred, or fixed. The way we run our societies around the world can quite suddenly and drastically be altered when we are forced to adapt, put aside our differences and work together against a common non-human threat. We have proved we can adapt; everyone alive today is here because they have the genes of countless ancestors who were the best of their generation at adapting to life's challenges. The genes of those who could not adapt, perished somewhere deep in pre-history, along with their obstinance.

As we leave one decade behind and move forward into the next, society will continue to change, I suspect increasingly rapidly. This is inevitable, and to resist it is folly. However, what every individual human on this planet has the power to influence, is whether the changes are born from sincere efforts to improve the lives of humans all over the world, in the present and future, or whether they are changes born from self-serving greed and corruption, without any consideration for long-term detrimental effects to human society.

Change is a fact of life, but we have to manage it carefully to ensure it is for the better and that it considers all of humanity fairly. It is our duty and responsibility as individuals to never accept change blindly because we think there is no choice. Yet, it is equally important we do not outrightly reject it because of nostalgia over ideals that may be outdated or unsuited to the modern world.

Society is not simple, and it is not binary, but too often humanity is divided as if it were. Simplification is tempting; we naturally tend to do it out of laziness where possible, but no one said working towards a better future should be a smooth journey of easy left or right turns. Complexity, integrity and hard work are safer. When we begin to notice complex matters being segregated into binary extremes, yes or no, black or white, left or right, with us or against us, there is a risk of absolutism, totalitarianism, civil unrest and ultimately dystopia. We should do our best to negate this risk by demanding a broader, open-minded approach to all matters political, welcoming debate from as wide a demographic as possible and shunning extremism in all aspects of our own lives. I believe binary division is one of the fundamental mistakes at the core of all social failures, and I will examine this belief throughout to demonstrate.

I humbly do not confess to be a professor or specialist of any subject matter I address throughout this essay, and you do not need to be either to appreciate the sentiments and ideas. All you need to be is human, with a desire to leave the world behind, when you depart, in a better way than you found it. Plato, a respected scholar of philosophy and one of the most erudite men of his time, dreamt of a utopia that included slavery! In as little as one hundred years time, many of the ideas I put forward will undoubtedly be considered as outdated as some of Plato's are to us, and that is fine. I do not arrogantly consider my essay some kind of timeless manifesto or gospel that should be religiously clung to, and I do not presume to have all the answers to society's great and many problems contained within these pages. It is merely about taking a philosophical approach to change and collaborating ideas that could benefit the future. With ideas that are sincere, selfless and fair, we can set goals and targets for the future. It is important that these goals should never be set in stone, always remaining malleable to prevent them from becoming dogmatic by nature.

It is not the responsibility of great public figures alone to shape history; every individual's actions can be just as important. Every human will have their own version of utopia with their own ideas to make society better, each as relevant as the next person's is, and they should all be heard and combined if we wish to create something truly great. To agree unanimously on everything is inhuman and unrealistic. However, if we only can begin to find common ground to build on, out of genuine care for humanity, not because we have our own selfish agendas, then we will be the first generation to do so and will take our first step towards a real chance at utopia in its truest sense of the word.

"...for the growing good of the world is partly dependent on unhistoric acts; and that things are not so ill with you and me as they might have been, is

half owing to the number who lived faithfully a hidden life, and rest in unvisited tombs."

-George Eliot, Middlemarch, 1871.

The above quote, from my favourite author, highlights so eloquently the vital role every individual plays in morphing and manipulating the relentless passing of time. Billions of humans who came before us who were seemingly unimportant, or have been totally forgotten to time, played a unique part in shaping the world they left behind, and we owe what we have today, for better or worse, to every single one of them.

Retaining humanity in utopia

"Observe now your own epoch as it appears to the last men. Long before the human spirit awoke to clear cognizance of the world and itself, it sometimes stirred in its sleep, opened bewildered eyes, and slept again. One of these moments of precocious experience embraces the whole struggle of the First Men from savagery toward civilisation. Within that moment, you stand almost in the very instant when the species attains its zenith. Scarcely at all beyond your own day is this early culture to be seen progressing, and already in your time the mentality of the race shows signs of decline".

- Olaf Stapledon, Last and First Men, 1930.

...The perfect person will not make the perfect society; it will be the perfecting of society that will one day form a better people - as close to perfect as humanly possible. This is the long way around, but it is the only right way around...

The pathways to utopia are many; yet to walk them straight and true, towards obscured horizons, as they convolute with the avenues of dystopia, has proved an arduous endeavour for even the greatest philosophers and political leaders that history had to offer. As the boulevards of dreams and nightmares interweave, the assumed amicable journey to utopia descends into a blind and treacherous fumble along the darkened walls of a labyrinth.

In the desperate pursuit of utopia, mankind scrambles down the rabbit hole, falling headfirst into the spiralling tunnels of the labyrinth. As our stamina and wits are tested to breaking point with dead ends, pitfalls, optical illusions and deceit, most of us will lose our way, go around in circles, give up, or worse, believe we have found a shortcut to utopia, when in fact we have unknowingly stumbled onto a dystopian expressway. The wolves in sheep's clothing that stalk the labyrinth are masters of deception, covertly moving the tunnels around, herding us towards *their* version of utopia. These wolves, the minority of the population who are psychopathic, sociopathic, and deluded in their belief that the end justifies any means, can gather millions of followers if their deception is devious enough and their propaganda is cunning enough. We, the gullible majority, follow blindly on a promise of something better, safer or more affluent than we have, not realising until it is too late that our leader's utopia was actually dystopia in disguise.

When the wolf reveals himself, it is already too late. We have been led into a hole too deep to dig ourselves out of, and the tunnels from whence we came have caved behind us. Trapped in dystopia, we are faced with a choice between compliance or outcast. In this forlorn, and hopeless place, most of us would bow to the order of authority in silent acquiescence to save ourselves, in spite of the future.

To navigate the labyrinth successfully, avoiding the wolves and pitfalls, we must be brave, rational and smart. Always do what we know is right, (not necessarily what we are told), and constantly remain vigilant for the biggest warning sign of a looming dystopian trap: the systematic removal of liberty. Freedom of speech, debate, critique, expression and individuality must be preserved at all costs. With intolerance we are divided, and with acquiescence we are conquered. No matter what, for the sake of humanity, we cannot allow this to happen.

The threat utopia poses is real, because the definition attributed to it varies wildly according to individual imagination. In a disturbed, corrupted mind, the lines of good and evil become blurred. Consequently, utopia has found itself at the centre of much controversy since the second half of the 20th century and it is no longer considered as seriously as it once was. The atrocities committed under the regime of the National Socialist German Workers' Party, (Nazi Party), in the years leading up to, and during WWII, demonstrated that the idealist, pre-war philosophical writers were way off the mark when they were envisioning the next millennium as a utopian paradise where genetic manipulation had become common practice in a world where war, crime, disease, birth defects, and human flaws had all long since been eradicated with science. Of course, the predictions did not come to pass; we have not eradicated any of these things, and eugenics is currently serving a life sentence for crimes against humanity.

With the luxury of hindsight, we have had plenty of time to contemplate the risks a society captivated with eugenics poses to itself and, on the most part, have concluded that eugenics, an idea explored by authors as prolific as HG Wells, in *A modern utopia*, is not something we necessarily need, or should want, for a truly utopian future. To practice eugenics on humans in an attempt to reform or improve society is doomed to failure. Ethical reasons aside, the idea is flawed because what is the point in trying to create the 'perfect' person if they are destined to be immersed in an environment/society that we have not managed to get anywhere near perfect?

When the very most basic needs of a human are not being satisfied, and our lives are threatened, nature will overpower any nurturing, and negative behaviours will prevail as instinctive, survival responses. We cannot deny our nature; panic, greed and selfishness are poised to pounce in all of us when we feel threatened. However, we can all ensure to take responsibility for training ourselves not to allow survival responses to rule us, thereby reducing the risk of our nature being exploited by an authority to withdraw liberty and free will from us - genetically or politically.

It should be clear to everyone that we cannot forcibly reduce these kinds of impulsive survival responses, just for the convenience of making a flawed society safer to live in, as this will only lead to dystopia. One also has to consider the risk of megalomaniac leaders taking control in a futuristic, utopian society, that had perfected humans via eugenics. Would people obsessed with control be able to exercise restraint in using their technology all the way to the logical outcome? To simply copy the genetic code of the 'perfect' person, further reducing risk to their authority that individuality poses. It would be rendering the human species merely a race of clones, with the same personalities and appearance, labouring to support the minority who deem themselves worthy of utopia's full benefits. Furthermore, a society obsessed with pushing eugenics to its limits could actually cap its potential. Isaac Newton is recognised as one of the greatest and most famous scientists of all time, whose very existence massively altered the course of history, and he was also likely autistic - an eradicated condition in a traditional, eugenicist's utopia. Stephen Hawking, another great mind, famous for contributions in science and mathematics, was afflicted by the motor neurone disease, amyotrophic lateral sclerosis, and therefore would not have been born into a eugenicist's world.

The decision to lock away eugenics, until a point when we are disciplined enough to use it responsibly, is a wise one; and promisingly proves we are far wiser now than we once were. The perfect person will not make the perfect society; it will be the perfecting of society that will one day form a better people - as close to perfect as humanly possible. This is the long way around, but it is the only right way around.

HG Wells wrote about the positive potential of eugenics in his utopia, but at the other end of the genre in Aldous Huxley's *dys*topian novel, *Brave New World,* Huxley recognised the dangerous potential of eugenics in a society where human breeding is controlled by an authority. Huxley himself was not necessarily against eugenics as an idea and considered positives too, as any intellectual would, but his predictive novel served as a cautionary tale to the obvious dangers of exploitation with this science. Huxley's novel was set approximately 500 years in the future, but in reality, it was only a decade after his writing, during the years of WWII, that the Nazis were performing human fertility experiments and attempting genocide on the parts of society they considered undesirable. Ironically, it is the Nazis who are now widely considered to have had the most objectionable personality flaws in history. The slippery slope to concentration camps, where these experiments were continued on a larger scale, began only two years after the publication of *Brave New World*, with the passing of a law in Germany for, "the prevention of genetically defective progeny". The consequence of the law was forced sterilisation of persons suffering from defects or illnesses that were claimed to be hereditary. This included people with learning disabilities, schizophrenics, epileptics, people who had lost hearing or sight, and people who had physical deformities. Forced human sterilisations were carried out by the Nazi government right up until the end of the second world war, with hundreds of thousands of people being sterilised. Human medical experiments and more sterilisations were performed during the war, at Auschwitz concentration camp, by Nazi doctors attempting to develop a method of mass sterilisation that could be used on entire populations. The methods trialled included administering doses of radiation and drugs. Although not lethal immediately, many of the survivors of the concentration camps, who underwent these horrific procedures, did develop health problems, such as cancer, as a combined result of exposure to the drugs and radiation.

Post-war, because of what came to light, eugenics went from an excitedly discussed future opportunity to a horrific taboo subject and a threat to humanity itself; and something that we cannot dare consider for application on human beings. The danger with eugenics stems from varying points of view. Who has the right to decide which characteristics are 'desirable' or 'better' for humanity? Even in the cases of people who suffer from severe disabilities, no one has the right to take away their chance to live their lives and have children, no matter what the risks of passing on that disability genetically.

So it does appear the reason utopia has come under fire is because of the definition many pre-war writers attributed to it, naively ignoring, or underestimating, the potential evil that could unfold in the futures they were describing. We cannot judge the concept of utopia too harshly however, as it is a human idea, and as we know, humans have extremely contrasting ideas that are open for interpretation and debate. What constitutes as utopia to one person, may be dystopia to another. An idea that may appear to have good intentions can always be exploited by the unethical, to be twisted for evil purposes, and the evil that humans are capable of must never be underestimated in any future planning. Some things our species has done, or has allowed to happen, would make our cave-dwelling ancestors ashamed to have us as descendants. Our shortcomings and poor judgement continue to this day. If some of the pre-war utopian writers were brought back to life today, I am sure they would be genuinely shocked and saddened to see that we have not lived up to the political, social or biological potential they imagined.

It is fair to say the idea of utopia is now regarded by many people as idealist or unrealistic, as the stereotypical utopia we tend to think of when we hear the word is a fanciful, unified society based on extreme ideas that contradict human nature. A place where ego is replaced with robotic, predictable, uniformed behaviour, and where anybody exploring individual opinion is treated as a pariah. It leads us towards the logical path to attain utopia being to alter human nature. However, this in turn then creates an unstable paradox, for to attain utopia we would have to tread a totalitarian tightrope, from which we could easily fall into dystopia with the slightest misplaced step at any moment. Changing human nature, by government force or scientific experimentation on human subjects is a sinister-sounding idea indeed and something that is clearly not desired by the majority of sane people. For this reason, some say utopia is an idealist's dream. A quixotic impossibility that has no place in reality; detrimental to society even. I say that it entirely depends on your definition of utopia.

If it is straining for the ideal world and perfect biological humans that the likes of HG Wells imagined, then yes, I agree this is not likely to succeed as a plan, simply because whilst we are trying to find an 'ideal' world and a 'perfect' person, ironically, we would be liable to destroy what makes us human, inadvertently forming our own dystopian society in which we would be trapped. Whereas, if we interpret utopia as a place more suited to human nature - something not too dissimilar from what we have today, only better, because we are all trained from birth to take responsibility for the next generation, then, just maybe, we will stand a chance.

My philosophy is simple: upon enlightenment of human potential, every man, woman and child on Earth should endeavour to avoid selfish, anti-social ways of life and instead do what they can towards changing society in small ways during their lifetimes, in order to provoke great and positive change for the future; giving our descendants the chance to live better lives than the generations before them. Despite all of our conflicting points of view, I am sure conceiving and nurturing a world where our children and grandchildren can have the best lives possible is one thing we can unanimously agree on, overcoming all of our petty differences to work towards. Of course, for a creature as complex as the Homo sapien, it is not as simple as agreeing on a vague idea. We need S.M.A.R.T targets, robust guidance and tenacious support to keep us in check. It will be difficult, and there will be sacrifices that may be too great for some to make, but the chance of utopia is the potential this essay is going to explore. I will present the most prominent of the problems that stand in the way of social advancement and offer logical solutions to overcome these problems without resorting to extremism, and being careful to avoid quixotism.

My intention is for this to be a straightforward, rational and persuasive essay that will be readable for an audience as wide as possible. Although fundamentally a futurist work, I will be examining the relevant past throughout. For any scholars reading who are specialists in each subject, please forgive the brevity of these examinations. The past is an invaluable aid from which we can absorb wisdom to guide our decisions in the present, in order to help us avoid retrogression and echoing past mistakes. However, in-depth historical study is not the underlying purpose of this essay, and when covering so many topics, (that each deserve an entire book on their own), it will be necessary for me to be concise with facts and economical with language to avoid losing primary focus, which is to create an action plan for humanity that avoids extremism and therefore, dystopia.

"Most people have found it necessary to concentrate on one or a small number of fields; yet the less a person knows about past and present, the shakier that person's judgement will be with regard to the future."

-Sigmund Freud, The Future of an Illusion, 1927.

The stirrings of utopia

"My friend...care for your psyche...know thyself, for once we know ourselves, we may learn how to care for ourselves."

- Socrates, 469-399 BCE.

...No doubt there were countless more throughout history whose genius could have changed the world for the better, had they not feared persecution for trying to do so...

For as long as humans have had civilisation, there have been those who dreamt of the perfect society. The dreams always vary, the possibilities and the degrees of extremism waver, but the fundamental principle remains the same: a yearning for something better than we have in our present time. The idea of a utopian society is by no means a new one. The word utopia was first used by Thomas More in the early 1500s. The ideals of utopia, however, go back thousands of years, envisioned by the greatest free thinkers of antiquity. Long before More's time, utopia was referred to as 'Arcadia' or 'Golden Age'. The Greek philosopher, Plato, would have us believe that we had attained this so-called 'Golden Age' before, with his famous account of *Atlantis*. A story that apparently came to Greece through the Athenian poet, Solon, from his time spent with the priests of Egypt. The story goes, that the Ancient Egyptians supposedly inherited knowledge of a great, long lost civilisation that was all but destroyed during a natural disaster, which occurred perhaps hundreds, or even thousands, of years before their first Dynasty was formed. There will likely always be debate over whether Plato's story was based on fact, or purely a creation of his own imagination. I do not wish to wade into this debate here, as it matters not how true it is. My reference is to point out that, whether a work of fact, fiction, or something in between, the tale is clearly intended to stand as a wise admonition to humanity. A tale Plato anticipated to be recalled by every generation, (as it has been), lest we forget how easily humans can become complacent and corrupted by luxury and power. With absolute corruption 'the fall of man' inevitably follows, and this is a social failure that is doomed to recur mercilessly if we do not recognise and confront the threats we pose to ourselves. So maybe the challenge is not attaining the 'Golden Age', but sustaining it, by maintaining equilibrium in all parts of society.

Undisciplined, equitable and rectitudinous leadership, society is doomed to naturally tiptoe into dystopia, no matter how good the intentions of its leaders, just due to fatal human flaws: greed, selfishness, aggression, lust for power and other undesirable traits our ancestors developed through natural selection, over the aeons where Homo sapiens were yet to reach the top of the food chain. When our ancestors lived in the competitive animal kingdom, where only the most ruthless would earn the right to pass on their genes, generation after generation, our ancestors *had* to be selfish to survive. Nature favours the selfish, and therefore selfishness is deeply inset into our genes, (as it is in every living creature's genes). That does not mean we have to let it rule us like it did our animalistic ancestors, who unlike us, had the luxury of ignorance as their defence.

Homo sapiens are the only known creatures to have ever developed the ability to envision and plan towards a better future far beyond their own existence. Even the closest ancestors, and closest cousins, of modern humans did not/do not have thoughts of the complexity required to set targets that will benefit the lives of unborn generations they will never meet. This is because survival and breeding are all they require to be successful species. However, as humans, we desire something greater than just survival. Therefore, whether we want it or not, we have a responsibility like no other creature that has ever lived on this planet. For some people, responsibility is a scary word, and perhaps they are right to be afraid; men such as More and Plato have attempted to describe what utopia would look like and how we should attain it, but it is alarming that even philosophers as wise as Plato fell short in their visions for the perfect society. Plato's *Republic,* for example, is his own blueprint for humanity and focuses on detailing the perfect society and the perfect person, or persons, to govern it. One does not have to stretch their imagination far to see his ideas in *Republic* align closely to what today we would call communism. Plato was judicious enough to realise no ordinary person would be capable of governing this kind of society, as the temptation to become corrupt would be far too easy for most. An elite, enlightened few, who had undergone years of philosophical training, and classical education, would be the chosen ones to govern such a society as 'philosopher kings'.

In Plato's utopia, knowledge is power, and those lacking in it would not experience the same benefits of utopia. Below the elite sociopolitical cognoscenti, the hierarchy would continue down the pyramid, supported at the foundation by slavery. I hope most people today would agree slavery does not belong in any civilisation, let alone at the foundations of utopia. The slaves are an attempt to solve a perplexing issue for any historical utopian; who, given a chance to be a component in the mechanics of an ideal world, would envision themselves performing the less vital, menial, monotonous or unpleasant jobs? Therefore, it was hypothesised society would require unambitious and apathetic 'worker bees' who never get ideas above their rank and would gladly bow in unquestioning acquiescence to their queen bee. For Plato, this solved the troublesome dilemma, allowing the pursuit of utopia for the minority deemed worthy, whilst the deliberately uneducated workers would labour to support the elite. To try and model human society on a bee colony, nature's ultimate totalitarian regime, is as far from utopia as we could possibly get; one leader who monopolises reproduction whilst controlling a sterile workforce. Although Plato's utopia scorns personal luxury and wealth, where one person should live like royalty whilst others live in poverty, the structure of his envisioned society is still hierarchical, with the benefits for those at the top of the pyramid being free education and clean, easy living, rather than material possessions or obscene amounts of wealth.

We do have an advantage now that Plato could not have dreamt of, which helps us to address the most troubling aspect of his historical hypothesised utopia - the requirement for slavery. In a future utopia, we can solve the slave worker problem, as we will be able to develop supercomputers, robots, androids and machines to perform the menial jobs that no human wants to do. This technology should absolutely be invested in and utilised to the fullest potential, not shied away from. I appreciate the technophobia and psychological fear response to machines that replace or out-perform humans, but if we think about the last couple of centuries since the industrial revolution, we discover there are many hundreds of manual jobs that do not exist anymore due to improved technology, yet there are even more jobs that have been created due to new technology. This is an unavoidable part of growth and development, and it is selfish to allow irrational technophobia and nostalgia to sabotage advancements for future generations.

Thomas More's view of utopia was similarly flawed, in that people would still have to work the gruelling and unpleasant jobs to keep everyone fed and clothed. His solutions were a combination of slavery and the idea that people would work their own trades as normal, but on top of that, they would simply have to take turns in doing their backbreaking duty in the fields labouring. In More's society, everyone should be clothed the same, in simple garments. Yearning for wealth, alcohol and material belongings, is forbidden. Even a kind of curfew where everyone should be home and in bed at a certain time was suggested, as a way to eradicate crime.

There are many contrasting religious groups in More's utopia, who apparently manage to co-exist in peace, including atheists, although atheists are merely tolerated whilst considered a precarious threat, as they have no fear of divine punishment, so apparently would be more susceptible to temptation and therefore, more inclined to break the law.

It is quite clear what classified as utopia to an Ancient Greek or even an English Tudor is going to be worlds apart from what we would envision today. I would go so far as to say Plato and More are describing dystopia to us from our perspective. This point demonstrates we cannot form our future utopian society on today's principles alone. The God-fearing starving peasants of 16th century England would likely have welcomed with open arms the kind of life More's book promised, but from our point of view in the 21st century, it sounds like misery. In the same way, we cannot assume that our descendants in the 22nd or 23rd century would be satisfied to live by our way of life today. It is vital we are forward-thinking and malleable in our utopian goals; that we dare to imagine what *could* be possible. That we are ambitious in what we can aim for and that we are not capping our potential by only considering what is realistic right now in our own time.

Francis Bacon proved this kind of forward-thinking possible in his 17th-century work, *New Atlantis*. His mini-novel describes a future society, living on an island, where science and Christianity coexist. Bacon's futuristic utopia had a Christian head of state, who would oversee all matters, scientific and religious, reserving the right to overrule scientific research, if it were to tread on the toes of religion. Of course, any writer of this period had to be tactful where the Christian Church was concerned, so this restricted his political imagination perhaps. However, the future inventions Bacon dared to dream of were utterly inspired. He accurately predicted, in the future, we would have air transport, supersonic travel, submarines, instant worldwide communication, synthetic people, and that we would be able to manufacture flavours and scents synthetically. Indeed, he also foresaw how scientific advancements could, unfortunately, be exploited by the immoral for the manufacture and deployment of weapons so powerful that they could decimate entire cities.

Francis Bacon was not the only one to explore the idea of human potential in science if left to flourish unhindered. Roger Bacon, (perhaps a distant relation), was one of the UK's first scientists. An English scholar and Franciscan Friar of the 13th century, and a disciple of the English philosopher Robert Grosseteste. Bacon chose to join the Church so he was able to freely continue his studies. It was the easiest way to freely educate oneself in the days when the Church was the centre of political rule over Europe, and were closely monitoring society for any movements that may pose a threat to their order. Although, even as a member of their own, Bacon's research and publications landed him in trouble with the Church. He wrote to Pope Clement IV, sending him research in philosophy and mathematics as well as demanding a reformation of education by removing the dogmatic obstacles standing in the way of knowledge. During Bacon's years there were many popes, and with Pope Clement's death he lost his papal advocate. It was the Franciscan Minister General, Girolamo Masci of Ascoli, (later to become Pope Nicholas III) who most likely condemned Bacon. The mistake of thinking that any leader of the Catholic Church would be allowed to compromise their organisation's order, by advocating 'dangerous' new ideas, cost him his freedom for the latter part of his life. The details are sketchy, but he was reportedly imprisoned or at least under house arrest for over a decade, only to be freed shortly before his death. Evidence of his crimes being his publications in science, mathematics, astrology and alchemy. He paved the way for the invention of the modern telescope with his invention of lenses to magnify and sharpen distant objects. He is a strong contender for the inventor of the spectacles and some even suggest his *Epistola de Secretis* contains clear predictive descriptions of modern aircraft, automobiles, ships, suspension bridges, submarines, and helicopters, long before Francis Bacon, or even Leonardo Da Vinci had conceived of similar ideas. Roger Bacon was a man of clear ingenuity who would have been a celebrated revolutionary and likely changed the world, in a secular society. But sadly, because his philosophies were considered heretical at the time, he was not greatly admired or influential. He was not even tolerated; accused of being a wizard by local simpletons who broke into his home and stole his scientific equipment, or so the story goes.

Roger Bacon had the courage to stick his neck out where others would not. No doubt there were countless more throughout history whose genius could have changed the world for the better, had they not feared persecution for trying to do so. There is no reason the industrial revolution could not have occurred at any point throughout the last several thousand years, other than the suppression of science and technology by oppressive leaders, in dogmatic societies, obsessed with preserving ritual and ancestral beliefs to the point where they fearfully rejected ways to improve their lives.

Roger Bacon's work on optics is a clear example of how successfully religious leaders can suppress invention because he was not the first to explore the practical applications that can come from harnessing the powerful relationship of glass and light. In the 4th century BCE, the Chinese philosopher Mozi was the first person to write down the principles of camera obscura - the natural optical phenomenon that occurs when an image is projected through a small hole in a screen and appears as a reversed and inverted image on an opposing screen. Later, but still over 200 years before Bacon's time, Islamic Physicist, philosopher and mathematician, Ibn al-Haytham, explained in his Book of Optics that rays of light travel in straight lines and are distinguished by the body that reflects the rays, and he was the first to point out that vision occurs in the brain, rather than in the eyes. Al Haytham was also the first documented person to dissect the eye and understand how it works, with lenses to focus light and a retina to receive and transmit the image to the brain via the optic nerve. The point here is, we have clear evidence that ancient humans understood the principles behind an invention as simple as the spectacles, yet it took at least 2000 years to apply it to create actual spectacles, binoculars and telescopes. A ridiculous time frame, by any standards, to get from understanding something to the point of application.

A worst-case scenario for a selfish society

Of course, not all scientific and technological advancement is great. Like many of his predictions in New Atlantis, the fears of Francis Bacon's superweapons would manifest in reality too.

At the turn of the 20th century, one of the greatest living minds on this planet had a thought process that came to him as thoughts come to all of us every second of every day. It came through differences in electrical potential from chemical reactions, transmitted via neurons, synapses and dendrites inside his unique, individual brain. Computing with natural electricity, produced from consumed ketones/glucose, this particularly complex thought would eventually prove to be simplified as the formula $E = mc^2$. Albert Einstein's theory of special relativity expresses that mass and energy are the same physical entity ultimately, and therefore can be changed into each other. The equation tells us that the increased relativistic mass of a body multiplied by the speed of light squared is equal to the kinetic energy of that body. This great discovery would no doubt have arrived with us sooner or later. It may even have been realised in the past and forgotten to time because ancient humans did not realise any use for it.

Unfortunately, the conduct of humanity, armed with this great knowledge, demonstrated we were not ready as a species to wield the responsibility of godlike power. We would be living in a very different world now if Einstein's equation became acclaimed just for making us comprehend how different the Universe is to how we perceive it through our human senses. But it is sadly infamous because of its association with the most destructive weapon produced by humans - the atomic bomb. To be fair to Einstein, it is unlikely that his equation was much practical use in designing the actual weapon. Nevertheless, his discovery made military scientists and leaders realise that such a weapon would be theoretically possible, and the equation did make an appearance in a 1945 report prepared for the United States government by physicist, Henry DeWolf Smyth. The US Manhattan project and the bombings that followed resulted in the instant deaths of hundreds of thousands of Japanese citizens in the cities of Hiroshima and Nagasaki, as well as countless more casualties in the years that followed due to the previously unseen after-effects of nuclear radiation on the environment. Leo Szilard, 1898-1964, was an Austro-Hungarian born, American physicist, and the man responsible for patenting the idea of a nuclear fission reactor in 1934. After escaping Germany during the rise of Hitler, (and encouraging others to do the same), eventually, he would find himself in the USA working alongside other scientists on the Manhattan project. A man of integrity, Szilard's only crime was perhaps naivety; that his protests against the use of the weapons on people would be enough to stop the bombs being used by the military on real-life targets. His hope was that a demonstration of the weapons in uninhabited areas would have led to the peaceful surrender of the enemy out of fear alone, without the need for any further loss of life. After the war, clearly haunted by what he helped create, Szilard remarked *"it is the tragedy of mankind"*, in response to scientific advancements being used for such evil. He even switched his field of focus from physics to biology.

Over seventy years later thanks to decades of tension and arms races, there are believed to be around 16,300 nuclear weapons, all possessed by just nine countries: China, France, India, Israel, North Korea, Pakistan, Russia, the UK and the USA. If any of these countries were to use these weapons with the intent to hit a populated target on our planet, it could be the beginning of the end for civilisation as we know it. If unleashed worldwide, the weapons the military leaders in these countries control could decimate the entire planet surface, eventually killing most of life on Earth. Only the hardiest creatures would be spared the purge of a full-blown nuclear world war, and the fallout that followed. It would probably be the shortest war ever fought, but the after-effects would be the longest. Potentially billions of years of evolution and progress wiped from history. Any large land animal survivors would suffer the effects of radiation the worst; during a nuclear winter that could last for decades resulting in a complete collapse of the food chain. The Earth itself would recover, with barely a scar to show from our self-inflicted attacks, and any left-over evidence of human endeavours would only take a matter of millennia to decay to dust. No one would know that we were ever here.

The above scenario is extreme, but even a less dramatic outcome where some parts of the world are less affected and pockets of humanity manage to survive, it would be close to impossible to start over with the ambition to get back to where we were, as the Earth is far closer to depletion now than it was in the past, in terms of natural resources readily available to mine, construct and power our way through another industrial revolution, as our ancestors did. We were lucky to get this far, triumphing through natural disasters over the aeons.

It could be that we only have one shot at getting this right, and it is clear we have no chance of reaching our utopian future whilst nefarious nuclear threats loom over us all. A priority must be the agreed disarmament of these discreditable weapons worldwide. We will pick up on this later, in the study on *war and peace,* to try and find a practical, realistic way to do this.

Ignorance, Xenophobia, War and Famine

The Four Horseman of the dystopian apocalypse are casting their malevolent shadows over our society. They personify the unacceptable disgraces of war and extreme poverty, (causing famine in some parts of the world), contrasting against the obscene wealth and gluttony in other parts of the world. This 'tale of two worlds' has been going on for generations, and we can no longer plead ignorance as our ancestors may have done. With television, schooling, internet, global travel and communication, we can quickly learn about what is going on over the entire planet. The causes of war and famine are public knowledge, yet we allow them to continue, accepting them as the way things are, carrying on with our heads buried in the sand, having the cheek to call ourselves civilised whilst doing so. Many of us do not bury our heads; sickened by the inhumanity, we do what we can to clear our consciences. We donate to charities that campaign relentlessly for crisis support, but despair that after decades of giving, the suffering remains. Sure, some great progress is being made with combatting world hunger, and public awareness has been raised massively in recent years. However, this is mostly due to the efforts of philanthropic individuals, rather than governments. Poverty in developing countries should be treated as an urgent international emergency by everyone until resolved, and this will only be accomplished by putting more pressure on world leaders who have neglected their duties for decades, passing on the responsibility to billionaires and charities who have picked up the slack but really should not have had to. It is mind-boggling that it has been allowed to drag on for decades, with no end coming anytime soon.

For the sake of those who are not aware: of the approximately 7.8 billion human beings on this planet, around 3 billion live in poverty. Contrary to what some may believe, famines in developing countries are not caused by world food shortages but by the political and social failures in these countries not being properly addressed, resulting in poverty. Even with our current flawed banking system and the global economy, there is ample wealth for everyone to be fed properly.

To demonstrate the obscenity of wealth in some parts of the world: In total it was estimated countries around the world splurged the equivalent of 1.68 trillion US dollars on military arms in 2016, an increase on 2015. The United States were at the top of the military spending league with a $611 billion spend. That was 36 per cent of the global total and over three times the amount spent by second-placed China. In 2018 the growing trend continued, totalling 1.82 trillion spent globally. Over half of this total is just from these seven countries: the USA, China, Russia, the UK, India, Saudi Arabia and France. If the trend continues, soon we will be spending over 2 trillion dollars a year just on military investment, with politicians pledging to spend more on 'defence' as part of their campaigns to gain political support! Who are we fighting against that we need to invest trillions of dollars a year? The answer is, sadly, each other. As if we are not all the same species, 99.9 per cent genetically identical and related via a small group of common ancestors, but still we cannot seem to tolerate each other, settling conflict with insane, murderous force. Meanwhile, 3 billion people are desperately just trying to stay alive living off the equivalent of less than a few dollars a day. This planet has ample resources for all of its current inhabitants, were they to be distributed fairly. The trillions of investment in the commodities of war are not showing a warranted return in stabilising the poorer parts of the world for the benefit of those who live there.

There is a potential 5th horseman of the dystopian apocalypse, which is over-population. Currently, the human population grows by over 200,000 people on an average day, so for every 100,000 people that die, 300,000 are born. Clearly, this is not a sustainable exchange. Now some readers may think our population growth dilemma will only escalate if we plan to eradicate war and famine. This paradoxical problem needs addressing, and I will do so in my study on *managing human population growth effectively*, where I will suggest there are humane solutions for combatting overpopulation, far less cruel than keeping nearly half of our fellow humans in perpetual suffering and misery in order to provide a balance so the rest can carry on with a 'worthwhile' quality of life, all be it with a tarnished conscience that their excessive luxury does not come without other's unwilling sacrifice somewhere else in the world. The most contemptible part of human society is the hypocrisy of the developed world's response to death, war and famine. For example, one 'celebrity' death in Western society creates more upset and gets more media attention than a combined one million child deaths from treatable illness in poorer parts of the world. Another appalling example of hypocrisy is the inhumane response from some people towards immigrants coming from countries decimated by war, hoping to find refuge in countries that are not negatively affected, domestically, by war and economic upheaval. It is seen as a threat and a nuisance by many people that they may have to share some of their accumulated wealth to help these people who have no homes to return to and are just trying to survive; yet, for those same selfish people to panic and begin clearing the shelves of groceries, ready to fight each other over the last pint of milk, all it takes is for a snowflake to fall in winter. Indeed the situation sounds dire, and there is no doubt it is a sticky situation and a deep hole of greed we have gotten ourselves into. With historic stalemates forcing arms races in financially capable countries to a ludicrous level beyond all sanity, and with a biased media manipulating global priorities, the world has gone mad. We are not too far gone, but the point of no return will come, and we are marching towards it faster than ever before.

So what is the plan?

The problems of society are extraordinarily complex having been allowed to fester and intensify for centuries. Building a utopian future for everyone where all of our species' problems are solved is deemed idealist and unrealistic, but we cannot just stampede on as we are, blinkered to the problems too difficult to face up to. It is not sustainable or humane, so what is the plan?

The world is not going to change overnight, that is for sure. Solutions to many problems will often just present a new set of problems with which to contend. Therefore, in some instances, the answer may simply be to look for the root cause of a problem and simply remove it. When it is not as simple as just finding and removing the cause of a problem, I will suggest achievable ideas to evade the horseman of the dystopian apocalypse, leaving us free to aim for the realistic concept of '**<u>H-utopia</u>**', with a real chance of attaining it one day. To set our sights on a utopian future where we still retain what makes us human; our character flaws, our free will, our chance to make mistakes, to learn and grow as a species.

As Plato taught us, a utopia in itself is a form of extremism, balancing on the verge of corruption, constantly liable to fall into dystopia. Therefore we should not aim for one. I propose, instead, we should aim for 'humanist-utopia' or (H-utopia): an altogether more realistic future society, fuelled by ethical, humanist ideals of the highest integrity. It needs to be a place that considers everyone, as a civilisation that is biased to serve the interests of certain classes or races over others will never be a great one. The neglected parts of society will naturally envy the privileged, and rebellious response will nearly always be the outcome, resulting in prolonged misery, and our species left doomed to re-live the cycle of losing its zenith near the point of attaining it, cursed by our own stubbornness to begin from savagery again and again.

Is this 'H-utopian' future realistically achievable?

It will not be easy. There are a multitude of complex challenges that will test our will power and human responses to the very limit along the road to H-utopia, but they all simplify down to one significant factor that has always troubled humanity right into pre-history: the short-term benefits of an individual are nearly always prioritised above the long-term benefits for the whole of the species, present and future. To put it another way, a human being, as a product of selfish evolution, finds it extremely difficult to endure a path that may be uphill and bumpy, even if at the top of the hill there lay a reward for the future generations. The smooth level ground is preferable to most people, even in the knowledge that after their own lifetime, the consequence of so many individuals lazily walking this easier path would be that it wears down to rubble, leaving only the uphill alternative available, therefore, removing the freedom of choice from their descendants.

The problem is a phycological one, and it is severe. To demonstrate, imagine a hypothetical plan by our scientists to discourage the use of mobile phones worldwide for five years, and a minimum of half of the Earth's population had to comply with the scientific advice in order to prevent a hypothetical catastrophe that *could* possibly occur in 500 years time if we failed. Undoubtedly, there would be almost unanimous protest, and we would not succeed in the sacrifice for our descendant's sake. Dooming future generations to misery is preferable to inconveniencing ourselves now for five years of our own lives. This example does not even seriously threaten our way of life or our food supply. Imagine if we had to make a real decision to benefit the future, such as, immediately stopping the use of our cars powered by fossil fuels, imposing limits on individual wealth accumulation, limiting each person to only one or two offspring, rationing food to only what we need, or stopping the inefficient practise of farming animals for our food. The 'every man for himself' attitude towards people of the future is not surprising when we consider the more disgraceful fact that we have little or no regard for people who are living, or more accurately, dying, in miserable conditions, in parts of the world that are suffering from long-term political and economic failures. We separate ourselves from the suffering with phycological barriers that make it easier to accept and live with, in the past dubbing underdeveloped nations, the 'third world'. As if they are not an equal part of our human civilisation that are living on the same planet. A planet that, by the way, loans its plentiful resources at no cost to all of us. We have the choice to decide how to control and distribute them, and we currently choose to do this unfairly.

In terms of physical barriers impeding the way to a better future, short of cataclysmic event or an alien invasion, there are no significant ones. Although, ironically, preoccupation with a global natural disaster to avert or an imminent alien invasion could turn out to be the best thing for world peace and collaboration! When confronted with a common enemy, even just unsubstantiated perceived threat, the human race would quickly forget all petty differences and become united like never before. So it is only our stubborn selves that have the power to stop us from attaining what we want for our children and grandchildren and so on. As a species, our not too distant ancestors' ignorance, greed, selfishness, intolerance, xenophobia and short-sightedness not only slowed progress to a minimum and made their own existence more miserable, but it has traumatised their descendants, and will continue to delay progress until we shake off the shackles of the past and make a positive and momentous change in the way our society works. With modern technological advancements, our lives in the developed world have become overly comfortable, and it will be harder than ever to accept any ideas that could threaten this easy, plentiful lifestyle we have grown accustomed to. It is important we philosophically and ethically train ourselves to adopt a mature and selfless reaction to innovative ideas that can benefit something greater than ourselves, as it is inevitable the difficult decisions will have to come sooner or later, and only with this positive attitude will our children live in a future free from coercion by a totalitarian superpower that *had* to assume full control to 'save us' from our ignorant, small-minded selves. The choice to do the right thing *must* come from the masses, not from a desperate struggling authority.

During this essay, I will outline the biggest challenges the human race must face up to, and I will argue that they can all be overcome with less pain and effort than one may think, provided that humans become prudent enough to master a balance between humanity and utopia. Remember, we are not aspiring for perfection, just something better and fair for everyone.

As Voltaire suggested in his 1759 work *Candide*, an 'ideal' world is not a realistic world. Even if it were possible, the inhabitants of such a world would have to forfeit what makes them human in order to resist becoming restless, when living in such an extreme contrary to human nature.

Products of time

"Equipped with his five senses, man explores the Universe around him and calls the adventure Science".

- Edwin Powell Hubble, 1889 – 1953.

...As an intellectual species, it is important that in all aspects of life we never hold ideas in such esteem that they become dogmatic; allowing theoretical prejudices to prevent further social and scientific advancements...

When attempting to understand how history formed the psyche of human beings, creation is a logical starting point. Let us begin by briefly reviewing the most widely accepted, scientific theories *currently* proposed for the origin of the Universe. Later we will move on to explore how the stirrings of spirituality became religion and the impact it had, and still has, on social development.

The humble beginning

13,800,000,000 years ago, (give or take 20 million years), it is theorised something extraordinary transpired: the Universe we exist in, quite suddenly, went from a state of infinite nothing, and became everything. At least everything that was required for the Universe to evolve into what it is today. All that was needed was a dimension with suitable laws of physics to force chaos into order. The time scales involved in the initial stages of the Universe are too minuscule to imagine and cannot be measured like time today is measured - with hours, minutes and seconds. It has to be calculated in a different way, known as 'Planck' time, where one Planck is written as 10-^{43} seconds. It was during this first Planck, that the four fundamental forces of nature came into existence in our dimension. Gravity, electromagnetism, strong nuclear force and weak nuclear force. By the time another Planck passed, the forces had already started to separate, with gravity breaking away first and then strong nuclear force, powering expansion. Energy and matter became distinct entities.

The primaeval Universe was an ocean of plasma, filled with

particles that interacted during highly energised collisions, creating matter and antimatter. When the opposing matter interacted, both extremes were annihilated and continued to generate new particles whilst the Universe was expanding at an unimaginable speed in every direction - faster than the speed of light during a period of 'inflation'. As temperature and radiation diminished, it is theorised that subatomic particles, such as quarks, combined together to form baryons (protons and neutrons), which then combined into nuclei through nucleosynthesis. After hundreds of thousands of years, the Universe cooled enough for the combined protons and neutrons to attract electrons and form atoms, then eventually elements. First, simple elements formed; hydrogen and helium, followed by lithium and beryllium.

When written as above, it sounds so quick and simple, but it took an estimated 200 million years for the Universe to find order out of chaos, allowing the first stars to form as gravity pulled the elements together at certain points in space. Hydrogen was, and still is, the most abundant element in our Universe. Fortunately, it is also the element which is the most quintessential for igniting a fusion reaction. The fusion process occurs when pressures and temperatures of a young star are high enough for the protons of the hydrogen nucleus to get close enough for the strong force to be able to over-power the electromagnetic force. This is called the proton-proton chain reaction, where two protons fuse to bi-proton or a helium 2 nucleus. The process requires the weak force of the Universe to stop the bi-protons decaying, to convert them into a neutron, and to form deuterium. This kind of fusion is what created smaller stars like our own sun. The type of star that does not burn out too quickly and the only type of star we know for sure allows suitable conditions and time scales on orbiting planets for intelligent life to develop.

What materialised in the early Universe allowed stars to form naturally, which in turn allowed life to spontaneously occur, (all be it after billions of years of waiting). The fact that hydrogen was the quintessential element for creating stars, and stars created just the right elements to form planets, and that our planet had just the right chemicals, materials and environment to spawn life, which eventually became us, all sounds suspiciously orchestrated - too perfect to be an accident that everything required to create us, occurred completely naturally from what was essentially 'nothing'. In reality, what we observe around us today, as incredible as it is, it is no more than a likely outcome, due to the fundamental laws of physics that happened to be present in our dimension right from the very beginning. It is entirely possible that an infinite number of other dimensions exist, with different laws of physics that are unsuitable for forming stars. Some universes may be utterly void, or remain totally chaotic.

There are many unanswered questions surrounding exactly what happened 13.8 billion years ago. Such as, did anything exist before that? We will probably never know all the answers with 100 per cent certainty. It is amazing we can look back that far and get any insight at all. Nearly 14 billion years is an unfathomably long time. As we have discovered, it is theoretically enough time for nothing, (where on a quantum level 'nothing' does not really exist), to become everything that is contained in the Universe today. Everything we can observe, touch, smell, taste and hear. It is even enough time for self-aware organisms to develop and become intelligent enough to realise all of this. We humans, like everything else in our Universe, are the natural, evolutionary, products of time.

We are living proof that given enough time, and perhaps infinite dimensional opportunity, anything is possible. The formation of stars, galaxies and planets like the Earth, with fully functioning eco-systems that are capable of producing life naturally, occurred just by nature exploiting the energy and forces present in the Universe and combining the raw materials that would have been produced during billions of years of fusion, in the bellies of long-dead stars, which, lucky for us, became supernovae.

When certain types of stars end their lives, the elements contained within, including heavy elements such as iron and gold, are not destroyed. Instead, they erupt into the vacuum of space to be re-cycled, one day becoming the materials needed for forming planets, and even making up the cells of lifeforms on any planets that are in habitable parts of their solar systems. Long-dead stars literally gave their lives so that we could live.

The planet Earth, and likely countless other planets throughout the Universe, provide a home where it is possible to nurture life, sheltered from the radiation of outer space. A safe Eden where the forces of nature and evolution can take the simplest cells made up of atoms, and transform them, (depending on environmental conditions and stresses), into a variety of life. Given billions of years, even something as complex as a human being, a blue whale, a dinosaur or a banana can all evolve from the same single-celled lifeforms. It sounds fantastic, and some people refuse to believe it, but we should not be so shocked that life appears in such variety or that intelligence like ours evolved. Producing life like ours is the easy bit, relatively speaking. For anyone observing the Earth, there would have been a tedious 4 billion year wait before visible to the naked eye life finally began moving around on the planet. The 600 million years after that, in comparison, raced by. The hard bit was over and life ran away with itself, overpopulating the Earth in every direction; land, sea and air. The lifeforms on Earth would have long ago bred themselves into oblivion if not for the natural balance nature administers with ruthless mercilessness. It is a humbling thought that all but 1 per cent of life between genesis occurring and now, has perished; with nearly all creatures going extinct during apocalyptic disasters or 'great dyings' over the aeons. The stubborn and determined survivors relentlessly squeezing through genetic bottlenecks, adapting, rising up, repopulating and flourishing again and again until we are left today with the chance descendants of those survivors sharing the planet, of which our species is one.

This all goes to show that both our planet and our Universe owe us nothing. The Universe on face value is not something that screams 'life' when observed. It is a relatively barren place; deathly cold, dark and radioactive. In space, one could travel for millions of years through the vacuum without bumping into anything alive or inanimate. It is by complete chance the laws of nature in our dimension allowed for us to be produced through incredibly longwinded, inefficient and entirely natural processes. Unfortunately, the same nature that gave birth to us can also consume us, and that is a far more efficient and thorough process that only takes an instant. The Universe is not *designed* for life; it just happens to have the physics that allowed life to evolve, (at least once), and has tolerated 1 per cent of it up until this moment. You do not need an understanding of quantum mechanics, (which negates the need for a creator), to use logic in order to conclude that this hostility the Universe shows to life is a sign that it is not designed specifically for it.

Creationists claim the Universe is too fantastic and impossible without a divine creator to engineer it. However, when we logically observe the nature of the Universe, it seems ludicrous that a divine creator would create with such inefficiency and leave so much to chance. Ask yourself: would a divine creator of a universe really wait billions and billions of years for progress to get to an interesting point, with sentient creatures finally emerging, only to let it disappear in an instant, never to be seen again? Asteroid impacts, magnetic pole shifts, chemical changes in the atmosphere, supervolcano eruptions, nearby supernovae, or a blast from a pulsating neutron star bathing the Earth in cell destroying radiation. Just to name a handful of natural cataclysms that have almost certainly happened in the past and will likely happen again in the future. The Universe is constantly threatening to kill its inhabitants. As I have already pointed out, more than 99 per cent of all species that ever lived on Earth are now extinct. Perhaps it is naïve presuming to apply the logic of human beings to God, but nevertheless, to think we will be the exception to nature's wrath is dangerously arrogant. For those who argue that it is impossible to get something like the Universe, the Earth, or a human being from nothing, simply do not appreciate the timescales involved. In a dimension with suitable laws of physics, 13.8 billion years is more than enough time. The laws of physics are of course perfect, because if everything was not perfect for us, then we would not be here to ponder it in the first place. If elementary particles and forces such as gravity are left alone to do their thing, in almost unlimited space, for this length of time, we end up with variety beyond imagination.

The problem is, it is such a long time since the Universe began, that even the cleverest human beings cannot possibly comprehend it properly. That is not to say it is all that incredible. It is just our human brains are not evolved to have to deal with imagining time to this extent - nowhere near it. It just does not serve an evolutionary purpose to be able to judge astronomical lengths of time. There is simply no need to conceptualise what billions or millions or even thousands of years feel like to endure, for an animal that generally lives less than 100 years. During the 13.8 billion year existence of the Universe, humans have only been on the scene for about 0.0014 per cent of it. We are newcomers who during our time in this Universe, which may only be a brief blink of an eye on the grand scale, are desperately trying to get some answers as to what happened before we were here and what will happen after we have gone. Still, many of us have the arrogance to think we are at the centre of the Universe and are content with keeping our lives simple by only considering the present epoch. Even the

Catholic Church does not attempt to claim the Earth is literally at the centre of everything anymore like some of our delusional ancestors did, but at least in a metaphorical sense many people, especially devout religious people, do believe they are still at the centre of God's plan. Some may feel they are born with a kind of God-given right to have dominion over the rest of life on Earth or that humans are God's gift to the Earth. Of course, this could not be further from the truth. I will try to put things in perspective with some gargantuan numbers, but first a quote from *The Shepherd Boy* by the *Brothers Grimm,* demonstrating beautifully the incomprehensibility of time, to the human mind:

"...how many seconds of time are there in eternity." Then said the shepherd boy, "In Lower Pomerania is the Diamond Mountain, which is two miles and a half high, two miles and a half wide, and two miles and a half in depth; every hundred years a little bird comes and sharpens its beak on it, and when the whole mountain is worn away by this, then the first second of eternity will be over."

VY Canis Majoris and UY Scuti – both are red supergiant stars estimated to be thousands of times the size of our sun. They measure billions of kilometres in circumference and would take centuries to do one flight all the way around, travelling in a rocket at the speed of sound; yet these insignificant specks of light are just 2 of approximately 1,000,000,000,000,000,000,000 stars in the Universe.

200,000,000,000 - the number of galaxies in the Universe is disputed and will likely change with improved observation, but for argument's sake, we will accept 200 billion galaxies in the observable Universe as an average estimation. Each galaxy can contain up to a trillion or more stars, many of which will probably have planets orbiting, a percentage of them much like Earth. The oldest galaxies in our Universe are thought to have formed around 13 and a half billion years ago, and some of the stars contained therein are nearly as old as the Universe itself. Whereas our own solar system is less than 5 billion years old and has only just had the time to evolve conscious beings that are able to realise where they really are, and contemplate the nature of reality.

1,000,000,000,000,000,000,000,000 – this is a very rough estimate for the number of planets in the Universe, based on extrapolating research done on exoplanets so far. This number translates as a septillion, but that is still not any help in visualising it. To realise what this number means, let us think about how many of these planets may be 'Earth-like'. A conservative estimate gives us a figure of more than 5,000,000,000,000,000,000, (5 Quintillion). That equates to more Earth-like planets in the observable Universe than there are grains of sand on all of the beaches on Earth, and it is almost certain that many of these Earth-like planets will have evolved some forms of life.

When put in perspective like this, it seems crazy that we have not already bumped into ET, right? Actually, not really. Again, this shows our inability to grasp huge numbers/distances. The fact is, solar systems seem to be distanced so far apart that any inhabitants would likely remain forever isolated by distances that could take decades or even centuries to traverse, travelling non-stop in one direction at 671 million miles every hour, (which is around the speed of light and the cosmic universal speed limit). That is just to reach the first nearest solar system with a potentially habitable planet. There would be no guarantee on arrival that the chosen destination even is habitable and that any voyagers risking the journey would not just end up stranded in space with nowhere else to go and with no hope of a return journey. So you see, even with one Earth-like planet for every grain of sand on Earth spread out across the Universe, the distances between each solar system are so vast, so ludicrously immense, that the chances are close to zero of happening upon a planet where intelligent life not only evolved but then:

1) Survived all the challenges an emerging intellectual species has to come up against, (mainly recurring natural disasters and getting along with each other).

2) Became space-faring and succeeded in its adventures, to reach another solar system with a planet whose inhabitants happened to have had all the same good luck and have been allowed to evolve to a highly sentient level.

We are probably far more likely to meet inter-dimensional beings than any of our galactic neighbours. If we did meet interstellar travellers, they would almost certainly have to be immortal cyborgs, or even completely computerised rather than the kind of short-lived fragile organic life we are used to here on Earth. In our current form, we are not built for space travel and even to traverse minute distances, (in galactic terms), such as going to the Earth's moon, takes years of planning, massive expenditure, protective equipment to survive the radiation and temperature extremes of space, multiple practice runs and failed attempts which can include fatalities, and even if the target is reached, no matter how careful the planning and engineering, there always remains uncertainty surrounding the possibility of a safe return journey. Another problem is, we do not live long enough to make distant space travel worthwhile. Even our closest stellar neighbour, Alpha Centauri, would take approximately 150,000 years to reach with the fastest rockets human beings have ever travelled in. Knowing this, it is unlikely any intelligent species would blindly send their people out into the Universe on a one-way trip, unless they had invented and perfected the theoretical concept of Einstein-Rosen bridge travel. Other wise known as wormholes - portals that link two points in space via a dimensional shortcut.

As if the Universe is not big enough, all of the above is just based on the observable Universe, which goes back in time by about 13.8 billion years. Beyond what we can see, there could be much more. It is entirely possible, and in fact logical, that we may live in a greater realm where there are universes all connected in a 'multiverse'. The Universe is almost certainly not all that exists; merely all we can observe. It could be that what we call 'our' Universe is only a tiny insignificant fraction of what exists beyond the event horizon.

Alien doppelgängers

With 5,000,000,000,000,000,000 Earth-like planets out there, just in the Universe we can observe, how likely is it that aliens could be biologically similar us? With so many chances, how predictable is evolution when subjected to comparable environmental stresses? This is something that has become a topic of considerable scientific debate. The only example of evolving life we have to go by is on the planet Earth itself. We can look for clues in species past and present that have evolved convergently. Entirely different lineages that have independently evolved to be analogous because of exposure to natural selection in similar environments. One of the best examples of this happening is observed with whales and dolphins, which are of course mammals but could easily be mistaken for being close relatives of fish because they are mammals that have evolved the streamlined fishlike shapes and fins that are best suited for marine survival. Convergent evolution occurs in plants too; at a glance, Euphorbia plants appear to be part of the cacti family, with their tough green stems and spines, but actually, they are not closely related. They have simply evolved similar in appearance, because both species' ancestors were solving the same survival problems with techniques for staying alive using the least water possible in the driest parts of the world, and avoiding being eating by small nibbling herbivorous creatures. These are just two random examples of convergent evolution, but there are literally thousands. If it happens in different parts of the planet Earth, then it is fair to say it probably would occur on Earth-like planets elsewhere in the Universe. Given similar amounts of time, similar geological and environmental stresses, and the same kind of luck Homo sapiens had, it is entirely possible that other hominid-like creatures very similar to humans could exist somewhere else in the Universe.

Let us not get carried away though, it is *possible* there are aliens just like us, but not necessarily likely. The variety on the Earth alone shows us there is more than one way to solve a problem, which is why for every convergent species, we can observe many that are not, and never have been, particularly similar to any other life forms on Earth. Some of the creatures of the long-isolated Australia and New Zealand are a living testament to this. The kiwi, kangaroo and the platypus all spring to mind. All evolved in habitats that are not entirely unique, yet they bare no striking resemblance to any other animals evolving in similar environments on other continents. So although convergence happens in evolution, it is not an inevitable or entirely predictable occurrence. There is a degree of chance, and we have to factor in other variables such as, how distantly these different species evolving in similar ways are related; if they are not too genetically dissimilar, then nature would be more likely to alter them in similar ways than it would creatures living in the same environment which are more genetically distanced. Life on a completely different planet, even an 'Earth-like' planet, would share no genes with life on Earth. Alien lifeforms may have radically different DNA, RNA or something completely alien that we do not even have a term for, to provide instructions for the building blocks of life to be assembled correctly. Therefore, aliens may respond to environmental stresses in completely different ways than we could ever conceive of.

There is also a huge amount of luck involved, as any single event from history can drastically alter the future. During the billions of years that elapsed whilst we were waiting to evolve, fate dealt blow after blow for the less resilient species. The Permian-Triassic extinction, at the time, would have been an apocalyptic hell for all creatures living through it, but it was beneficial for the species that became dinosaurs. Nature allowed dinosaurs to rule the Earth for 165 million years, but they could only avoid *their* fate for so long before they were dramatically annihilated in the form of an asteroid, that slammed into what is now the Gulf of Mexico, approximately 66 million years ago. It was the climate change brought on by this event that would finish off the dinosaurs, as well as many other species, but luckily for us, not the little furry creatures whose descendants spent the following 66 million years becoming hominids, as well as countless other mammals of course, most of which do not exist anymore.

With a deepening understanding of the past and the Universe we occupy, our humility intensifies. Humans have had a much-needed reality check over the last hundred years, and much of what our ancestors held sacred has been shattered. With the increasing frequency in scientific revelations, this will continue to be the case for decades to come, I am sure. Our observable Universe was comfortably small before 1924, the year in which astronomer Edwin Hubble announced to the world that the nebula known as Andromeda was, in fact, an entire galaxy. We now know that our Milky Way galaxy is just one of hundreds of billions of galaxies in the Universe. For our more distant ancestors who lived before the time of Galileo and Copernicus, the Universe was even smaller still. Most humans believed the Earth was the centre of all creation and everything else revolved around it. Human beings are naturally curious creatures and craved answers, but wistfully, they simply had no physical way of observing beyond what their own senses and logic could tell them. It is tempting now, with our scientific instruments and overblown human ego, to think we are the pinnacle of evolution, living in these 'special times' where we appear to know almost everything. As it happens, we are just passing through a time that will likely be regarded as ignorant to our descendants as the people of the dark ages seem to us. We have been fortuitous enough over the last 13,000 years to live in a relatively undisturbed period, in terms of geology. The last ice age finished, and since then we have escaped global catastrophic events long enough to become technologically capable of generating electricity and manufacturing the materials needed to create complex scientific aids, such as electron microscopes, and the Hubble Space Telescope. Only with this technology are we able to observe and confirm for certain what we could only ever have theorised before.

The Quantum Universe

Ex nihilo, (out of nothing) - creating something from absolutely nothing is a power only God is said to possess. A quantum fluctuation in a vacuum is not merely synthesising, using pre-existing building blocks to make something. It is *literally* something tunnelling into existence from what appeared to be absolute nothingness. For many people, this is understandably hard to accept as a real phenomenon, but this is, again, due to our inability to even begin to grasp the timescales and sizes involved in the Quantum Universe. 0.00000000000000000000000000000000000000001 of a second is the time it takes for a pair of virtual, 'zero mass' particles to pop in and out of existence in the quantum realm. I am talking about sizes trillionths of a centimetre. They are unmeasurable, even on the nanoscale. Quantum mechanics is so mind-boggling, and the sizes and timescales involved at the quantum level are so unimaginably small, that even the theoretical physicists who devote their careers to it, do not fully understand it. So what chance have the rest of us got? In science, it is quantum mechanics found to be responsible for our entirely natural beginnings, and it is quantum mechanics that truly negates the intervention of a supernatural creator. Therefore we have a duty to at least try and understand it, to teach it, and to improve on the current models. To make it easier to appreciate quantum mechanics, it would be helpful to first gain a full understanding in all areas of mathematics, including geometry, matrix algebra, group theory, differential and integral calculus, and vector calculus. I, for one, certainly do not have a full understanding in all of these areas, and I know I am not in the minority. Nevertheless, let us attempt to delve into the Quantum Universe and attempt to wrap our heads around exactly what our reality is.

It has been said that our instruments for observing reality have been built perfectly focused, but will never help us to perceive it clearly, as reality is strangely blurred by its very nature. When we get down to the most fundamental processes taking place in the Universe, they do not make sense to our brains. Brains that are programmed to navigate reality as we perceive it through our human senses. The brain assembles signals received through our sense organs, which have evolved with the primary purpose of keeping us alive long enough to reproduce, not for being able to interpret the Universe as it really is, by deciphering nature's code on a minuscule scale.

The nature of reality simply cannot be fully explained by local models of classical physics, so as tricky as it is to wrap our heads around, at some point, we have to turn to the Quantum Universe to give us a purely scientific answer to creation. Just because something does not make sense to us, it does not mean it is supernatural in origin. Our ancestors believed everything was influenced by the gods, but as our species has advanced scientifically over the millennia, we have systematically robbed divine power of its apparent supernatural control over nature. We have explained the origins of, illness and disease, the weather, natural disasters, the stars, and the evolution of life. We have pulled back the curtain further and further until all God possibly has left to take credit for is the origin of the Universe itself, which we have not fully explained to a satisfactory level yet. However, with the Quantum Universe, we are closing in on delivering the final blow to the comforting reassurance of the divine creator. The origin of the Universe has been the hardest part of nature to uncover, as we cannot see it directly like we can bacteria under a microscope or fossils in a museum.

We must not be too hard on ourselves for not fully understanding quantum mechanics. We cannot expect the brains of a member of the ape family to have evolved to fully understand and accept something on an invisible level, when the primary purpose of the brain is just survival. To keep the host alive, through the trials of the third-dimensional plains it dwells in, just long enough to mature and pass on genetic information to the next generation before it is lost forever when the host body dies. In the same way human brains have not needed to evolve to comprehend the immensely big numbers and distances such as trillions of years or lightyears, the brain finds it equally difficult to imagine the almost infinitely small. The very smartest of us can calculate the mathematics and work out theorems, endeavouring to articulate what it means in words to the rest of us, using imperfect analogies to help us picture it as best as we can, but no theory is 100 per cent proof when it comes to the unseen. Perhaps to fully understand nature is just not something life is meant to do?

As if our own observable Universe is not big enough to overwhelm us, working with the idea of parallel universes, there is the 'Many Worlds' theory of quantum mechanics. This brings a whole new meaning to the word cosmic. Suppose that for each possible outcome of any given action, the Universe splits to accommodate all decisions, with each possibility, no matter how seemingly insignificant being played out. Technically, this theory takes free will out of the universal equation, as it suggests that no matter what we choose to do, the very act of choosing will create a universe to decide every possible alternative. The ultimate form of self-preservation; even if I chose to destroy the entire Universe, I could rest assured that another universe was created where I chose not to! It would mean we are all creators of universes, every second of every day. Even for quantum mechanics, this theory comes across outlandish.

If we wind ourselves back in for a moment and examine a more universally accepted and actually provable interpretation amongst quantum physicists known as the Copenhagen interpretation of coherent superposition. First proposed by the brilliant physicist Niels Bohr in 1920, it has perplexed physicists and philosophers alike since. It tells us that fundamental particles do not decide on one particular state, but are simultaneously in all possible states, that is until they are observed, at which point they are effectively forced into choosing a single possible state. As weird as this seems, it has been proven. One famous experiment worked by firing out electrons to impact on a surface that was partially blocked by another surface of the same size with narrow vertical slits that should allow some particles to pass through to the back. The particles which impacted on the back surface left a formation that would leave one to interpret them as travelling in waveforms. However, when the experiment was repeated and the firings were observed one at a time, the superposition collapsed and the quantum particles were forced to choose a single-particle state, forming a pattern that would suggest they were particles. So electrons were behaving both like waves and particles, depending on the level of observation.

There is a famous thought experiment that demonstrates quite effectively how even large objects can exist in more than one state until they are observed. The experiment was introduced by the Viennese physicist Erwin Schrödinger in 1935. It goes something like this: if you were to place a live animal, (famously a cat in Schrödinger version), inside a box for one hour with something that had a 50 per cent chance of being triggered and killing the animal, but you had no possible way of knowing what was happening inside and no way of knowing if the device had been triggered, then for that hour, the animal inside the box is technically in a state of both living and dead. There is no definitive state without the conscious observers in the Universe looking and forcing the Universe to make a decision on the fate of the boxed creature. If no one ever looked, the state would never be determined. This has been likened to the old philosophical question: *if a tree fell down in a forest with no one in earshot, would it make a sound?* The tree impacting on the ground would generate energy signals. Some of this energy would be what we call sound waves, but without a listening device or sense organ to let the waves in to meet receivers, and a brain to then decode the received waves, then the answer to the question is no, there would be no sound as we know it. However, it is important we do not confuse this with the event not occurring, just like we must not confuse the Universe with not existing until it is observed by conscious beings. The events are real, and the information being sent out into the Universe is real. The observation or the listening is interpreted by our brains as best as they are evolved to do so. The same is true for taste, touch, smell and sight; the information is received by sense organs and nerve endings, but all assembled in the brain. Ironically, even sight occurs inside the pitch dark recesses of the skull where no light penetrates. When we look at something, what we see is a lightwave reflection, captured by the sense organ housed in our eye sockets, sent via the retina along the optic nerve to be assembled into an image that consciousness has evolved to comprehend, for survival purposes, through natural selection.

Superposition is just one weird implication we have to deal with when it comes to quantum mechanics. Another bizarre product of the Quantum Universe is 'quantum entanglement'. This is a phenomenon where pairs of particles are generated and interact in such a way that the state of each particle is determined by the other, regardless of their proximity; even if at opposite ends of the Milky Way galaxy, they would still be affected by one another. Albert Einstein famously dismissed the idea of separated objects sharing a condition or state, calling it "spooky action at a distance." However, physicists have since demonstrated the reality of quantum entanglement. It was the physicist John Stewart Bell who devised a means of testing whether or not particles connected through quantum entanglement really do communicate information to one another "spookily", faster than the speed of light or, as Einstein argued, that the outcome was predetermined at some point in the past and there was no communication taking place. That is not to say Einstein, a classical physicist, was against the new age idea of quantum physics, quite the contrary; he was an advocate. It was just that he believed it to be incomplete and was not happy with the idea that the Universe was fundamentally random, law-defying and 'fuzzy' by nature.

Bell's intention was not to disprove Einstein but to find a way of differentiating between Bohr's and Einstein's models. Bell's theorem actually depends on *hidden variable theory,* developed by Einstein. According to Einstein, nothing can travel faster than the speed of light. However, quantum mechanics appears to allow information to do just that, between two entangled photons. Einstein did not want to accept this, so responded with hidden variable theory. According to quantum theory, particles remain in constant and instant contact with each other, no matter how far apart they separate. Hidden variable theory allows two entangled particles to have specific values upon creation, removing the need for them to be in communication across time and space. What Einstein, and other proponents of hidden variable theory, did not want to accept is that perhaps nature just is not meant to be understood by humans. The nature of the Quantum Universe does not owe us a clear black and white explanation that is convenient for us to understand in our minds. The hidden variable theory is just an attempt to make sense of something that does not make sense to us, but we end up going around in circles because the hidden variables then require their own set of hidden variables. If we just accept quantum theory as it appears on the face of it, then it removes the need for a deterministic interpretation of natural phenomena, and we are simply left with an understanding of particles and particle behaviour based upon statistical probability.

In his analysis, John Bell derived formulas dubbed the 'Bell inequalities'. Probabilistic statements about how often the spin of two particles should correlate with one another if classical probability were at work. However, the Bell inequalities were violated by quantum experiments, meaning one of two things: either physical reality was failing or the theory of locality was wrong. The logical answer of the two was that in the very most fundamental quantum movements occurring in the Universe, local theory does not apply, thus apparently proving quantum entanglement, or "spooky action at a distance", to be correct and therefore cause and effect is not limited to the speed of light on the quantum scale. There was a third option, that Bell's test experiments had flaws and were not 100 per cent accurate. However, more air-tight and loophole-free tests have been done since Bell's time, and still, for now at least, they continue to appear to confirm quantum entanglement violates Einstein's locality.

We are at a crucial point in history, where the quantum world is liaising with our computer science capabilities, and we will discuss the applications of quantum computing later on, but for now, consider the fact computers were only invented within the last century, and the extraordinary rate at which they have advanced, and still are advancing. Once computers surpass their creator's intelligence and processing power becomes great enough, the human programmers will inevitably begin to explore the possibility of creating a simulation universe, by entering all of the quantum laws of physics into a computer programme and letting it play out. Multiple simulations could operate simultaneously, but for at least one of these, we would certainly choose laws to mimic our own Universe exactly. In a simulation, we would have to enter constants or limits anyway, such as the speed of light or absolute zero temperature at which atoms stop moving. Time, however, would not be a constant. Time is relative, and as the observers of a simulation from the outside, our time would not move at the same rate as any consciousness that evolved inside the simulation. When we consider this, is it beyond the realms of possibility that we are already existing within a simulation created by another race of beings who already attained this ability before us? Is it in fact almost certain that if such a thing were possible, we would not be the first to do it? Furthermore, such an advanced civilisation may not be limited to a mere 13.8 billion years like we are. The creator's 'real' universe could be trillions of years old for all we know, and it would only have taken one civilisation in that universe to begin running simulations to make it almost certain that we are in one of them. Applying this logic, it is infinitely more likely we are living in a simulated universe than a real one, and this could explain why when we try to understand the Quantum Universe it appears 'fuzzy' by nature? It would be impossible to simulate the complexity of the Universe with a normal computer, or even a quantum computer, for that matter. However, there is a hypothetical way of running such a simulation, proposed by Robert J Bradbury (1956-2011), with his concept of a Matrioshka brain. It is a layered spherical brain-like megastructure of immense computational capacity, built-in space and powered by a fusion engine. What if it were proved our Universe *was* created, not by God, but by the inhabitants of another universe? Furthermore, who is to say *their* universe would be real and they themselves were not inside their own simulation, creating simulations within simulations. Scientists and philosophers alike could debate this forever, as well as the potential consequences on society of learning we are sims and not 'real' creatures. Considering the entire Universe and everything in it is made up of invisible information, that we know exists but cannot see, at some point, we have to define what 'real' is. The fact we are conscious, evolving, sentient, sensory beings living and breathing in an environment that we can influence, makes it reality, surely? If it turned out we are living in just such a simulation then it would instantly solve many problems in classical and quantum physics that cannot currently be explained. We can trace the Universe to an apparent beginning, at which point we have the bizarre period of exponential expansion, known as inflation, where the Universe grew faster than light speed. At the instant of the Big Bang, everything happened so law defyingly quickly, it is almost as if the Universe was simply 'switched on'. If we choose to accept we are in a simulation, suddenly everything becomes simple to explain; the Universe is like it is because that is how the simulation is programmed to be. For many scientists, this is akin to giving up and saying 'God did it'.

Currently, when we observe something that defies previous laws, physicists create new theories to fit around the observation, with mind-boggling mathematics and a new set of laws. We know inflation must have happened, but we do not know why and, admirably, scientists can admit that. In 1998 the Hubble Space Telescope observed something else defying what was previously believed: observations of a supernova proved that in the distant past, the Universe was expanding slower than it is today. Contrary to the logic that after an initial explosion of matter, gravity will slow it down. But no, it is actually still accelerating, 13.8 billion years later, and so we explain this with 'dark energy'. Dark energy is nothing more than a mysterious name for an invisible driving force that is countering the effects of gravity. Along with dark matter, we estimate these two unknowns make up around 95 per cent of the Universe. What we can observe in the Universe: the Earth, planets, stars, dust, physical matter, is only 5 per cent of what the Universe is. We do not know what phenomena dark energy and dark matter are, but we do know that without them, there is no Universe.

Avoiding dogma in science

The lesson we must learn from this particular study is, as an intellectual species, it is important that in all aspects of life we never hold ideas in such esteem that they become dogmatic; allowing theoretical prejudices to prevent further social and scientific advancements. Scientific premises are being disregarded, updated, or improved upon all of the time as our capabilities increase and our experiments and observations achieve higher degrees of accuracy - for instance, English physicist J. J. Thompson won the Nobel Prize in 1906 for his work which revealed the electron to be a particle. In 1927 his son, George Thompson was part of the team that determined it to be a wave, later winning him a share of the Nobel Prize! Alternative theories and improvements in science tend to spark excitement and debate, rewarded and recognised with prizes. However, when we attempt to apply the same developmental philosophy with religious beliefs, it is not met with the same kind of open-mindedness and celebration. Unfortunately, quite the opposite and a son contradicting his father's beliefs, in the way George Thompson did, would bring shame, not pride. We have to be careful to avoid this kind of arrogance and ignorance in science if we wish to continue progressing.

We have seen there is clearly far more to the beginning of the Universe than we currently understand. The 'Big Bang' theory, with inflation theory attached to it to solve the uniformity problem, has been largely accepted for decades as the explanation for the origin of the Universe, but if it turned out to be an incomplete model, or just completely wrong, then no genuine scientifically minded person would cling to the old theory with dogmatic stubbornness when presented with overwhelming evidence to the contrary.

We are possibly on the verge of just such a revolution when it comes to the origin of the Universe. In recent years the Big Bang theory has been attracting greater scepticism, and the 'Big Bounce' theory has been getting a lot of attention. The idea is that a universe, once it has initially come into existence via a quantum fluctuation, is then immortal, self-reproducing and oscillating by nature, with each bounce being greater and lasting longer than the incarnation that preceded it. For many scientists this is a more logical theory than a universe originally starting from an insanely dense singularity and suddenly inflating for the first and *only* time, at an apparently arbitrary traceable point in history, to become the insanely enormous Universe we live in. We can only trace back to the beginning of our observable Universe, we cannot see what came before, but this has not stopped us hypothesising. The idea that the Universe is cyclical and undergoes rebirths, for argument's sake, every trillion years or so, is by no means a new idea. The Ancient Egyptians and Babylonians held this view, as does the ancient Hindu religion, still to this day; it describes the Universe as an eternal cycle of creation and destruction. It is fascinating that science is now inclining back towards the big bounce theory which has its origins in ancient times, historically expressed as the Uroborus or Ouroboros paradox with the symbol of a snake devouring its own tail, (originally a dragon in Chinese mythology, and also expressed as the mythical phoenix in Ancient Greece, burning to ashes and being re-born from the destruction). Did our ancestors know something we do not or was their ignorance of quantum mechanics leading them to the only logical explanation being an immortal, self-preserving Universe? Perhaps we have been overcomplicating things.

The Big Bounce theory, incorporating the Big Crunch theory, implies that our Universe expands for 100s of billions of years until it becomes very old, very cold, and the patient, relentless gravity finally has its chance to overpower the weakening mysterious forces driving expansion and everything begins to recede, collapsing back down to a dense singularity that either implodes on itself, much like we observe with supermassive stars that become black holes, but then it simply bounces back again, re-using the same dimension, before it ever gets to the point of implosion. To avoid inevitable implosion, we have to throw classical physics out of the window at this point and rely on the quantum forces at work, on the incredibly small 'Planck scale', to save the Universe from total annihilation.

In the 1990s physicist, Werner Israel came up with a solution to the problem of entropy dissipation that previously appeared to make it impossible that a universe could be oscillating by nature. Israel's theory was to do with the magnificent power of supermassive black holes. As the Universe contracts, the last things to merge are what remains of galaxies, at which point the background radiation of the Universe would become hotter than stars and dissolve everything that was left, until all that remained in the Universe would be the supermassive black holes at the centre of galaxies and the enormous built-up radiating powers trapped within them that had been trying to escape at the speed of light since being sucked into them. The instant these black holes overlap, still hours before the end of the Universe was due to occur, the gravitational forces would be so uncontrollable that the rest of the big crunch would effectively be brought forward ahead of schedule and the Universe would instantaneously collapse to the familiar singularity of the Big Bang theory, in the shortest amount of time allowed by quantum mechanics to the smallest size allowed. At this bizarre point, the Universe avoids complete destruction by the trapped powers that had been radiating outwards, hovering in between the black hole's two event horizons, being suddenly released all at once, bouncing back outwards into the un-resisting void. The universe is re-born even more powerfully than it was during the previous inflation, perhaps destined to expand slightly more each time this occurs.

A black hole by definition is a point in space where a star has collapsed to a singularity, and its gravity is so strong that the escape velocity to pass the event horizon and move beyond its relentless pull would be faster than the speed of light and therefore not possible for even light to break free. This means singularities contained within black holes are frustratingly forever cloaked and cannot be observed. However, we know singularities exist, and for a long time, we have been adamant our Universe began with one. It is entirely logical then that the singularity of a black hole is related to the singularity of the Big Bang. We can also use logic to hypothesise that at the other end of every black hole that sucks all matter in, we would find a 'white hole' that spews energy out, into a new quantum field, perhaps spewing it out faster than the speed of light as we know it in this dimension. If singularities occur when stars collapse, then of course we should expect this happens, (and on a more powerful scale), when an entire universe collapses, and supermassive black holes merge. All forms of energy at this stage in the life of the Universe would be re-cycled as time begins all over again; the same universe, but re-born like a phoenix from its ashes, again and again, possibly forever. If this theory is correct, it could mean our Universe is staggeringly older than we thought. Perhaps hundreds of trillions of years old. Black holes, (or white holes, depending on your perspective), could be the parents of the Universe. If this is true then consequently anything that *could* happen, probably already *has* happened. There almost certainly would have been planets similar to the Earth, with creatures like us, living identical lives at some point in the eternity that was the infinite past and *is* the infinite parallel. Remember, just in the current incarnation of our observable Universe alone there are an estimated five quintillion Earth-like planets currently in existence.

Whatever is responsible for the Universe, whether divine or natural, it does not owe us a clear and simple answer. We are being forced to the limits of our mental capabilities, straining to explain a bizarre reality that our brains simply are not evolved to comprehend in the slightest.

Regardless of whether we ever attain all of the knowledge of creation, to be able to theorise and devise experiments that drawback the curtain to reveal the nature of the illusions our senses deceive us with, is a testament to human ingenuity and imagination. We should be immensely proud of our species in this respect. With the knowledge, wisdom and technology we now have at our disposal, I do feel that we are ready to pursue the age-old goal of a utopian society, with a realistic chance of actually succeeding, on the condition we aim for 'H-utopia' as I have defined it.

Ironically, since we have had the science to disprove God, and have been living in a time where many humans no longer fear their every action is being judged to determine their fate in the afterlife, our species has become more civilised and tolerant towards each other than we were in our horrific God-fearing past, where humans practised, seemingly without conscience, regular and widespread atrocities such as slavery, torture, gruesome execution and genocide; things that our zealous religious ancestors appeared to relish in, but we struggle to stomach even hearing about today. That is not to say we are all squeaky clean now, or that a decline in the belief of divine observation is the only factor to consider in the decline of heinous evil, but it is an interesting comparison and, at the very least, proves that fear of divine judgement was never a successful deterrent for evil.

Who said one person could not make a difference?

Not guaranteed as a deterrent for wrongdoing, but certainly a motivation to do good actually tends to be the opposite of ignorance. Every so often, nature gives us a genius, or prodigy, whose individual existence changes the course of history. Geniuses not only give us revelations in science and technology, but equally give us political, philosophical, artistic, and literary inspiration, with their intentions often being selfless; wanting nothing more than peace, progress and prosperity for humankind in return for sharing their extraordinary gifts. The pen truly is mightier than the sword, and even in the fictional genres, literary geniuses have the power to resonate throughout time, immortalising themselves by shaping history with their influential, satirical, often predictive writings that spark cognizance within us by tactfully highlighting the flaws in society, and helping us dare to imagine the possibilities of the future. How different would the world be today without the fictional inspiration of authors such as Charles Dickens, George Eliot, Thomas Hardy, Alexandre Dumas, Leo Tolstoy, Mark Twain, Jules Verne, and many more, influencing and inspiring generations of people with their powerful words?

Influential geniuses highlighting the flaws in society can be found much further back than the authors of the 19th century of course. If we travel further back in time to the explosion of philosophy, credited to the Ancient Greeks of around two and half thousand years ago, we find ourselves at a time when the question of what makes men great was first being pondered and recorded. Later the craze spread to the Roman empire, with great emperors such as Marcus Aurelius becoming self-proclaimed students of philosophy in an attempt to become worthy and wise leaders for the greatest empire on Earth. Despite being one of the most powerful men who ever lived, Aurelius managed to stay humble, and devoted to his people. This is what made him one of the greatest leaders in human history. Arguably, never has one man with such power come so close to embodying Plato's description of a philosopher-king.

One such individual responsible for sparking the intellectual explosion in Ancient Greece was Thales of Miletus born circa 624BCE.

Thales could be credited as the first true atheist scientist. Dissatisfied with the previously told stories of mythology and the idea that gods are responsible for everything, Thales chose to believe in the forces of nature over the supernatural. He introduced geometry and astronomy as a proper science to Ancient Greece, accurately predicting a solar eclipse and speculating that the moon is a sunlight reflecting satellite. Another intellectual pioneer was Pythagoras of Samos. This ancient Greek philosopher is renowned for his mathematical, political and religious teachings, and is the influencer for other greats such as Plato, Aristotle and Euclid. Euclid, often referred to as the "Father of Geometry", is the author of perhaps the most important mathematical textbook of all time, *The Stoicheion, (The Elements)*, which includes a collaboration of the mathematical realisations that had taken place in ancient Greece. These include the work of Pythagoras as well as Hippocrates, Eudoxus, Theaetetus and Theudius. Euclid was able to rework the mathematical concepts of his many great predecessors into Euclidean geometry that is still relevant today. It was not until the 19th century that non-Euclidean geometry was even hypothesised by the historically underrated geniuses, János Bolyai and Carl Friedrich Gauss. János Bolyai 1802 – 1860, is the official discoverer of non Euclidean geometry, although child prodigy, Carl Friedrich Gauss, 1777 – 1855 claims he had already hypothesised it years earlier but had not published anything for fear of the controversy it would cause, and there is evidence to back up this claim. One of Gauss's students, Bernhard Riemann, 1826 – 1866 should be equally credited for expanding on the ideas of non-Euclidean geometry, to lay the foundations for Riemannian geometry, and algebraic geometry. All of the above mathematicians should be household names for their contributions to understanding the mathematics of the Universe. Albert Einstein, one of the most famous household names, was able to develop his theory of general relativity only because of the influence of many, far greater, mathematicians that preceded him. Just as Euclid combined the explosion of intellect from his predecessors into one neat and tidy theory thousands of years earlier, securing his own metaphorical immortality.

Archimedes of Syracuse, another great mind, considered one of the greatest mathematicians ever and dubbed one of the first engineers because of the practical uses for his genius. He was hinting at calculus around 1500 years before it was perfected by the likes of Isaac Newton.

He is also credited with approximating the value of Pi to 3.14159 during his work on measuring circles. He famously jumped out of his bath yelling "Eureka" after contemplating the displacement of objects in water and discovering the law of hydrostatics, and he was possibly the first to use exponentiation (powers) for expressing very large numbers. E.g. 10^{20} being equal to 100000000000000000000. His inventions include the compound pulley, the hydraulic screw, and 'death ray' which used mirrors to focus the sun on enemy boats. Because the practical applications of his genius were useful in warfare, he was employed by the state of Syracuse to help with their defence during the Roman conquest of Sicily in 214 BCE. Not enough is known about his personal life to be sure, but it is a fair assumption that Archimedes' documented lacking social ability, coupled with his obsession with numbers, are indicators that he may have had high functioning autism. Possibly what today we would label as Asperger Syndrome. His obsession with numbers was so intense that it was probably responsible for his untimely demise. During the capture of Syracuse, he was reportedly more interested in a math problem he was working on than the invasion of his city and home, apparently defying Roman soldier's orders to come with them, because he could not be disturbed until he had solved the problem. Although it must be noted this is not corroborated historical fact, just a story and there is another version of the story that says he did follow the order to leave but not without gathering his mathematical equipment first, and this was the reason he was killed. What is certain is despite orders not to harm Archimedes, one of the soldiers killed him anyway, and it was possibly for his defiance or lack of social understanding.

Although we have the Ancient Greek's to thank for a lot of our mathematical knowledge being written down and passed on, if we delve even deeper into history, we discover they were clearly influenced by the much older Ancient Egyptian people who clearly had their knowledge of geometry to absolute perfection in order to achieve such precise pyramid building. The source of this knowledge may be found with a fairly well documented historic and influential genius known as Imhotep, who lived in ancient Egypt over 2000 years before the great Greek mathematicians were even born! The son of an architect and the first in a long line of master builders, his best-known work which still stands today is King Djoser's Step Pyramid at Saqqara. He was so respected in his own time for his many talents that he became a fully-fledged Deity, immortalised as the God of wisdom and medicine, clear evidence of humans bridging the phycological gap between themselves and the gods they worshipped. Imhotep was a priest, a vizier to multiple Pharaohs, a physician, a poet, an astronomer, a mathematician, and an architect. This original master of all trades was a one-stop shop for providing everything required to create the foundations for the building of a great and wise civilisation. When completed, the Step Pyramid rose 204 feet high and was the tallest manmade structure of its time. Djoser was reportedly so impressed by Imhotep's creation that he disregarded previous protocol that only the name of the Pharaoh should appear on their monuments and honoured Imhotep's name by inscribing it also. It is possible Imhotep's designs are the architectural basis for all pyramids built in Ancient Egypt, and the construction of the monuments at the Giza Plateau would not have happened without his earlier influence. World history would have been extremely different without this one man. Imhotep's great revelations were not just in architecture; he also understood disease and infection to be naturally occurring, not punishments sent by gods as was the prior belief, and that he could treat many ailments with medication. He was practising and writing about the subject of medicine two millennia before the 'father of modern medicine', Hippocrates was born.

There is no sure way to measure the Intelligence quotient (IQ) of long-dead individuals, but we can estimate. Every so often natural-born polymath geniuses of such extraordinary calibre, like Imhotep, seem to materialise in a place and time they do not appear to belong. In 1452 in the town of Vinci, Italy, a child was born. Although the father was a wealthy legal notary, the child was born out of wedlock to a peasant woman named Caterina. He would grow up to be the greatest artist who ever lived - estimates for the IQ of Leonardo da Vinci range from 160 all the way to 220. Whilst most people know da Vinci for his priceless masterpieces, he was also an expert in mathematics, geology, cartography, and engineering. His inventions and detailed drawings of them are utterly inspired for his time.

Another notable case of a serial inventor is the Serbian scientist Nikola Tesla, also born into fairly humble beginnings in 1856, Smiljan, Croatia. His father was a priest in the Serbian Orthodox Church, and his mother managed the family's farm. It has been calculated that his IQ could have been around the 200 mark also. Considering how many inventions and discoveries he made, such as the remote control, electric motor, the laser, and, (depending on who you ask), the radio, this is probably not an exaggeration.

Sadly for every genius allowed to flourish there have no doubt been countless more whose talents have been squandered. There have been many well-known, but also ordinary people with IQs of 160 plus, even 200 plus, and do not think for a moment that this is a modern phenomenon or sudden turning point in evolution. As we have seen, there have been geniuses of such calibre born for millennia around the ancient world, and perhaps even deeper into the past, that have been lost to history completely, because their talents were not appreciated as important by the ordinary people of their era. Would a hunter-gatherer turned farmer of 10,000 years ago really be interested in prime numbers or the fundamentals of calculus for example, if presented to him by his child who happened to be an autistic savant? No doubt the obsessive nature of this kind of natural genius, focusing on something seemingly fruitless, instead of learning to farm, would have been viewed as potentially harmful to their way of life and discouraged by the family members of average cognitive ability.

Even in more recent, recorded, history, being recognised as a genius was no guarantee of greatness. One such individual was Democritus, another ancient Greek philosopher, known in our time for his formulation of an atomic theory of the Universe. Along with his shadowy lesser-known mentor Leucippus, who is credited with spawning the idea of the atom, his speculation on the nature of atoms is not far off our contemporary understanding of atomic structure. For this reason, Democritus is considered as more of an early scientist searching for factual truths on the nature of reality rather than just another philosopher. It was likely because of this that he was largely ignored in his own time. Fellow philosopher Plato, reportedly despised him and unfortunately, only fragments of Democritus's vast body of work survived to our time. We do know that the theory Democritus held is that everything is composed of atoms, which are physically, but not geometrically, indivisible. He also hypothesised that atoms are indestructible, infinite in number, constantly moving and between them is empty space. With no adequate tools of observation or experimentation available, his theory could never be proved or disproved in his own time and therefore was of little interest.

A more recent example of lost genius is the tragic, cautionary tale of William James Sidis, born in America in 1898. His parents, both intellectuals, wanted to create a revolutionary genius with their son, and they probably thought they had succeeded at first. With a supposed IQ over 250, William by age seven was already a linguistic genius, capable of speaking six different languages on top of English, including Latin, Greek, Russian, Hebrew, German and French. On top of that, he was already completing High School level studies. He was accepted by Harvard University at nine years old but had to wait to mature emotionally before attending at twelve after he gave his first lecture on four-dimensional physics. A consequence of all this pressure was he was never allowed to be a child. After the most promising start to life a genius could hope for, he did not get on well with his peers at Harvard, and as an adult, he travelled around taking menial jobs where he could. He was said to be generally miserable, and to have had a child-like demeanour. He did write some books in his life in which he does briefly scratch the surface on what we now call black holes but other than this there is nothing really noteworthy to speak of. If we take his IQ score as fact, he may have officially been the highest-ranking intelligence who ever lived; yet he died of a stroke at just 46 years old, a clerk, with nothing to his name and no contribution to science or humanity beyond what a person of average IQ could offer.

The financial strains of modern society, formal education, and parental pressures train us, against our nature, to be specialists, to choose a vocation and stick to it, forcing geniuses into boxes. For example, the brilliant mind of Ludwig Van Beethoven decided to create music and only music, even after going deaf. Whereas some of the high IQ geniuses of the more distant past freely composed music, studied the stars, invented, designed buildings and painted masterpieces. Ludwig Van Beethoven was from a very musical family and his father, Johann, had decided his son would be a prodigy following the successful footsteps of Leopold Mozart's son, Wolfgang. Unlike with William Siddis, the parental pressure and guidance in this case obviously paid off, and Beethoven is a household name as one of the best composers of all time, but no one knows what else Beethoven and countless more specialists could have contributed to society if allowed to freely express themselves in more than one area as Imhotep did.

Just as geniuses such as Siddis do not necessarily contribute to humanity, people of average intelligence do not necessarily pass the world by without contributing great things. We do not all have to have extraordinary superhuman IQs to make major positive contributions to humanity. All you need to change the world for the better is an open mind and integrity. We can become overly obsessive trying to categorise and define degrees of genius and let it determine what an individual is capable of, but a high IQ does not necessarily indicate a smart and productive person and likewise, a lower IQ does not necessarily mean someone is not capable of displaying great ingenuity. An IQ is just calculated from a standardised multiple-choice test after all. We should not hold the IQ rating in such high esteem that we automatically bow in deference to those who rank highly whilst sneering at those who rank low. Although good at assessing how we use our reasoning capabilities and working memory, they are not able to assess our ability to use our brains in real situations to theorise and invent with originality and creativity.

Furthermore, one would assume that geniuses making scientific revelations at the forefront of society would have helped to overcome stagnation in societies caused by religious preservation, but as we have seen with Imhotep in Egypt, he only strengthened it if anything, by bridging the gap between mortals and the gods. Imhotep himself was a devoutly religious man and would likely have been regarded as physical, walking proof that the gods were watching over the Egyptian civilisation with approval, by sending him to Earth so he could aid them in accomplishing what would have been viewed as godlike miracles at the time.

Since the 'fall of man' the withdrawal of God from human affairs has upset religious people. Prophets, spirits, angels and saints serve as emissaries for God, and purported encounters with them are latched onto as evidence of a divine presence still watching and intervening from time to time, rather than the contrary way of looking at it - that humans had no need for the divine and could achieve miraculous things all on their own.

It was not until the invention of modern-day observation equipment, such as the Hubble Telescope, and the undertaking of incredible engineering projects such as the Large Hadron Collider in Switzerland, that geniuses have had the resources available to pull back the curtain, penetrate the fabric of space-time and reveal a Universe more bizarre and extraordinary than anyone could have imagined.

Having all of the answers to our origins is not guaranteed to create peace or unity amongst all people. There will always be disagreement, and debate and there are billions of devoutly religious people in the world who do not entertain even well understood scientific breakthroughs, or at least do not accept them as evidence against their creator; and they do not have to, for peace and unity will not come from cold hard science alone, there are many aspects that must come together to unite all of humanity in spite of contrariety.

Religion, and what place does it have in the future?

"Finding that no religion is based on facts and cannot be true, I began to reflect what must be the condition of mankind trained from infancy to believe in error".

Robert Owen, 1771-1858.

...The fact scientific knowledge was celebrated by a spiritual people thousands of years ago, evidenced in monuments such as Stonehenge, but was not officially accepted by the Catholic Church until 1992, demonstrates that it is not group spirituality that clashes with truth and science, it is specific organisation leaders, inconvenienced and threatened by the truth, who despise it...

A dictionary definition of the word religion states: *The belief in and worship of a superhuman controlling power, especially a personal God or gods. Perhaps based on Latin religare **'to bind'**.*

Ignorance of our ancestors

Where did we come from and why are we here? Due to flawed logic, our ancestors thought they had answered with certainty the riddle of our creation. Apparently with relative ease, and very little debate or rational observation of the world around them, they arrived at the conclusion that the human race was of recent origin because it was noticeably advancing in knowledge and technology during individual human lifetimes. Therefore, humans could not have been around for that long or the species would have progressed much more.

With Christianity, the leaders took this oversimplification of human origins and progress a step further, with Bishop James Ussher confidently, and very specifically, dating Genesis to the night of October the 22nd, in the year 4,004 BCE. There does appear to be a lack of clarity over whether this was the creation of life in general, just human life, or the creation of life and the actual Earth itself at the same time. Physical surroundings, the mountains, the land and the ocean change very little in a human lifetime, so it was suggested they had existed forever, or they had been created at the same time as life to give living creatures a home. The 'minor' details obviously were not that important though. God created everything and that is all that mattered. To question this divine fact was heresy, punishable by torture and death for much of written history.

Thank goodness, not everyone was happy with the notion that the Universe had a beginning like this. We have to give some of our ancestors credit for thinking outside of the box. Some fascinating religions historically acknowledged the Universe's extreme age, with Hindu philosophies describing something that could be likened to the Big Bang and Big Crunch cycle theory, chronicling timescales significantly closer to reality than the Bishop Ussher's embarrassing estimation. The Greek philosopher Aristotle thought it perfectly possible that the Universe had existed forever, evolving naturally, and had not been created by divine beings. He even offered an explanation to the flawed logic that humans should be more advanced if they had been around longer than a few thousand years. Reasoning that we may have been growing more advanced in the distant past but that natural disasters had repeatedly set civilisation back to the beginning and we had to start all over again. Despite being logical and plausible, this theory did not catch on, as the Genesis myth of the Old Testament did. Perhaps because this godless explanation offered no comfort to a species undergoing the long process of coming to terms with its own mortality during a time when life was brutal and short for most. In comparison, a belief in God and the afterlife offered much comfort; an eternity of reward in 'heaven', reunited with deceased family and friends, (so long as you lived a good and moral life, practising your religious rituals and ceremonies, without question of course). This is much more attractive than an eternity of nothingness; and with no technology available to prove the science behind any alternative theories, religious belief prevailed for a long time. When the technology became available, the oppressive religious organisations had grown so powerful and widespread that they were able to suppress, with force, any emerging contradictory theories. For hundreds of years, religious organisations and cults thrived whilst the uneducated masses and budding scientists alike had nothing to gain and everything to lose by going against the religious regime imposed by the heads of state or cult leaders. The debate continues even to this day and age. Aristotle's logic and thousands of great minds after him still have not defeated the deep inset ignorance of our ancestors.

A brief history of spirituality

Unearthing the roots of spiritual stirrings in human history is no easy task. Every emerging culture around the ancient world had their own rituals, sacred sites, carvings, cave paintings and stories, implying a general, worldwide belief in unseen supernatural forces or beings. The fact that spirituality appeared around the world in cultures that had no contact with each other does suggest it is a natural part of development for a creature whose intelligence evolves to a certain level of self-awareness and becomes conscious of its own inevitable mortality. Our ancestors had the mental capacity to begin pondering the nature of reality, but did not yet have the scientific capability to confirm theories; nor did they have the language ability to greatly debate theories amongst one another. Our evolving ancestors' tens of thousands of years ago could not possibly have comprehended what nature really is, so they adopted a belief in the supernatural as a way of satisfying curiosity for the time being. If we push back as far as we can in terms of physical evidence, it seems that much like the human species itself, religion came out of Africa; with one of the oldest confirmed sacred sites, that was evidently dedicated to rituals, being in the Tsodilo Hills, Botswana. Artefacts uncovered by archaeologists at the site confirm it was in use as far back as 70,000 years ago. There was no evidence found suggesting a settlement; therefore, it was most likely visited as a place of worship or ritual, with the apparent 'deity' being a giant python shaped rock formation. As further corroboration, the Tsodilo Hills are still sacred to the indigenous people today, who believe the site to be the home of the gods, with the snake figure being the creator or ultimate original ancestor of the human race.

With a belief in the supernatural, came the possibility of an afterlife, where one could meet their maker. The custom of death preparation, burials and ceremonies became an overwhelming part of early human society. Even in Palaeolithic times, people were burying their dead, sometimes with artefacts and tools that they would presumably need in the afterlife. Further back in time still, before Homo sapiens began the practice of burial, there is evidence Neanderthals buried their dead over 50,000 years ago, proving that symbolic thought is not unique to modern humans. The evidential remains of a series of small fires discovered within a dolomite hillside in Spain, suggests Neanderthals even held funerals. The prehistoric fires just happened to be surrounding a spot where the remains of a Neanderthal child were unearthed. Alone, this is not a confirmation of funeral fires; however further evidence of ritual is present. There were symbols left at the site also. The horns and antlers of Rhinos, Aurochs, Bison and Deer were placed around where the remains were discovered.

For further insight, we can look to rock art for clues into our ancestor's beliefs on the nature of reality. Rock art has been found on every populated continent on Earth. The rock art in Europe was becoming quite sophisticated around 18,000 years ago. Examples found in the Franco-Cantabrian region, (southeast France and north Spain), are particularly abundant and interesting. This is because, during the late Upper Palaeolithic, this part of Europe was densely populated with herbivorous species. So it is not surprising that our hunter-gatherer ancestors would naturally have settled here, and they developed into quite an impressive and talented colony.

Some of the most sophisticated, and enlightening, artwork can be found in France, north from the Spanish border, in Lascaux Caves. The artwork there has been estimated to date from between 17,000 and 18,000 years ago. Realistic animal paintings depict the prey that our ancestors hunted. There is more to the rock art at Lascaux than just hunting rituals though; with impressive patterns that some have interpreted to be fertility cycles, models of the cosmos and even a crude version of the creation myth. There are even theories that some caves were used as sensory deprivation temples, perhaps to initiate Shaman. Rock art, the practice of shamanism and burial rituals show that our ancestors clearly had an obsessive preoccupation with spirits of the dead, both human and animal. This fascination with death and life cycles was constructing the foundations of early religion.

Around 12,000 years ago, hunter-gatherers began making the transition into farmers and builders. One of the most impressive and oldest constructions on Earth that still stands today is Gobekli Tepe in modern-day Turkey. The main structure is estimated to have been completed between 11,000 and 12,000 years ago, and its purpose is deduced to have been a place of pilgrimage because, just like the python rock in Botswana, there is no evidence of a settlement on-site, so it is deduced this was somewhere our ancestors would have made a point of visiting, but not lived at. Some of the monuments at Gobekli Tepe are as tall as three men and as heavy as three elephants; this was the work of a determined and convinced ritualistic people. It would have required intense labour, a large workforce and would not have been undertaken as a light-hearted project by an uninspired people without conviction. The stone monuments contain beautiful carvings of almost demonic-looking creatures such as snakes, spiders, vultures, scorpions and lions. These creatures are perceived by humans as formidable predators, not prey. There is debate over the true purpose of the site, with theories and interpretations ranging from a cathedral, a skull cult, a hunter's burial ground, a temple where shamanistic rituals or ceremonies took place, even the mountain location where modern agriculture and civilisation was birthed and taught. This last theory does not seem to suit the stone carvings. At least not for a primary purpose, but it may hold some credence; whoever built it was in the perfect environment to find the raw materials and livestock for farming. Furthermore, it has been proven that settlers who lived only around 20 miles from the site began to domesticate sheep, cows and pigs as far back as 10,500 years ago. There is also evidence they grew domesticated strains of wheat. Gobekli Tepe may have been built by the hunters, during a stage where they were transitioning into farmers and builders, to honour and commemorate their ancestral hunting roots. A burial ground for fallen hunters is suggested because of the imagery; some ancient cultures did believe that flesh-eating birds such as vultures would literally transport the bodies of the dead up to the heavens, piece by piece. Similar carvings of vultures are found in Syria from around the same time. So it seems the site may have been the work of a widespread developing civilisation who chose this location away from their settlements as a place to honour the spirits of their heroic hunter ancestors, and possibly to communicate with them, and/or spirits of dead animals in shamanistic rituals with mass drug and chant induced hallucinations. It is clear that humans were becoming increasingly anxious about their own mortality around this time and maintaining a connection with the dead would have been an obsessive preoccupation that might just have been motivation enough to build megalithic structures such as Gobekli Tepe.

If we travel further to the east and forward in time, China's Yangshao culture was creating its own ideas of spirituality around 7000 years ago, (still predating Mesopotamia and Ancient Egypt). The Neolithic people of the Yellow River region exhibited their strong belief in the afterlife by developing intricate burial rituals. One of the oldest sites uncovered was the Banpo village, where they buried their dead with pottery containing food, utensils, jewellery and icons depicting formidable predators and mythical creatures, much like the creatures depicted at Gobekli Tepe. The dead were carefully placed with their heads facing the same way, always towards the setting sun. The devotion shown towards their dead is made clear with the considerable resources and efforts that went into death ceremonies. Food and precious jewels were buried in large chambers, with shelves for the items to be carefully placed near the body. This practice is not exclusive to the ancient Chinese, of course. Thousands of years later, the ancient Egyptians did the same thing, only far more elaborately. Time consumingly mummifying the bodies to preserve the mortal form of their Pharaohs for the afterlife and placing them in large decorated tombs with obscene amounts of gold and treasure. With the arrival of more complex societies, such as Egypt and Mesopotamia, we finally had the invention of writing and these spiritual rituals and ideas that had been floating around, passed down for millennia orally were at last compiled and written down, in works such as *The Pyramid Texts, the Kesh Temple Hymn* and *The Epic of Gilgamesh.* Over the years, the stories told had become very elaborate and embellished but nonetheless were sacred and respected as absolute fact. The stories were woven into books that bound society, serving as inspiration/moral guides. These original religious books and the stories contained within have continued to be passed down, re-written, embellished, refined, restructured, and modernised all the way down to what we have today. Fundamentally, many of us still practice the same worship of the creator, and the performing of rituals for honouring the dead, that our ancestors began at least 70,000 years ago in Africa. We just have modernised versions of the practices, to fit around modern life, and have compiled the stories into various books such as the Bible that are at the core of modern religious organisations. With the invention of writing and books, spirituality truly became organised religion.

The scar on the mind of civilisation

One particularly interesting and recurring story that crops up again and again in the ancient world, and is pretty much universally accepted as being based on fact, is the story of a great flood, which probably occurred around 5700-5600 BCE. The timing would coincide with glacial melting that caused a colossal breach in the enormous enclosed Lake Agassiz of North America. This date would explain the abandonment of proto-cities in modern-day Turkey, such as Çatalhöyük that was occupied by as many as 10,000 people for around 2000 years, from around 9500 years ago until an estimated 7700 years ago. The Great Flood is a scar on the mind of civilisation that has never fully healed, and the agriculturalist city building survivors of this traumatic event probably originated from settlements in Turkey not too far from either the Mediterranean Sea or the Black Sea, (which would have been considerably smaller bodies of water, before the rise in sea levels, than they are today). By all accounts, the flooding was incredibly sudden and destructive, rather than a gradual rise in water level. Any humans who experienced the flooding first-hand and lived to tell the tale would probably have had to of been seafaring and expert shipbuilders.

After losing almost everything during the episode of natural disaster, it is a strong possibility that this previously localised society spread out, teaching and rebuilding their civilisation in many parts of the ancient world to re-spawn and preserve their lost culture, all the while drilling the cautionary tale of the flood into their descendants, passing it down orally until writing was invented and it could be preserved. With the invention of writing, the flood legend, which by this point must have been extremely embellished, was woven into epic tales as a warning about the mercilessness of nature and wrath of the gods. The single original society spreading out from this cradle of civilisation is one explanation for why there are so many similarities in religions, buildings and cultures that developed around the ancient world after 7600 years ago. It is more logical than lots of separate groups of isolated people simultaneously coming up with the same ideas and stories. Durably constructed megalithic monuments dedicated to ancestors and gods, built to withstand the test of time, (and any further natural disasters), began to appear all over Europe, North Africa and the Middle East. The Great Pyramid and the complex at the Giza Plateau stand proud to this day as a testament to the capabilities and determination of the builders. For some researchers, the fact the Ancient Egyptians demonstrated incredible architectural capabilities very early on in their history suggests maybe they inherited some knowledge of civilisation from these mysterious migrating flood survivors of pre-history. There is even new archaeological and genetic evidence that suggests Stonehenge in England may have been constructed by people of Turkish ancestry. Even today the story of the deluge is still being retold with the most commonly known one being Noah's Ark. Stories such as this, that demonstrate the wrath of God when he is displeased, are a significant driving force when it comes to forming a God-fearing population that is easy to manipulate into compliant behaviour. This trick would have been worked out millennia ago by the leaders of these great civilisations who wished to centralise their power for a more effective ruling.

Whilst on the subject of Stonehenge, regardless of who built it, it is absolute and literal rock hard proof that the people of 5000 years ago clearly understood several things: the procession of the equinoxes, that the Earth was not flat, and that it revolved around the sun. Yet it was not until the 1500s that this was being re-discovered by Nicolaus Copernicus and later confirmed by Galileo Galilei. The re-discovery was not welcomed by the Church or its God-fearing followers and consequently Galileo, much like Roger Bacon, spent the latter part of his life under house arrest, forced under threat of torture by the Roman Catholic Church, during an inquisition, to recant his science. Unbelievably, it was not until 1992 that Pope John Paul II finally had to officially admit Galileo was right. The fact scientific knowledge was celebrated by a spiritual people thousands of years ago, evidenced in monuments such as Stonehenge, but was not officially accepted by the Catholic Church until 1992, demonstrates that it is not group spirituality that clashes with truth and science, it is specific organisation leaders, inconvenienced and threatened by the truth, who despise it.

Smoke and mirrors

The evolution of spiritual belief can be separated into several distinct stages of development that likely find their common ancestor in shamanism, which is possibly the oldest form of routinely practised religion. Based on a belief that everything is infinitely conscious and has a spirit that can be communicated with, shamanism was prevalent in Africa, Asia, Australia and the Americas at least as far back as the start of the Neolithic. It could have originally evolved from accidental experiences with nature's hallucinogenics and/or physical or mental medical conditions afflicting the 'chosen one'. A shaman did not simply decide to become a shaman, they were 'chosen' by the spirit world, either from birth or sometimes after a near-death experience. Out-of-body experiences and trances that helped an individual to disconnect themselves from reality could have been triggered in the hippocampal-septal region of the brain via hallucinogens, rhythmic auditory stimuli, fasting, sensory deprivation, social isolation, prolonged physical stress, meditation, or even severe fever; all enhanced by mental/physical illness. There is an insatiable human yearning to be reconnected with the spirits of lost friends and family. Having seemingly found a way to achieve this supernatural feat through shaman, our ancestors clung to the rituals and refined the practices to perfection.

This depth of emotional attachment to others is unique to human consciousness, and shamanistic rituals would have been a great comfort for creatures becoming too intelligent for their own good, in terms of being faced with accepting the harsh reality of their own mortality. Although viewed as an extremely primitive practice, shamans delivering this deeply spiritual experience, in a trance-like state, remain to this day in some tribal cultures, believing the practice is the link to the spirit world and that they are capable of not only contacting the dead but also healing the sick and controlling the weather. Because of this extraordinary power the shaman is seen to be wielding, they command a high level of authority and respect in their tribal group. This respect and control that the shaman earns, can stem from a fear that they could, if provoked, use their 'powers' for evil purposes on any member of their society who steps out of line or breaks the rules.

The shaman's contribution to a hunting group is normally their 'gift' alone, and they are not expected to join in with hunting and gathering; relying on the rest of tribe to bring offerings back to them. The social authority of the shaman is demonstrated through the practice of always giving them the best cuts of meat and the inedible ornaments from the animals as decorative gifts. Rarely is the shaman contradicted, nor is any negative opinion expressed regarding the legitimacy of the practice by the rest of the tribe. This is how the concept of the shaman survived: by becoming exempt from, or at least intolerant of, criticism, much like modern religious organisations. Any murmurs of non-belief in the shaman could easily have been quelled by the shaman publicly 'cursing' the non-believer, followed shortly by the untimely, mysterious demise of the unfaithful sceptic, (murder by poisoning most likely). This is the stirring, not just of religion, but of the hierarchy of society in general. By exerting authority and delivering wrath when appropriate, the many would allow the few to control them with a deception perception of power. Contemporary shaman have even been known to profit from their services. The Evenki of northern Siberia traditionally would pay shaman with live animals as a kind of taxation for their continued services. The Evenki offer an insight into how archaic beliefs can be passed down in undisturbed areas indefinitely. The word shaman is an Evenki word that was actually introduced to the modern world by them. The belief persists amongst the Evenki that all natural phenomena are a materialisation of spirits, and that the spirits can be influenced by shaman attaining their hypnotic state during rituals. They believe they can positively affect everything their society depends on, including hunting, herding and health. Even after a successful hunt, the shaman would be needed to stop the spirits of the killed creatures seeking revenge on the hunter who killed them. So you see the hunters could not even eat their meals without the shaman first saving them from an invisible threat.

Throughout their history, the elaborate costumes and theatricals of shaman, all contributed to the otherworldly experience they provided. Depending on what part of the world they were from a shaman usually wore ornamental clothing, adorned with the parts of animals that were not edible such as deer horns, bird feathers, bones, or fur. With these parts they constructed entire outfits; everything from horrific looking headgear constructed with antlers, decorated sceptres or staffs, all the way down to fancy footwear resembling hooves or claws. The dress code varies from region to region, but the recurring theme was animals - specifically, the prey. The eccentric look complemented the dramatic production, which included chanting, singing, dancing and drumming. The ceremonies would have been at nightfall, lit by fire to add a degree of ambience and mysticism. As the cloaked figure would dance around the fire, his eccentric clothing and shiny items would cast reflections and shadows, coupled with the rhythmic banging of drums and rattling of other makeshift instruments; this would have excited the spectator's imaginations, creating optical illusions.

We may think of the shaman as a mark of a very primitive

people, but even today all over the developed world we have something quite similar, that vulnerable and desperate people will pay good money to enlist the services of. They are known as psychic mediums - individuals who, not unlike shamans, claim to have the ability to enter the spirit world and act as an intermediary to help the rest of the living communicate with the dead and exchange messages. The medium often performs in a sensory deprived environment - either in silence or with a monotonous humming and the séance often takes place in a darkened room, with participants eyes closed. They may even use significant objects to summon certain spirits.

Mediums, conjurers, shamans, witches, wizards, sorcerers, necromancers, clairvoyants, whatever you want to call them, history is absolutely saturated with accounts of humans said to have had these kinds of magnificent magical powers at their disposal, yet there is not a shred of solid evidence of anything supernatural ever occurring anywhere ever, only numerous examples of how susceptible humans are to delusion and how easily the vulnerable human brain can be fooled by illusion and hypnotic manipulation - especially in a sensory deprived environment. This is not to say all have been fakers or con artists; self-delusion is a powerful thing too, and many most probably believed they really had these supernatural talents. There always has been a need for these people to act as a buffer between humans and cold hard mortality, and it is only natural people would step in to fulfil the role society demanded. Where there is opportunity, there are opportunists. Some may profit from it, some may do it for protection, some purely out of the goodness of their hearts, because they like providing comfort to others, or because they truly believe in it, but one thing is certain, these individuals have always been there to fill a psychological void, and they likely always will be.

Forming a better relationship with death for a safer future

So, the shaman provided a comfort perhaps for our ancestors, but how can we calm the innate fears caused by death in modern society, to ensure these fears cannot mentally enslave us, or be exploited to justify heinous evil? Depending on where you live in the world, death, or more accurately the expression of grief, will be celebrated with varying rituals and therefore subject to varying levels of exploitation: contrary to the West, where funerals are incredibly sombre affairs and mourners predominantly dress in black to show respect, in China, mourners wear white, and often employ professional wailers at services to represent the emotion of family members, particularly the younger generation who may feel embarrassed to show what are perceived as weak public displays of emotion. In Japan, death is perceived as liberation, and over the top outbursts of grief are not appropriate as these would undermine the strong belief that life is cyclical rather than linear. The dearly departed are remembered during a three day long Buddhist-Confucian holiday, Obon, or Bon, during which the spirits are said to return to their homes. As with Buddhist's, mourners in the Hindu faith also generally wear white. The cremation ceremony is formal attire, but they dress casually for the wake. In Hinduism, the deceased are believed to be liberated 13 days after cremation at the end of the mourning period. Muslims, much like Catholics generally opt to bury their dead rather than cremate them, due to the belief that they will need their bodies again when resurrected on the day of judgement. Muslims are buried facing Mecca, and a mourning period of up to 40 days follows a burial.

Death etiquette and customs vary wildly, but the common theme that links nearly all cultures is the belief that we are never gone, and that our souls and/or bodies will return to life in one way or another. Every major religion gains and reassures billions of followers with this comforting claim, and yet there is not one scrap of evidence to prove this claim. What is evident, is that deep down many extrinsic religious followers whose religious acceptance appears to be motivated by pragmatic considerations, such as the personal emotional benefits, rather than true belief in the divine, are clearly plagued with doubts, otherwise we would not witness such widespread hysteria in the face of death. Furthermore, if it were a fact that the comfort of the afterlife significantly reduced fear of death, then we would expect to observe atheists everywhere going mad with fear. This is not the case though; many studies and polls have shown atheists are actually amongst the least anxious about death. If we dig a bit deeper what we find is that it is not so much a fear of death but rather a fear of the unknown which determines the level of anxiety. How well we are trained to cope with things that are new, or different to what we are used to, can help to reduce this anxiety.

With any kind of uncertainty, there is always going to be a degree of apprehension. Religion cannot offer comfort for the unknown, only an arrogant assertion to know for a fact what is coming. The end of life is a frightening prospect for most because it is a new experience; we do not know for sure where we are going. If a person is dying, they may endure endless physical pain and disability for a long time, but even this is seen by many as preferable to actually dying because what comes next is entirely unknown. It could be something better, but is has an equal chance of being something unimaginably worse, or it could just be nothingness, an empty void of non-existence for eternity. What can relieve anxiety of the unknown is training an open and rational mind that is accepting of multiple beliefs and options. A mind that is actually excited about embracing new discoveries that may overwrite older beliefs, instead of fearing and rejecting them before they have even happened, just in case it is something upsetting. Sadly, many people assume that facing death without religion renders life pointless, but I, for one, would rather be faced with infinite opportunity than a gamble that I have backed the wrong horse my whole life. What is logical, is that any divine creator that created something so capable of critical thinking would certainly not punish its creation for exercising this wonderful ability as much as possible during its lifetime, and such a life would definitely not have been pointless.

Death will come to all living things, and it is upsetting in some degree to all. It unifies us as a species, but it also fiercely divides us as we disagree over what death means and the dread around it has been exploited to scare and manipulate people into submission since the dawn of time. It is this fear that our ancestors no doubt used to justify their behaviour and blood lust during vigilante witch hunts, looking for a monster to blame for their misfortunes, all motivated by irrational trepidation, they killed innocent people that we now know could not possibly have been witches because logic and science dictates there is no such thing. Regardless of what you may think, we are not too different from our ignorant ancestors. You only have to browse through some comments on random social media posts to see there are fearful and hateful individuals desperate for a witch hunt, and one can easily begin to imagine these individuals dressed in colonial attire grabbing their pitchforks and partaking in these cowardly witch hunts where a hundred simpletons chase down a single innocent scapegoat.

Whether it is faith in a shaman, or an obligation to monarchy, offering up loyalty and/or freedoms in return for protection and survival is a deal our ancestors have always made, and we continue to make without even realising it. One important thing to take away from this is that life and living are two different things. Freedom of thought, critical thinking, equality and liberty must be retained at all costs. As upsetting as death may be, as long as there is new life, it will never be the end. The importance of having a healthy relationship with death and the unknown must not be underestimated if we wish to reach H-utopia, as unless we work on our anxiety we will always be crippled by it and easy to manipulate by opportunists offering comfort at a cost, and there will always be a demonised enemy for us to attack in order to save ourselves. Fear of death is arguably the biggest threat to H-utopia, and the most likely reason we will end up in a dystopia. Luckily, it can be overcome, as each and every one of us has the power to change our mindset.

Organising religion

Other spiritual precursors to modern-day religion are astrolatry and veneration of the dead. Astrolatry is literally worshipping celestial bodies such as the moon and sun as actual conscious gods. Perhaps the most well-known example is seen with the ancient Egyptians, who worshipped their Sun God, Ra.

Ancestor worship, veneration of the dead, paying respect to the spirits of forefathers, combined with life cycle and fertility appreciation. All of the above are precursors to religion, and we know these were practised all over the world, far into pre-history, evidenced in cave paintings and in the most ancient of monuments.

One of the oldest civilisations, the Çatalhöyük people, buried their dead beneath the floors inside their dwellings and their 8000-year-old 'Great Mother' goddess figurine found at Çatalhöyük is possibly one of the oldest examples of a society worshipping a deity in human form. The female seated mother figure appears to have its origins in Palaeolithic Western Europe, with similar figures found in excavations in Germany that date to at least 35,000 years ago. At Willendorf in Austria, three of the so-called 'Venuses' were discovered in an archaeological excavation of what was a temporary settlement that was in use approximately 25,000 years ago by a tribe of hunter-gatherers. The fact there were multiple statues of the same distinct design, with exaggerated breasts and thighs, suggests this was not just one individual's artwork or self-portrait, but actual evidence of communal, ritualistic practice. The Venus mother goddess survived tens of thousands of years through proto-civilisations, such as Çatalhöyük, to later appear in early Greek, Spanish and Italian cultures, making it the longest reigning worshipped deity of human form, passed down from our ancestors an incredibly long time ago. The culture at Çatalhöyük, much like the ancient Greeks, also worshipped the Bull, as a symbol of masculinity, which has been depicted in human art for approximately 52,000 years, with the earliest example seen in Lubang Jeriji Saléh cave in Borneo. Ancestor worship continues, to an extent, to this day. We still honour our dead with elaborate, often expensive, ceremonies and we still make regular 'pilgrimages' to visit the burial sites of long-dead relatives.

Most religions can be simplified into one of the following three accepted categories:

Polytheism - a belief in many gods. The earliest confirmed practice of polytheism, that still exists today, dates from at least 4500 years ago in the form of Hinduism. The Bhagavad Gita revealed that many gods were subject to a supreme Brahman God. Polytheism was practised throughout antiquity in Egypt, Greece, Rome, Assyria, Babylonia, South America and many other places. The ancients viewed their gods as being in control of everything, from rainfall and the harvests, to fertility. Unfortunately, some of these polytheistic people believed they had to sacrifice animals and/or each other in horrific, bloody ways to appease their gods. It was the Greeks and Romans that developed polytheism into a pantheon of gods and goddesses. Both cultures had the same gods but under different names. The Greeks had Zeus, and the Romans had Jupiter. In Greek mythology, Poseidon, the brother of Zeus, was worshipped as god of the sea and the Romans worshipped King Neptune as god of the sea.

Pantheism - the acceptance that the entire Universe and everything contained within *is* God, originated in the beliefs of some African, Asian and Native American cultures. Then appeared later specifically in Ancient Egyptian religion, as well as forming the systems of belief in cultures of the far east in the form of Buddhism, Taoism and others which have shamanistic roots. There is something quite positive to be taken from this doctrine, if it is viewed from a secular perspective. It is quite right that we should be in harmony with nature. Humans are no different than any other animal, we do not have any more right over this planet than any other creatures who evolved here, and we should do our best to live in peace with our fellow inhabitants, sharing the plentiful resources fairly. The ideals of Pantheism without the divine aspects can be adopted by the humanist or atheist for the formation of a well-rounded and moral human being.

Monotheism - the belief in only one all mighty God. Ironically there are several of them, (which is the cause of much conflict, and is responsible for the deaths of hundreds of millions of people over the last couple of millennia). The Judeo-Christian-Muslim religions all argue that their God is the only God. The common ancestor of these monotheist religions was formed in approximately 2000 BCE, with Abraham. The relationship between God and his creations became far more intimate with the invention of monotheism. God even began to personally address and influence certain 'worthy' individuals through the nation of Israel. The Jewish Israelites escaped from slavery in Egypt and journeyed to the promised land, led by one of these honoured individuals. It took 15 centuries for various authors to complete the chronicles of the Old Testament. Christianity was born during the period of the Roman Empire, with the story of Jesus Christ, the long-awaited Messiah. After Christ's crucifixion, resurrection and ascension into heaven, the Christian church grew in His name, and the New Testament was written. Islam appeared approximately 600 years after Christ when Muhammad began preaching in Mecca. Muhammad believed he was the pre-eminent prophet of God, and his teachings became the Qur'an.

There are over 4000 religions, and I cannot claim they all fit into these categories neatly. I am going to add a couple of exceptions that do not quite fit the categories:

Cannibalism cults - there are cults that believe they must consume the heart and brains of their dead, in order to keep their spirits alive and free. Unfortunately, this has resulted in fatal Creutzfeldt-Jakob disease being prevalent in cannibal cults in the past.

Scientology - a belief that humans have reactive minds that respond to life's traumas, clouding the analytic mind, and this keeps us from experiencing true reality. Members of the religion 'audit' themselves to find the sources of trauma, with the aim to neutralise them and attain a spiritual state known as "clear." The church of Scientology promotes the idea of an ancient intergalactic civilisation who were destroyed and became "body thetans," which continue to latch onto humans causing mental and physical trauma, which can be removed via the Scientology auditing process. The process is usually charged, and at no small fee.

Of course, 'profit' really is the key difference that separates organisations from general spirituality. With the emergence of religions based on polytheism and monotheism, there came an opportunity to exploit innocent followers beliefs for profit and political control, expanding the organisation just as one would with any other business. Unfortunately, this was often at the expense of scientific advancement and social development in the afflicted cultures. These negative effects of religious oppression are best observed in Ancient Egyptian society. A brilliant race of people who were incredibly sophisticated and skilled for their time; yet became almost stagnant, in terms of progression, for over 2000 years because of obsessive religious conservatism passed down from father to son, strict indoctrination of the next generation and treating their leaders as gods incarnate all ensured no one would question the authority or the status quo. The preoccupation with death and the belief in gods of the old kingdom was so intense that it ruled peoples lives and civilisation advanced very little, at least compared with what it could have if they had evolved into a secular society, more tolerant to new ideas.

The accomplishment of the Great Pyramid at the Giza Plateau is one of the greatest projects ever completed by hand. Mainstream archaeology tells us the 2.3 million blocks of the Great Pyramid were quarried, transported, cut and placed by hand over a period of just 20 years, with incredible precision, and with chambers and shafts that demonstrate an extremely advanced knowledge of mathematics and architecture. Not to mention the construction of two further colossal pyramids and the Great Sphinx that make up the complex at Giza. We are taught that these fantastic pyramids are tombs for the Pharaohs, and it is widely accepted that the Great Pyramid was the tomb for the Fourth Dynasty Egyptian Pharaoh Khufu.

Whether the monuments at Giza were built as tombs, a

necropolis intended for elaborate death rituals, or for some other purpose, is still the cause of much debate, but whatever their original purpose, it stands as a testament to the advanced knowledge and capabilities of this civilisation at a very early time in its history. The Ancient Egyptians peaked early, then apparently lost the knowledge or the motivation to construct such things again, or to flex their scientific and creative muscles further. This is a clear example of where a religious obligation is prioritised above everything else and is powerful enough to halt progress indefinitely. Egyptian religion is an ancestor of many modern religions so if the Ancient Egyptians had evolved into a purely scientific and secular people, who knows what they may have discovered and what kind of a world we would be living in today. Imagine where we would be now if the industrial revolution had happened over 2000 years ago.

The oppression continued in the rest of the world during the millennia that followed the end of the Egyptian dynasties. The most successful and dominating organised religions still exist today, now boasting billions of members all over the world. Even today, as a society starting to break free of the religious bind imposed upon us by our ancestors, we are still hampered by countless generations of dogma, oppression, child abuse, and self-comforting delusion. Progress has been slow, however, it is evident when we take a step back and observe the timeline of spirituality throughout human history that, particularly in the developed Western world, humanity has worked its way through the stages of belief quite steadily. In biological and geological terms, almost instantaneously we have gone from worshipping comets, moons and gigantic celestial fusion reactors, to praising a single creator, (a creator we vainly tend imagine in human form in most modern religions).

Religion was formalised, with the invention of the written word, in various religious texts and books, which tell the incredible tales of messiah figures who saved us in the distant past and are foretold to return again. These holy books, compiled entirely by human authors, some of which never even met or lived at the same time, detail fascinating accounts of supposed historical events, (that at best will be distorted truths), intertwined with moral ways to live our lives, such as the Ten Commandments. I would be shocked if any human being would need to consult their Bible, or Qur'an or Torah, to know right from wrong and be inspired to do good only because of the threat of damnation if they do not. If this is an individual's motive, then they would be paying an insult to their wise and all-seeing creator, thinking that He would not see through this kind of cowardice.

Actually, we do not need to be bribed with promises of heavenly reward to do good on Earth. Altruistic behaviours are genetically built into us, from millions of years of primate evolution, where cooperation, relying on friends, family and even strangers was important to the survival of primate's genetic lineage. We may not know how we are related to a stranger, but we know that we are of the same species and therefore logically must be pretty closely related, at least 99.9 per cent related genetically in fact. The feeling we get from helping someone in trouble is euphoric. The deepest motives are subconscious of course, but it is beneficial genetically speaking to save someone's life who could possibly share our own genes, or to help someone out for no reward, as long as the payoff is not losing our own life and risking our own genes. This kind of behaviour separates mammals from other creatures on Earth who would not put themselves out in the slightest for the sake of saving a distant cousin from being eaten by a predator. Mammals are considered sentient, they feel empathy, and make conscious decisions to help others for no immediate, selfish reward. Altruism has even been observed across mammal species; there have been instances where dolphins have saved humans from shark attacks, putting their own lives at risk in the process. Why would they do such a thing? Because they are sentient creatures and because their mammalian genes drive this kind of altruistic behaviour subconsciously.

Nowadays, although there are over 4000 religions practised all over the world, the predominant ones, that boast the most members, are Judeo-Christian-Muslim. They practice monotheism, one God and one primary holy book containing stories and values that are heavily based off of much older religious movements, which neatly evolved to become Judaism. In Africa and the Far East, polytheism is still practised widely. Hinduism, Mahayana, Confucianism, Shintoism, to name a few.

In more isolated parts of the world, we are given an intriguing insight into how religions that speak of physical encounters with God may have come about deep in pre-history. In ancient times the primary means of transport for most developing cultures would have been by foot or on animal back. The capabilities and knowledge of civilisations would have been growing at varying rates all over the world, so when they did meet up, the ones that developed fastest could appear like gods to the ones that developed slowest. Even in the 21st century there are islands with indigenous populations that are completely cut off from the rest of civilisation, uninfluenced by science, but not necessarily uninspired by technology.

So-called 'cargo cults' is a phenomenon witnessed best with the Melanesian islanders in the years during and after WWII. The indigenous peoples observed first-hand the godlike, technologically advanced nations coming to their islands. The Japanese and allied forces arrived on these islands, with a multitude of supplies, and they mingled with the islanders. The vast amounts of military equipment and supplies that both sides airdropped to troops on these islands completely changed the lifestyle of the native islanders, many of whom had never even seen other humans before, let alone tinned food, tents, clothing, medicine, and other 'exotic' goods which all arrived in large quantities for the soldiers. From the islander's perspective, the gifts were dropped from the heavens. The soldiers would share the airdropped goods with their island hosts, and the islanders idolised them for it. The 'John Frum' cult is one of the most long-lived and is particularly interesting; formed on the island of Tanna, Vanuatu. The natives worshipped certain Americans having the name John Frum or Tom Navy, who they claimed had brought goods to their island during the time of WWII, and who they identified as being divine entities, destined to return to them again one day in a sort of 'second coming'. The 20th century saw rapidly increasing global transport, via airliners, and ships, thanks to transglobal trading. Hence, the formation and documentation of such cults, increased.

This was by no means the first time religious movements by a primitive people have been created, or enhanced, by misunderstood encounters with other humans. An example of something similar occurring in the more distant past is 'White Gods'. There is strong evidence that cultures of the 'New World' were visited by seafaring Caucasian races from Europe in ancient times, and that they were known as 'White Gods' because of their pale complexion and blue eyes. This is based on 16th-century accounts of the Spanish conquistadors being greeted as divine beings by the peoples of the New World, adamantly believing their gods had returned. A misunderstanding like this presents an opportunity for exploitation of natives, and it is certainly a trick that has been pulled off more than once by individuals in the past lacking integrity. Even today, our mental image of God is human in form, so it is not surprising that primitive people would mistake more technologically advanced humans for gods.

Now back in the 21st century, we are in the process of coming to terms with a fifth and perhaps final stage of belief, (or more accurately, non-belief), in the form of atheism - the rejection that the existence of the Universe requires any supernatural or divine intervention, and can, in fact, be wholly explained scientifically. Atheism accompanies humanism nicely, encouraging people to do something meaningful and for the greater good of humanity with their own lives, whilst welcoming scientific advancements, showing compassion to fellow humans, and living rational lives. This way of life was inevitably going to be the next natural progression that comes with increased intelligence and scientific advancement. Should we wish to reach H-utopia, we need to embrace this way of thinking and make a decision to do one of two things:

1) Fully embrace atheism and science whilst rejecting religion.

2) Embrace an omnistic agnosticism, humbly accept that we cannot know everything for sure, cannot force beliefs on one another and become fully tolerant of all peaceful ways of life.

Option two is clearly the one most suited to H-utopia and the option I am an advocate of. Regrettably, it is not as simple as choosing option two, as even this open-minded and accepting option does not suit the proportion of individuals who practice **fundamentalism**. When we hear the word 'fundamentalist' in the context of religion, many people's thoughts jump immediately to al-Qaeda, and to 'Islamic' terrorists who commit murder, in the name of God, against the gluttonous Western world's 'fair-weather' worshippers. However, every country and every religion has its fundamentalists. To pardon, or turn a blind eye to one, whilst condemning another, using it as a scapegoat for religion in general is an injustice that will only fuel further hatred and violence against innocent people. We must recognise all fundamentalism and the different risks it poses, doing our best to negate those risks in the future.

Even Buddhism, that has a reputation as one of the most peaceful religions, contained within its half a billion plus followers, has its fair share of fundamentalist members. In Burma, 'hard-line' Buddhists have targeted Muslim minorities, led by nationalist Buddhist monks of the group Ma Ba Tha. The group's leader was even imprisoned for inciting violence against innocent Muslims. The intolerance of Islam is further demonstrated by Sri Lankan Buddhist organisation Bodu Bala Sena - a right-wing group that claims to protect the rights of Sinhala people, but in actuality they have targeted the Muslim minority of Sri Lanka, protesting the building of Mosques and wearing of the Burqa. So you see, no religion is exempt from the dangers of fundamentalism, and they are all connected by one thing: a determined intolerance of other people's rights, arrogantly believing themselves to be the absolute holders of truth. In actual truth, fundamentalism stems from a fear response to losing one's religion, hence why Christian fundamentalist churches in America have been on the rise whilst the followings at traditional churches have been dwindling for decades. For many of the devout, it is becoming 'all or nothing' in a final attempt to preserve age-old cultural practices in a world where science and technology advance every day in the opposite direction, systematically robbing God of His once all-mighty power over humankind.

To be fair, not all fundamentalist religions attract physically violent members. Fundamentalism can be attractive because it makes life simpler. Everything is far more black and white when we get down to fundamentals, and certain groups offer emotional comfort and security to those overwhelmed by the complexity of the modern world and the unrighteous paths it can lead people down. An example of peaceful Christian fundamentalism is observed with the Protestant Amish, who opt for simple living, free from modern electronic conveniences and technology. With Jehovah's Witnesses, we see a religious order that accepts the Old Testament of the Bible to be literal, with its leaders even predicting the 'end times' on multiple occasions throughout the organisation's history. Jehovah's Witnesses also refuse to give indirect acts of worship to any Pagan gods, choosing to abstain from all rituals and celebrations that Christianity 'contaminated' itself with when absorbing Paganism, including the Christmas winter solstice festival, the birth of new life at Easter time in spring, and even birthdays. Jehovah's Witnesses 'recruit' new members by approaching people either in the street or by going house to house, making small talk, casually discussing the daunting problems in society that affect us all, and subtly offering their organisation as a comforting solution. This method of recruitment, (or conversion from traditional Christianity), is particularly successful with the emotionally vulnerable - people who have recently suffered the loss of a close relative for example. The promise of being reunited in God's Kingdom with lost loved ones is nicer than the alternative cold, hard reality of death being eternal nothingness or something unknown.

Of course, people are not born fundamentalists; they are intensely conditioned, usually as children or during times of mental vulnerability. To try and un-condition millions of fundamentalists is a pointless exercise as the phycology that allows for fundamentalism is deeply inset. A fundamentalist truly believes their way is the only way to heaven, or attaining heaven on Earth. They believe the coming of God's kingdom on Earth is imminent, and when it arrives there will be an end to poverty, suffering, inequality, exploitation, hunger, homelessness and all of the other overwhelmingly unjust things in the world. Fundamentalist or not, we can all agree on wanting a better world like this, but the dispute is how to achieve it. Ironically, it is the convenient strategic divide imposed upon us by religion that has stalled us reaching this better world, (H-utopia). Contrary to what many people may think, it is not religion that divides us though. It is intolerance towards one another, and trying to push faith on others, that leads to violence and fierce divide. It is vital we find peace in accepting the beliefs of others, so long as they are not hurting anyone, as only from accepting that others are going to have varying beliefs can we push through the barriers of prejudice. We are often too quick to point the finger of blame anywhere else than at ourselves, and religion has made itself into a scapegoat for violent acts because the followers of religion are often less tolerant toward other religious groups than any atheist is towards all religion in general. Blaming religion for death is the same as blaming a gun for shooting someone. The inanimate object is harmless on its own. Only when an unstable person wields it does it become a threat.

Secularism, and morality without religion

An age-old quest for our creator has led us to an incredibly strange end, and for many people, it is understandably unsatisfying. Earlier on, we considered how our Universe is almost certainly not the only universe; perhaps an almost infinite amount existed before and/or exist parallel in other dimensions. Aristotle mused that an eternal existence made more sense than a created one, (he can be pardoned for not having access to physics on a quantum level). We are now sure that our Universe is not eternal and actually had a beginning around 13.8 billion years ago, based on expansion rate, although we have learned it may be cyclical by nature, rebirthing at the point of destruction via quantum processes which are not yet fully understood. Furthermore, it is theoretically very possible that the Universe originally came into existence via a quantum fluctuation, and therefore did not need a supernatural entity to create it. The temporary change in the amount of energy in a point in space is explained and theoretically accounted for in Werner Heisenberg's uncertainty principle. This allows the creation of particle and antiparticle pairs of virtual particles. Although virtual particles popping in and out of existence may sound like science-fiction, and for some may be harder to accept than the existence of God. Whether we like it or not, it is based on fundamental mathematics, and it is currently the best explanation for how universes could come into existence from nothing. We also reviewed the theory that 2nd generation universes may come from their parent universe's own kind of reproductive systems, via black/white holes or some other, as yet, unknown phenomenon.

A religiously inclined person may ask at this point what the difference is between a God we cannot see that exists outside of our normal Universe and virtual particles we cannot see that exist outside of our normal Universe? The difference is, we can see evidence of virtual particles and, despite their name, they are indeed real particles. Quantum mechanics actually requires momentary violations of conservation of energy. One particle can become a pair of heavier particles, (the so-called virtual particles). The virtual particle almost instantaneously re-joins the original particle, as if it had never been there at all.

Even if we can accept all this science, and do not *need* religion for its original purpose, which was to explain the origin of the Universe, can it still be of use in helping us to maintain peace, law and order?

Anyone who argues we need the threat of eternal damnation to keep us from sinning or acting immorally, clearly is deluded. We only have to look at history over the last thousand years to see this argument is complete nonsense. I do not know how many atheists have killed in the name of their belief, but I suspect the number will be close to zero. If we look at how many deaths have been caused, justified or enabled by religious obsession and intolerance, on the other hand:

The Crusades – fought between Christians and Muslims, there were eight major crusades that occurred between 1096 and 1291. These ruthless conflicts enhanced the status of European Christians in the fight for land in the Middle East.

Thirty Years War - lasting between 1618 and 1648, is one of the longest and deadliest of all European wars, with millions of deaths on both sides of the conflict.

French Wars of Religion – occurred during the reign of the Catholic King Francis I. As the Protestant Huguenots gained influence and began displaying their faith more openly, Catholic hostility increased and incited many civil wars that took place between 1562 and 1598.

First and Second Sudanese Civil Wars – the conflicts were ongoing between 1955-2005, (with an eleven year gap that lasted between the two wars from 1972-1983). The root causes of the civil wars were political and religious. Partly where Sharia, (Islamic), law was being imposed on non-Islamic peoples. The death toll ran into the millions.

Lebanese Civil War – 1975 -1990 was a conflict between Sunnis, Shias and Christians.

Muslim Conquests of India – lasting for centuries and sometimes referred to as the Hindu Holocaust. The Muslim conquests lasting up to the 16th century, were for Hindus, a horrific and endless slaughter. Entire cities were lost and the populations decimated. Those who escaped death at the hands of the invading Islamic soldiers were deported as slaves. There are accounts depicting literal hills made of Hindus skulls. No one can know for sure the death toll, but it runs into many millions, with accounts of 50,000 men, women and children being slaughtered at a time. Without doubt, this relentless genocide was one of the most tyrannical, long lasted evils, imposed from one race of humans to another in written history. Why? The conquerors justified their actions, claiming it their religious duty against non-believers, shamefully using the Islamic faith as a flag to cloak themselves.

Congolese Genocide - the 19th century Belgian King, Leopold II, transformed the entire Congo into his own personal domain. He was responsible for an estimated 15 million deaths, and it is strongly agreed that it did constitute genocide. This sounds like an epic and diabolical legend from the times of old where our ignorant ancestors did not know any better but in fact, this was in living memory until recently, only occurring at the turn of the 20th century! Needless to say, this embarrassing atrocity on the face of modern humanity is left out of mainstream education in the Western world. The official story for Leopold's unfathomable actions was to protect the natives of the Congo from Arabic slavers, and for the Christian missionaries to 'welcome' the natives to Christianity. Leopold made a fortune from exploiting the natural resources of the Congo, that the natives were forced to harvest. The ones that did not work hard enough were beheaded.

Armenian Genocide – another 20th century disgrace, where attempts have been made to quietly sweep it under the rug. The Armenian people resided in relative peace in the Caucasus region of Eurasia for around 3,000 years. In the 4th century AD it became the first nation to make Christianity its official religion. During the 15th century, Armenia became part of the Islamic Ottoman Empire. Although it tolerated religious minorities like the Christian Armenians, they were treated as 2nd class citizens, who had less legal rights and had to pay higher taxes than those who were not Christian. At the turn of the 20th Century and with the start of WW1, the Turkish sided with Germany and the Austro-Hungarian Empire. At the same time, Ottoman authorities declared holy war against Christians, and in 1915 the Armenian genocide began with the arrest and execution of hundreds of Armenian intellectuals. This was followed by Christian men, women and children being turned out of their homes and sent to walk naked through the desert, without food or water, until dead. Many were also drowned, crucified, thrown off cliffs, and burned alive, just for identifying as Christian. The world watched the ongoing suffering for seven years until it finally stopped in 1922, by which time an estimated 1.6 million Christian Armenians had lost their lives, and many more orphaned. Kidnapped children were spared death, but forcibly converted.

Aztec human sacrifice – gruesome human sacrifices were a part of Aztec religious ceremonies that were, ironically, meant to appease their gods by feeding the sun with human hearts in an attempt to spare their civilisation from death. The actual number of people sacrificed is much debated. It could have been as many as 250,000 a year killed during these ceremonies. Although this may have been greatly exaggerated by the Christian Spanish conquistadors, who saw the chance to benefit from making the natives seem more barbaric than they actually were. Even if we go with the lower estimate of 20,000 per year, it is still pretty horrific, and incredibly they did it to their own race of people, who were hunted down and brought back to Mexica-Tenochtitlán for the sacrificial ceremonies. This is an extreme example of the dangerous power religion wields over the devout, determined and ignorant.

Spanish Inquisition - started in 1478 in Spain. Anyone who was not loyal to the Roman Catholic church could be accused of heresy, and the punishment was being burnt at the stake. Not only Protestants were targeted but also Jews. The rulers of Spain, Ferdinand and Isabella, called for the Inquisition, to discourage belief of any religion apart from Catholicism, by intimidation and extermination, if need be. Amazingly the Inquisition carried on, to some degree, until as recently as 1834.

The Northern Ireland Conflict - the root cause was political, however, the opposing sides were majority Catholic against majority Protestant. Exploiting contrasting beliefs for political gain is nothing new.

This is by no means a comprehensive list, and I am not claiming that religion was the only factor involved by any means in all of these. However, it is an enabler, or at least a justification, for those participating in the atrocities. It is impossible to know exact figures, but an educated estimate based on the above and the many other conflicts not detailed here would total somewhere in the region of a quarter of a billion untimely deaths, in the name of religion, throughout recorded history. Whether self-inflicted, such as the Aztec's suffering, or persecution of certain people, just because their religion was not deemed as worthy as others, such as the Holocaust, targeting, amongst others, the Jewish peoples during WWII.

So why has religion, that is supposed to preach peaceful living, made us commit such heinous evil against each other for thousands of years? We are human, and one of the great things about being human is, we are all very different. We all have vastly different opinions, ideas and a desperation to seek the answers to our questions. Religious organisations however are not famous for tolerating opinions, new ideas, critical thinking or answering questions with any deep thought. The organisations would not have survived to modern times if they did.

Religion is more than just the worship of God; it is a definition of how its followers live their lives. Followers of the same religious organisation will generally live their lives in a certain way. What they wear, what they eat, how they act in society, the places they meet to worship and socialise, their views towards others, towards women, children and animals will all be similar. The religion of a devout follower forms their personality or identity, and people in a community with similar identities form a bond; a kind of unconditional kinship. Billions of us have been segregated into these religious 'teams' across the world. In its simplest form, it is called tribalism. Of course, people will support the person from their own tribe when he or she is challenging another person from a competing tribe, regardless of who is right or wrong, or whose motives were good or evil, (which are different depending on one's perspective). The opposing person's team naturally retaliates, verbally and/or physically, inciting communal violence and abuse. If we escalate that up to a grander scale, wars break out. Even people of the same basic religion have justified violence against each other in this way. An obvious example is Protestants versus Catholics, both of the same basic religion, but the small differences continue to divide them fiercely to this day.

So the problem does not lay with religion *per se,* but rather the way religious organisations have *had* to conduct themselves in order the survive the test of time. I.e. absolutist and intolerant of individual, creative ingenuity or rational questioning. It is entirely possible atheists could become motivated to kill in the name of their theories, if they were to start identifying with one another by dressing the same, forming their own language, believing the same scientific premises and refusing to change these ideas, disregarding any new discoveries, even in the face of new evidence. Perhaps splitting into two atheist factions. For example, one faction that believes in the quantum fluctuation and one that believes we are in a simulation, created by an inter-dimensional species from another universe. The reality of this happening though is slim as this is just not how atheist mindsets work. Generally, the atheist holds Humanist values, is scientifically minded, logical, and they embrace new discoveries, even if they contradict older beliefs. The atheist is constantly evolving, and therefore not at risk of becoming set in a rigid identity, and the atheist will generally have a more rational, peaceful reaction to debate. If there is a disagreement during a debate on the nature of the universe between two atheists, they can rise above the disagreement remaining friends or associates with one another, agreeing to disagree until further evidence provides more definitive answers. What is more, there is no evidence to say that atheists live any less morally than a religious person. Below, (in no particular order), are a secular, ten commandments that everyone, regardless of age, gender or ethnic background, can surely agree on:

1. Be tolerant of others and do not allow personal fears to manifest as hatred.
2. In everything you do, ensure it does not cause suffering to others.
3. Respect the Earth and all of its living occupants.
4. Welcome knowledge and education like the most precious gift you could receive.
5. Do not hold any belief so strongly that you could not disregard it should it be proved wrong.
6. Live ethically and with integrity, doing what you know to be right, not necessarily what you are told.
7. Support those who need your support, seeking no reward or recognition.
8. Acknowledge wrongdoing and make every effort to put it right.
9. Exercise forgiveness, not vengeance.
10. Exercise scepticism before accepting facts.

Personally speaking, as a Humanist individual, I am tolerant of all beliefs and ways of life, however, I am not tolerant of any root causes of human suffering or deliberate sabotage of our future potential for any one individual's selfish reasons, and consequently, I have become sceptical of blind faith to anything with proof, particularly organised religions that have historically committed terrible wrongs in the name of their rigid fundamentalist beliefs.

It would be fine if religion did not cause humanity a problem, but in its current form it always has, and that is because the primary focus of the organisation leaders has always been profits and power, rather than helping its followers to attain genuine and peaceful spiritual enlightenment. To add insult to injury, these organisations even claim tax exemption which has enabled them to influence massive amounts of the economy. So long as there are religious organisations praying on human weaknesses, people are always going to die in the name of them. To be fair to the few that do manage to avoid starting conflict, the vast majority of deaths are specifically related to the three predominant monotheistic organisations, and it is no coincidence the organisations with the most violent histories are the dominant ones today.

I think it is going to be more challenging for us to reach H-utopia whilst religious organisations continue to segregate us, just because they attract fundamentalists who, by definition, cannot find tolerance and peace with their fellow man. However, we cannot expect everyone to abandon their beliefs overnight just for the pursuit of 'H-utopia'. Total abandonment of belief in this way would not be a desirable thing in any case; a fickle person willing to give up on something just because they were told to is not admirable. I do believe the dissipation of rigidity within organised religions will ultimately come naturally with further education, cultural mingling and scientific enlightenment. Perhaps over the next three or four generations, if we continue developing linearly, religion will return to its pure spiritual roots.

It is important religions continue to be studied by everyone, unfiltered and without bias, out of historical respect and to help learn about ancestors. Culture is important, as the role of culture/religion is, and always has been, to protect us from the raw forces of nature, especially the prospect of death, as well as to unite us peacefully. A general spirituality fulfils a phycological need, cushioning the blow of the cold, hard, and often cruel reality of the natural world, but without the accompanying violence of fundamentalism or tribalism. It would be psychologically damaging for many people to entirely remove spirituality from our society. Studying all cultures and beliefs will give everyone a chance to come to their own decisions when presented with all of the different options from an openminded viewpoint, and because no one would be obliged to choose purely due to peer pressure or ancestral guilt, the divides in society would begin to disappear. There are lots of positives to come from spirituality, and even if we do eventually abandon organised religions entirely, that would not mean we would be unable to continue to draw positive aspects from religion.

The strong divides religion creates in society and the blinding of reason it causes are the targets to be eliminated, not spirituality itself, and we achieve this through education from an open-minded, philosophical, secular perspective. Being secular is being tolerant and respectful to everyone irrespective of the religious beliefs of others and also to allow people to freely educate themselves on matters spiritual and non-spiritual. Secularism is not a direct attack on religion as is a common misconception. For instance, it is possible to be a religious/spiritual person but at the same time, believe society should practice secularism when educating its children, in order to avoid breeding dogmatic ignorance.

Secular childhood

In the 21st century we like to think of ourselves as a mature and logical species of high intellect. Yet, all over the world we are still forcefully indoctrinating our children with ancient superstitions and rituals, that are hideously outdated, preventing them from learning about other ways of life as *equal* to their own, because they are told their ancestors' way is the *only* way. We generally accept all other modern advancements and improvements: plumbing, driving cars, using electricity and fossil fuels to power our cars and heat our homes, watching television, using computers and mobile phones to communicate across massive distances in seconds. We tend to get frustrated when our technology becomes outdated, and when a newer model is available we simply must have it, yet we are as stubborn as a mule when it comes to maintaining a belief system that is outdated by thousands and thousands of years! Yes, it is respectful and interesting to learn about our ancestors' beliefs and practices, but for goodness sake, we should not force our children to carry on practising them literally, without even a say in the matter. This is at best, hindering their development and learning, at worst, child abuse, fuelling xenophobia and crippling social development. It is time to take a stand for the sake of society, and more importantly, our children and their sanity. To make the decision to raise our children as tolerant agnostics in a secular environment, allowing society to develop and progress naturally unhindered for the first time since the dawn of civilisation. This is one of the most important steps we need to take in order to reach H-utopia.

As I have said, this does not mean completely abandoning religion; a thorough religious education should be encouraged, just not in a biased way. Children should be encouraged to study all religions and beliefs, alongside scientific ideas that argue against the requirement for a divine creator, such as naturalistic evolution and quantum mechanics. After a thorough education, children should then be allowed to come to their own conclusions, without feeling any guilt imposed by their authority figures, and this is the vital change we need to make. Who knows what fantastic scientific and spiritual breakthroughs could come from the next generation if they are being raised in this way.

This is easier said than done though. Generally speaking, even a convinced atheist parent would allow their child to go forth with an unpolluted mind, give them the chance to study all aspects and points of view, both scientific and religious, and then let them make a logical, well-informed choice as to what they believe about the Universe, without fear or prejudice surrounding their decisions. Whereas, many devout Catholic, Islamic or Jewish parent's would not be comfortable allowing their children the same opportunity. In a devout home, the child would be raised biased from birth towards their parent's way of life and would of course, accept their parent's beliefs on good faith as absolute fact. Often children will even be sent to single religion schools to make sure they are only mixing with likeminded individuals, reducing their exposure to diversity and debate, so as not to confuse or distract them too much during the vital early years of development. Imagine you spend the first 16 years of your life believing something to be fact, because the people you have the most respect in the world for, (your parents), told you it was fact, strengthened by only mixing with peers who had the same kind of upbringing. Now, as a young adult going out into the world teeming with diversity, you are bombarded with all of these conflicting points of view. This is what happens to millions of young adults from devout families. It is overwhelming, confusing and just easier all around for most people in this situation to bury their heads in the sand, rather than face the debate, and defy their parents and ancestors. Until recently, this was a pretty effective form of oppression, but nowadays, with the internet, every child growing up has access to a world of knowledge and culture. Billions of online videos, forums, articles, documentaries, eBooks, TV/film productions, music, social media, and all available to access without even having to leave the comfort of home. Parents are losing the control they once had over the diversity of what their children are learning. In the developed West, we are seeing a big increase in the number of young people who now identify as agnostic, atheist or 'no religion', who would previously have casually identified as Christian, purely because their parents were raised as Christian, (even if they did not practice Christianity or go to church regularly).

Religious organisations are not stupid, they have recognised the threats posed to them by the politically correct, *millennial* way of learning and thinking. This is where xenophobia raises its ugly head again; devout religious, (or just patriotic), people can feel threatened by political correctness and therefore reject it, remaining 'set it their ways', sometimes coming across racist, even if they did not intend to, further delaying social development by fracturing society. Christian organisations have been quickly trying to adapt to cater for the 'millennial' generation in a desperate attempt to prolong their survival. Christianity and Catholicism claim to be comfortable now with the theory of evolution, the fact that the Earth is over four and a half billion years old, and even the possibility of alien life. Not because they are comfortable with this awkward admission, but because they *have* to be okay with these incontrovertible truths, in order to be taken seriously and stand any chance of surviving the 21st century. But when these truths undermine the principle teachings of their earliest scriptures, the hypocrisy of the 'U-turns' may be damaging to the organisation's reputation, and eventually, they are going to fall apart, crumbling from the foundations into a more generic spirituality, rather than any specific organisation. To allow this social development to occur would be good for humanity, good for peace, but obviously bad for business for those who benefit from the immense power and wealth these organisations have accumulated over the centuries. General spirituality is peaceful as it does not strongly segregate us as organised religious groups do.

Christianity can now accept that the Earth and humans are not the centre of the Universe, but it does not change the fact, in the not too distant past, people were discredited, threatened, tortured, burned alive for daring to suggest what is now 'officially' fine by the Church. There is still a long struggle ahead, but the path we are walking is definitely heading in the right direction. I do believe spiritualism and atheism would be able to coexist nicely in H-utopia without conflict arising. To train the next generation as tolerant agnostics, rather than indoctrinate them as extremists out of fear, which can only lead to hatred and suffering. Perhaps one day we will be able to completely cut off these vague religious labels that define who we are, and truly free ourselves of the bind that has prevented us from embracing each other for longer than history can remember.

Preparing H-utopians with education, parenting and child development

"The object of education is to prepare the young to educate themselves throughout their lives".

- Robert M. Hutchins, 1899-1977.

...The world will not change for the better in the future, and we will never attain H-utopia if the children being raised now are carrying forward problems of past generations into the future. We will always be doomed to go around in circles in an insane society of dangerous, socially inept, self-sabotaging people unless we commit to mentally strengthening our children during their most impressionable years...

As part of our action plan for building the foundations of H-utopia, we desperately require a re-evaluation of the importance we place on thoroughly educating and training people. Combining this with a reformation of school systems, and a setting of clear goals for establishing the correct environment and behaviours in schools and other training facilities.

Delivering a high quality of education for everyone, regardless of wealth or social status, is a primary focus on our action plan. We have a responsibility to ensure we are creating an engaged and calibrated population, properly prepared to lead us into H-utopia, whilst overcoming obstacles and challenges that the future will bring, and accepting change with a mature and wise approach.

Setting children up for success, psychologically

The two most important things to teach the next generation are **open-mindedness** and **integrity.** With these two attributes alone trained to children from a young age, future generations will succeed where we failed, make the right decisions where we made the wrong ones, and accept one another as we could not. Equally as important as training the right attributes, we need to drastically reduce **intolerance** and **acquiescence** from society, as much as humanly possible. With intolerance we are divided, and with acquiescence we are conquered. Unless learning environments, both in the home and in schools, fully estimate the importance of reducing these two traits in children, whilst encouraging open-mindedness and integrity wherever possible, then we will fail on our journey before we have even taken the first steps.

In most schools, there is currently a lot of emphasis on memorising specific knowledge in the traditional subjects, such as mathematics, literacy and science. The primary role of a teacher is to prepare children to achieve the highest ranking possible in these core subjects when being tested on them. However, education only focusing on traditional subjects is not fulfilling anywhere near its capacity and therefore limiting humanity's potential.

Schools are the seeds and roots from which we grow the minds of the next generation. The input children absorb during this crucial time in their lives will directly impact how well they live their lives and how successfully they function in society. To create successful H-utopians, development of the young human mind needs to cover training in the following areas:

- Creativity.
- Cognitive ability.
- Recall/memory training.
- Mental health, self-care, fear and stress management.
- Speed of thought.
- Decision making and rationale.
- Ability to separate fact from assumption.
- Physical motor skills.
- Logical thinking.
- Integrity.
- Ethics.
- Open-mindedness.
- Teamwork.

However, before children can learn effectively in any areas, they need several things provided as a foundation:

- Sleep/rest.
- Sunlight.
- Nutrition.

- Hydration.
- Love.
- Social skills.
- Personal coaching.
- Independence.
- Responsibility.

Sadly, even these basic needs are not provided to many children. In this section, I will address some of the most significant educational maladies, suggesting remedies for them.

Making children responsible for their actions, and responsible for their own lives from a young age will have a major positive impact on their independence and social skills as an adult. As parents, we should not speak for children as much as we tend to. Any opportunities for children to take the lead in social interactions during early childhood should be encouraged. For example, allowing children to communicate their own health problems to a doctor, or to perform their own transactions in shops when buying toys; handing over their own pocket money to the cashier and accepting the smaller amount of money back as change. All of this will improve their self-confidence, social understanding and independence. When a child does something wrong, parents should discourage the behaviour; discuss with them rationally why it was wrong and respond calmly whilst resisting the urge to 'react'. As adults, we can become aggravated by misbehaving children, and although it is unhealthy to hide all emotion from them, we must exercise restraint and respond with rationale, not react with aggression. To react aggressively to someone so much smaller and more vulnerable than ourselves is cowardly. Not only is this detrimental to a child's mental health, but it may also have lasting effects that resonate throughout society forever. At the root of many violent criminals who have committed atrocious acts, we find a childhood deprived of love, brimming with abuse, both mental and physical.

It is during their school years that children first learn to socialise away from parents, set their own goals and priorities, choose their own friends, adopt their own philosophies and form a relationship with non-parental authority figures. Of course, parents play a massive part in their own child's development, preparing them for school, and life beyond; training tolerance, respect, empathy, discipline, integrity and determination. It is vital to continue supporting and building on these positive foundations throughout childhood. Although all too often, the opposite is true, with parents' own prejudice, intolerance, ignorance and irrational fears being programmed into the next generation, as immortalised in the Pink Floyd song, 'Mother'. The aim of rearing pre-schoolers, one would hope, is to develop children who will respond well to the school system and avoid the pitfalls that come with socialising independently for the first time. A well prepared child from a tolerant and supportive home will tend to be confident, disciplined, have a good work ethic and will be less susceptible to the dark side of socialising, such as peer pressure and bullying, which go hand in hand to feed a negative and disruptive environment.

Being liked or feeling a need to fit in with a group or 'clique' can bring out the worst in some children and if these weaknesses in character are not remedied, then the flaws are often carried into adulthood, forming an unpleasant, anti-social person lacking integrity and self-confidence. With the invention of the internet and social media, bullying is not just limited to the school playground anymore. The abuse can haunt a bullied child's every waking moment, even when at home they are not safe from the cyber bullies hate campaigns, gossiping and tormenting. The primal, selfish mentality of a bully is relentless, in extreme cases, even pushing their victims into suicide for a power kick. It is sickening that some of the culprits in such scenarios do not even show empathy or remorse for an act so evil. Ironically, the bully's motive is often fear; of not fitting in, not being liked, or being bullied if they are not the bully themselves. Sadly, there are some genuinely, mentally unstable children whose traumatic home life provokes them to act out in an aggressive and hateful manner, but peer pressure is the enabler that normalises the behaviour for otherwise mentally well-adjusted children. Children become socially influenced to participate in bullying, without feeling much guilt for their poor judgement and decisions because *"everyone is doing it"*, or they are just relieved it is not them being targeted. When phrased in this way, it sounds very absolutist - bully or be bullied, but it is not a binary choice, and it is certainly not a choice that is supposed to be made by children. This lack of integrity and individuality is a parental failure materialising in real life at a child's earliest stage of true independence, and when system failures in schools allow it to escalate out of control, it is sometimes too late to save the bully from themselves; anti-social bad habits and personality flaws are, to an extent, tolerated in children as an expected inevitability, but this acceptance of parental failure has potentially dire consequences for society and should not be brushed off so lightly.

If caught early and properly addressed, bullying behaviours can be corrected quickly. How discipline is implemented is important in order to effectively deal with this type of anti-social behaviour. Parents who are not trained in child phycology may struggle with the right course of action, or perhaps feel denial that their child is at fault, ignoring the warning signs that their child is developing into an intolerant human being, failing to correct the problematic behaviour and further enabling their child's wrongdoing. Some parents may swing to the other extreme, embarrassed by their child being called out as a bully, they resort to 'eye for an eye' punishments to shame their own child, as an overcompensating form of public discipline to demonstrate their parental disapproval to any judgemental onlookers. For instance, posting an embarrassing picture on social media of their child or posting a video of themselves ranting at their child. This bullying of children by adults as a punishment is far worse than children bullying each other and may offer some insight into where these behaviours stem from. This is definitely not the right thing to do as it will only fuel resentment against authority and feed the negativity of the bully. Instead of dishing out this 'Old Testament' style punishment, the focus should be on instilling empathetic responses and making amends; showing that actions have consequences and acting out is not cool. This is where parent and school collaboration needs to improve, and counselling sessions need to take place in the form of 'coaching plans'. It is important that misbehaving children are 'coached' and not 'counselled'. The word 'counselling' comes with a stigma that provokes instant judgement and enforces a negative message onto a child. It is very easy to oust a bully and penalise them, suspend them from school, or expel them, but this only moves the problem around in society. Failing to correct the course of troubled children will only result in more socially inept adults and criminals materialising amongst us in the future. This short-term thinking and laziness when passing problems around, rather than facing into them head-on, is a failure very early on in society that exposes our future as vulnerable, by leaving fate to decide the outcome of the next generation's mentality, and levels of criminality.

Instead of fuelling resentment against authority by going full attack against the identified anti-social behaviour, if we can get the misbehaving child to open up and discuss the consequences of their actions, taking the time to adjust their perspective and really empathise with their victims. If a bully can be made to realise what they are doing is socially unacceptable and cannot be tolerated, then this is actually enhancing the child's Emotional Intelligence Quotient, EIQ, which will prevent further bullying, whilst also reducing other kinds of disruptive behaviour too, resetting children on the right course to a better future.

Coaching plans agreed with parents and one to one meetings, without the parents present, may get to the bottom of some root causes for the bully's conduct; it is essential that it be determined what triggers any incidents of anti-social behaviour and to find a reason, not an excuse. There is no excuse, (and it is vital this is understood by children), but to properly administer a remedy, we must first diagnose the ailment, whether it be jealousy, frustration, anxiety or something else. The information gathered during these coaching sessions will allow schools and parents to come up with an appropriate discipline plan and to make the child face up to responsibility for their own actions. Although not practising an eye for an eye, punishment does need to be suited to the crime. Even inherently good children can do bad things and will make poor choices. This is where it is important that instead of criticising and overreacting, we have to help them realise what they have done is wrong and that they must take responsibility for rectifying it in any way appropriate.

Corrective actions should be instilled into children all through their childhood anyway for wrongdoing. For example, if a child says something rude to a person, they should be told they must apologise. Or if they deface someone's property, they should have to put it right. If they take something from a sibling without asking, they should have to return it and apologise. Sometimes it will be effective to remove privileges at school or in the home, such as sports clubs or video games. In the case of cyberbullying, the logical punishment is to remove the use of the internet for a time, or the device being used to access it. As long as the timeframe they are losing the privilege for is communicated clearly and stuck to strictly, this will be a very effective punishment. Equally, we must remember to praise children when they do well and be sure to tell them *how much we like it when*...they share their toys, for example, or when they do something kind or selfless.

Parents can be very upset and in denial when their child is in trouble at school. Of course, no parent wants to be invited for a meeting at school because their child has been identified as disruptive or a bully. It is not that uncommon for most children, even the well behaved ones, at some point to at least have joined in with some degree of bullying, so parents should not take offence and enable the behaviour by blindly defending it out of parental pride. Instead, at this pivotal point in a child's life, the most important thing is to respond positively and take action. Discover the root cause, whether that be peer pressure, a response to being bullied themselves, or a form of relief from tension. Whatever the reason, schools will have a disciplinary policy/plan, and it needs support from parents at home too, or it will not work. This is the most important step to ensure the life lesson is learnt and the bad behaviour is stopped; for the parental figures to show their child that even they cannot rescue them from the consequences of their own poor choices. Parents can do their best to make sure it does not ever get to this stage by showing a keen, regular interest in school life. Doing this will make it far easier to identify the warning signs, such as their child becoming stressed by peer pressure, or demonstrating envy. Only once the motives are understood, can that child's authority figures truly have a positive influence. A bully is nothing without peer pressure to maintain a gang or clique, and this will be more difficult if parents and schools are targeting peer pressure as a root cause of social degeneration.

It is important we do not overstep boundaries though and interfere with forming friendships. A common mistake is parents making judgements on families they do not know and trying to choose their child's friends for them, based on adult relationships or prejudices. Children feeling pressured to be friends with peers that they are not necessarily emotionally suited to, can force children to pretend to be someone they are not, via parent induced peer pressure. So long as we are teaching our children right from wrong, we must trust them to make their own decisions using their instincts when it comes to making friends, they will be the right ones for them at the time. If they turn out to be unwise, then this is a life lesson opportunity.

A brief history of education

For education to fulfil its potential and do its job with maximum efficiency, there should be little expense spared in making sure schools are the best state of the art environments imaginable, with the right people in place to teach and lead. However, when we explore how schooling has changed since its mandatory introduction, we find initiatives are surprisingly small and uninspired. In turn, this has a negative effect on student attitude towards learning. This engrained lack of enthusiasm for learning will likely stay with a person for the rest of their lives, which makes uninspiring, poorly equipped schools a serious, ongoing social threat.

For nearly a thousand years the wealthy elite were educated by private tutors, and at universities such as Oxford in England, and the University of Bologna in Italy. For the majority of the population, education was unavailable; and free public schooling was not widely available until the second half of the 1800s. This was even the case in the most developed parts of the world at the time. In England, the formation of 'ragged schools', an innovation of John Pounds, (1766-1839), accentuated the benefits of schooling everyone, not just the wealthy. His initiative would eventually lead to free schooling in England for every child. John was an altruistic individual who personally searched the streets of Portsmouth, England, taking dozens of children who were poor and homeless off the streets and into his school, where he taught them 'The three Rs' of education, reading, writing and arithmetic, giving them prospects to improve their circumstances. For millennia it was not even deemed worthwhile, by world leaders, to educate the lower class working citizens in the way that John took the selfless initiative to do. After all, the work that the majority people were going to be doing, when old enough, did not require them to be literate, or even to think for themselves, (better that they did not in many cases). So why waste time and money schooling the lower classes, many of which were statistically unlikely to survive childhood anyway, due to poor living conditions? An unfortunate attitude and yet another example of how our species has relentlessly held back social progress for everyone, like it did not really matter, in exchange for private, selfish gain for the minority.

In England, as with most developed countries, in the 21st century it is now a criminal offence not to send children to school, at least primary and secondary school, between the ages of 5 and 16. We trust that the law is there to protect our best interests and wellbeing and that school, as a public, government implemented service has been designed and tested against all other possibilities to be the most efficient that it can be at its purpose, which is, turning our children into adults with the skills, knowledge, motivation and direction to succeed to the best of their abilities in this life. But does school actually do this?

For hundreds of thousands of years, humans educated themselves through free play, exploration, hunting, storytelling and surviving. This is how we are evolved and adapted to learn best. Roughly 90-95 per cent of our species' time on this planet has been spent as hunter-gatherers, learning all that was needed about the world by experiencing it first-hand and mimicking elders. This carefree age came to an end approximately ten thousand years ago, with the invention of agriculture. When tribes exchanged hunting for farming, they inadvertently started the ball rolling on the path to becoming labourers and industrialists, enslaved by economists. After wandering the Earth freely for hundreds of millennia, humans settled down and got to work. There was no time in this new world for frivolous play, adventures, and daydreaming. Individuals who preoccupied themselves with such activities would have been considered detrimental to the new profit-driven society.

Following the abandonment of the nomadic way of life, maturing generations had to dedicate much of their time to learning the intensive, time consuming and monotonous skills that were required to yield successful crops. Farms teaching agriculture were perhaps the first kind of fixed learning environments and lessons would have been long and arduous. It was a worthwhile and desirable thing to be a farmer at this early time in human society, as it offered a big advantage over those who could not farm. Competing members of the species would depend on farmers for their living, and this is more true today than ever, as much of the world's food supply still comes from traditional farming. For the thousands of years that followed this revolutionary new way of living, the energy of children and young adults was exploited to be used for labour on farms across Europe. The next big change came at the dawn of the industrial revolution. The newly constructed mills and factories needed a workforce of strong, energetic children to boost their profits by keeping labour costs low. Still, the level of education beyond required practical skills was kept minimal, and this was intentional. The factory workers did not need creativity, literacy, ambition or great intellect. Men, women and children alike became dominated by inhumane, tireless machines. In the pursuit of economic and technological progress, people were seen by industrialists as mere parts of the machines they had created. It was not uncommon for children young as four years old to be worked to exhaustion in polluted factories. Obedience, punctuality, discipline and the ability to follow simple instructions to complete the repetitive tasks was adequate. Idleness replaced cruelty as the worst sin and terrified, impressionable children were even taught how much their judgemental Lord despises idle hands, as part of their 'Sunday school' education. Thankfully, this social martyrdom in the name of economic progress came to an end at the dawn of the 20th century, as technology advanced further and industry continued to be revolutionised, people were freed from enslavement and were given the opportunity to study for wider career prospects.

Some parts of Europe and some American states recognised the importance of education and introduced mandatory schooling as early as the 17th century, however, it did not become widespread until the 19th century. As the nation that had been leading the way in industry, I am going to use the UK as an example. At the end of the 19th century with industry growing and technology advancing faster than it ever had before, many of the farming and factory jobs that had supported families for generations were becoming automated, and with the 20th century looming it could potentially have left a massive workforce obsolete and unemployed. To avoid a multi-national crisis, it became a necessity to properly educate the population in preparation for a wider career opportunity. It took until the 20th century, but finally, there was free, compulsory education all the way up until teenage years in the UK. It was provided with good intentions to give children all the opportunities possible, whilst shaping them into moral, intellectual, competent and capable adults. Compared to today's range of vocation, school curriculum was initially narrow. For girls, the focus was reading, writing, housekeeping and needlework. Clearly, the curriculum was designed with some pre-determined conclusions about what girls were 'meant' to do after they completed their mandatory schooling.

In 1911, the census recorded the population of England and Wales at over 36 million, with a further 9 million people across Scotland and Ireland. With over 45 million people packed into this small nation, there was a realisation that some serious social issues needed addressing on a national level to avoid a crisis. Apart from educating children thoroughly, there were many other positive welfare decisions made in this period, including old-age pensions, maternity leave, child welfare, healthcare and unemployment insurance. Between 1901 and 1921 there was increasing widespread utilisation of technology. The technological improvements were faster in that 20 year period than they had been in the previous 200 years put together. Electricity, radio, motor vehicles, aeroplanes, were all becoming commonplace.

It was during this explosion of mass production that some unscrupulous individuals across the developing world saw an opportunity to become obscenely wealthy and had begun mass producing bombs, handguns, artillery, military vehicles, an other commodities of war, stockpiling them, ready to sell to both sides of any conflict that may arise. They had built the supply, now all that was needed was the demand, in the form of a prolonged and global conflict. All of the above was exploited to the fullest in making an unprecedented worldwide war, on an industrial scale, possible. During the horrific years of WW1, 1914 to 1918, there were obviously economic constraints and cutbacks to all the non-essentials of society that were not directly related to winning the war and saving lives back home. Children's education once more went to the back burner whilst the grown-ups of the world settled their differences in a war so abominable, it was responsible for the deaths of at least 16 million people. Over the duration, that averages out at 70 thousand people a week dying as a result of the conflict. Following WWI, an already suffering economy was devastated further by the 'Spanish Flu' pandemic, that tore across the world in 1918/19 killing at least three times as many than had died in the war. With no antibiotics to treat secondary bacterial infections, even otherwise healthy young people were not spared, which is why the mortality rate was around 10 per cent. Although primitive antibiotic treatments, such as applying various moulds and plant extracts to wounds when treating infections, were practised at least as far back as Ancient Egyptians times, people did not know the infections were caused by microscopic bacteria that can spread via the blood throughout the whole body, and it was not until 1928 that penicillin was first discovered by Alexander Fleming. The most fatal pandemic in history, 'The Black Death' which killed over half of Europe's entire population at the time, would never have occurred if the people of the 14th century had antibiotics. More than anything else in history, (with the exception of perhaps plumbing/sanitation and heating), antibiotics are significantly responsible for the population boom of the mid to late 20th century. In between fighting each other in WW1 and WWII, humans won the war against nature's number one ally in population control, bacteria. Until 1928, infections that we now consider straightforward to treat, such as bacterial pneumonia, were the number one cause of human death in the developed world. It was not until the second world war was nearly over, and the population began to boom, that it became necessary for education to be taken seriously again and compulsory secondary school leaver age was raised to 15 in 1944. By the 1970s it was raised to 16, where it still stands today in the UK and many other countries. Although, since 2013, to combat unemployment after leaving school, further education is now enforced, unless the school leaver has an apprenticeship or work placement already arranged to occupy themselves.

With the rise of schooling in the 19th and 20th centuries, the design of the classroom became a reflection of the child's workplace, adopting methods that had been used in factories. Those initial ideas, despite long since outdated, have never left the school system entirely and are still present in many schools to this day. From the layout of the classroom, (rows of desks reminiscent of production lines), to how the children must address the teachers, "Yes Sir" or "Yes Miss". There is strict routine, and a timetable enforced by a ringing bell to signal lunch/bathroom break or the end of the workday. Think about how many modern workplaces still have a ringing bell or designated timeframes to eat? There is even a strict, often monochrome, uniform policy in many schools around the world.

Schools are not reflections of the modern workplace. The curriculum is much broader than it was 100 years ago, with creative subjects such as art and music becoming part of mainstream education. However, tedious repetition and memorisation of a very rigid curriculum, in the core subjects, appears to be what counts above all else. In the UK, the most important part of school is achieving the highest number of General Certificates of Secondary Education in the GCSE Examinations taken at the very end of the final school year after around twelve years of preparing and practising for them. Final year examinations have been removed in many countries and, I will get to reviewing the success of this initiative shortly.

Exams rely on repetition and memory rather than genuine intelligence and/or creativity. Children from exam-focused schools leave with a piece of paper containing a handful of numbers determining how competent they are *supposed* to be at each subject that they took an exam for. The pressure that is put on children to achieve the highest number possible is considered unacceptable by many parents and teachers alike. Even more unacceptable are the standard attainment tests, commonly known as SATs, taken by ten-year-old students at the end of primary education. Many children will move into secondary education under the impression they are already failures because of these tests. The most imaginative children, whose instincts urge them constantly to play freely and explore the world on their own, are effectively crushed during their school years. They have two choices on how to react to this kind of strict structure. Either rebel or do their best to comply and struggle, whilst pretending to be something they are not. Children are not meant to be in this kind of environment, just as they were not meant to be working in factories or labouring in fields. Right into the 21st century, free will was being, literally, physically beaten out of children by teachers and schoolmasters. The cowardly abuse was not just tolerated by the governing bodies and parents alike but seemed to actually be encouraged, as it was believed to be beneficial in the long run. To quote: *Proverbs 13:24 - "Whoever spares the rod hates his son, but he who loves him is diligent to discipline him"*. In England, it was not until 1986 in public schools, and 1998 in private schools that corporal punishment was finally banned in England. This was 200 years after Poland set an example as the first country to ban it. The level of psychological damage done to generations of children over the last 200 years whilst schools were failing to deliver on their good intentions, is irreversible. For a long time, the most memorable lesson children learnt in school was, it is acceptable to commit verbal and physical assault to those more vulnerable than you. Shockingly, corporal punishments are still legal in some parts of North America and Australia, whilst remaining commonplace in a number of African, Asian, and Middle Eastern schools.

Ongoing failures in the post-industry classroom

Although inflicting physical abuse on students has been illegal in most of the industrialised since the beginning of the 21st century, it is still in living memory for many people, and the mentally damaging effects remain circulating in society.

The damage to children now is mental rather than physical; this is mostly due to the very nature of school, rather than any deliberate mental abuse. Learning is challenging, and harder for some than others. Children whose learning styles are so strongly revolved around play and who struggle to adapt to classroom settings are labelled, diagnosed and sometimes medicated. Most children, even those who are naturally book smart and desperately try their very best, for fear of disappointing their authority figures, will find school a hard and stressful time, due to the competitive strain the current school system can put on students. Even from as young as four-year-old classes, the students are quickly segregated into ability groups, (sets), based on teacher assumptions of what children are capable of. Children placed in the lower sets have automatic constraints placed upon them, capping their potential, and only need to achieve to a level of what is expected from a lower set child for the school to be deemed as succeeding. What is more, it is not done discreetly; the children are well aware they have been put into this hierarchy. The 'smarter' children will often take great pleasure in letting the 'underachievers' know this. The children at the bottom become anxious, the ones at the top become egotistical and narcissistic, and the ones in the middle will often suffer too, from a lack of attention. So we have 4 year old children who have only been at school for a matter of months and they are already having their future decided for them and are developing mental health issues and/or personality disorders. Yet, these procedures are something that all children are forced to abide by and get used to. The ability sets are an attempt to solve a practical problem, even in private schools there are ability sets and this is because the funding, time and energy needed to develop tailored learning for each and every student individually is deemed too great and complex, so it is easier to group children together and tailor the learning to 5 or 6 small groups instead. In the past, lower sets have even been refused exam entry to avoid them dragging average school test scores down.

To be classed as achieving, there is a way children are told to learn and a deadline of when they are told they need to have learnt it by. Lessons are very specific, rigid and do not change all that much over the years. Teachers have a small amount of leeway in their own classrooms but at the end of the day they have to teach the curriculum and most will opt for the 'old school' or by the book way for an easy life. No one learns to the best of their ability like this, though. It is known that even adults do not learn well, or trust information given, from someone they do not like or do not respect. This is the same in the workplace. People work for people - working hardest and with the most initiative for bosses who they respect and want to impress, or to help succeed. Some inspirational, passionate, talented and emotionally aware teachers will realise that it is important to be respected and liked by their students to get the best out of them and will dedicate a lot of time to get to know each individual child's learning style and alter their approach accordingly, but this is challenging in large classes, even with an assistant.

Some teachers may use more innovative techniques, such as explore and play, to get children engaged and focused during lessons that are very theoretical. However, generally, this is not allowed as a theme but rather just as a novelty every now and again. Sadly these teacher's spirits will be easily crushed by budget constraints, overpopulated classes, disapproval from lazier, envious colleagues or by the knowledge that when the students progress to the next year, their new teacher will only revert them back to 'old school' anyway. One good apple in a dozen is not enough; the rot of the others will consume the individual.

So one change we need, to assist in our goal of developing H-utopians through education, is a re-defining of the teaching profession, including a reformation of teacher training courses at universities, followed by a retraining of all current primary and secondary educators to calibrate on new methods.

There have been attempts to reform schools, but they have as yet not been fully successful. Montessori schools, for example, are considerably more aligned to human nature, and the students tend to respond well to this. However, the schools have received criticism for not preparing children thoroughly enough for traditional examinations with their more relaxed approach. Envisioned by Dr Maria Montessori, she developed a child-centred approach that takes into account the development of the child, psychologically, physically, socially, emotionally and cognitively. The key principles are hands-on learning, through cooperative and self-directed activities. The child gets to make the creative choices in their learning; the teacher just encourages age-appropriate, fun activities to guide their choices. If nothing else, children coming from Montessori schools will come away with an invaluable principle that will keep them welcoming learning with open arms for the rest of their lives: learning is associated with fun and positive feelings. Whereas the children in traditional schools, especially those who were not traditionally book smart and struggled with exams, risk coming away having realised learning is tedious hard work, feeling resentment against the authority figures who failed them, and will perhaps then be inclined to reject further teaching and knowledge, even forgetting what they did manage to memorise in order the get the highest possible number in their final exams. **If children leave school only remembering one lesson, it needs to be that learning is fun**.

That is not to say that school should not be challenging for students, but it should be equally challenging and rewarding for their teachers and if the only criticism of the Montessori approach is that it does not prepare children properly for traditional exams, then maybe it should be the exams that go? I would go so far as to say exams are detrimental to society; children are taught to fear exams, (or at least to fear failure of them), and therefore they fear education, becoming angry at themselves for failing and hateful towards those who succeed. This causes a dangerous resentment of the very thing that can save society and ensure H-utopia is realised.

The blame for turning schools into 'exam factories' lies at the feet of power-hungry, vote chasing politicians who instruct governing bodies such as, the Office for Standards in Education, Children's Services and Skills, known as Ofsted, in the UK. Because Ofsted are forced to serve government policy set by ignorant politicians who have become so focused on statistics and figures, such as attendance, exam results, and school league tables, to impress voters with conditioned, old fashioned values, that they have forgotten the little human beings the numbers represent. They have forced schools to prioritise getting statistics to look good over genuine human development, (and compassion, when it comes to childhood illness). This has reduced educators to data performance managers rather than what they should be, which is inspirational and malleable trainers that have a genuine intellect in their chosen fields. As a result, it has left less time in the school timetable for anything not directly related to passing standardised tests and an unfair amount of pressure being put on children by overly stressed teachers. Furthermore, schools that have previously attained a rating of 'good' or higher in Ofsted's vague rating system, are perhaps only inspected for a single day every few years, and the school is pre-warned about the visit when it does come. This renders the inspections near enough pointless and as a result, schools with behavioural issues, substandard teaching and inadequate staffing are slipping through the net undetected for years at a time, potentially failing generations of students. The headteachers or principles, motivated by a fear of potentially losing their livelihood if they do not pass the inspections, will pull out all the stops for a visit, making the school appear to be running extraordinarily well, only to relax back into complacency after the visit.

Home-schooling is becoming increasingly popular, with an increasing number of parents taking their children out of school, choosing to home-school them instead. The reason? A lot of the time it is out of desperation because their children are developing mental health issues from the horrors we have discussed so far. Although home-schooling may be a quick fix to solve some of the problems raised for an individual child, I do not believe it is the right solution to home-school our children, as the social aspect and time away from parents is an important part of development that children just will not get if they are staying at home. Besides this, at some point, home-schooled children will inevitably have to re-enter the world they have been withdrawn from. We cannot hide individual children from society's problems and expect them to go back into a flawed society as adults, trusting them to adapt healthily. Instead, we need to face up to the many problems now, demanding reform and better regulation by authorities.

Doing it right - what can we do to help produce H-utopians through education?

So it is very easy to point the finger at who is to blame: uninspired or lazy teachers, complacent headteachers, self-serving politicians, uncaring government bodies obsessed with statistics, a lack of funding and improper training. But what can we do to fix all of this? Let us not overcomplicate things; the vision statement is simple: create a better society through better education by making the basic standard of education high across the world for everyone. High standard of education allows for a well-balanced, well-adjusted people to function and be happy in society, and in their interpersonal relationships. Furthermore, a better focused and consistent education system is less likely to fail when it comes to discovering and nurturing geniuses, so they will be free to contribute their full potential to society.

How we make this vision a reality starts with setting simple targets. In matters academic, physical, social and emotional, we should be setting tailored targets for fulfilling potential in individual children. It is vital the actions needed to achieve these targets are specific, measurable, achievable, realistic and time-bound, (S.M.A.R.T). Most importantly, the desired goals of children are discussed and agreed during regular one to one coaching sessions and aligned with parents during meetings, so the learning remains relevant and consistent at home.

There are many success stories from countries around the world that have trialled various ways of educating their citizens, and it has paid off. We can draw wisdom from these and combine all of the great ideas to agree on global standards of education, with the aim to produce a focused and cooperative civilisation. Here are some examples of a progressive approach to education:

- In the USA and Taiwan, there are no final year school exams. This seriously reduces the burden on teachers and students. Instead, credit is awarded for projects, initiative, and completing school work. In the USA there *are* tests such as American College Testing (ACT) and the Scholastic Aptitude Test (SAT) that universities may require to evaluate candidates, however.

- In Denmark, education at every level is free of charge, and high schools place great importance on vocational subjects that focus on preparing students for real-life responsibilities and occupation.

- In Singapore, schools have moved away from repetitive tasks to concentrate on cultivating life skills, teamwork and building a moral conscience so that the country produces responsible citizens. Lessons in moral science, music, art and healthcare are of vital importance.

- In Finland, the school starter age is seven years old, and school days are only five hours long. As one of the top performers in education globally, schooling is shorter than in most countries, but evidently, it is more efficient.

This does not help the rest of the world who remain stuck in the past with an authority intent on preserving outdated practices and principles based on misplaced trust in statistics. Perhaps education is too important to be left to individual governments picking and choosing its own rules and setting its own standards.

An option for the future could be to establish a global council of accomplished, innovative educators and phycologists from the world's most academically successful countries, who could decide the standards for education, removing the blame and the burden of trial and error from individual government authorities, who may be scared to take risks incase they compromise their political status. The benefits and drawbacks of specialists making political decisions relevant to their field, instead of politicians, is something I will come back to later on.

There are so many practical changes we can make to enhance the efficiency and productivity of schools right now, and I will suggest a handful of ideas that are totally achievable and realistic. They are by no means completely original or brand new, some are even already in place in certain forward-thinking countries, but they should be implemented in every school worldwide; there are millions of like-minded individuals crying out for reform, and this just goes to show how blatant it is that schooling is being done wrong and it is something we simply cannot afford to get wrong any longer. Much of this is going to be down to the governing bodies and world leaders, to realise what is important, take some risks, follow good examples, and channel the funds desperately needed into schools. Nothing can be more important and beneficial in the long run, than getting the education of our citizens right. Investing in better education now will reduce strain on health and social services, as well as lowering crime rates, slowing population growth down to a sustainable level and ultimately producing a more successful civilisation for the future. Education is our number one ally for helping us to reach H-utopia, if we use it to its potential.

Setting children up for success, physically

First and foremost, children need feeding nutritious meals for breakfast and lunch to be able to maintain optimum levels of concentration throughout the school day. Every day, across the world, many children are sent to school hungry, with no food, not enough food, or not enough money to purchase a school dinner. Some schools may provide free school dinners for certain age groups, but currently, there is a stigma around free school meals because only children from poorer families are entitled to them. There is an opportunity here to solve a social issue and remove this stigma by allowing all children a free breakfast and dinner at school. There is no extra money to be found by governments or parents to do this. The parents should save money theoretically by not having to purchase breakfast and lunch for their children five days a week. Instead, the school buys it, with government money collected as additional taxes. The money comes from tax-paying parents, and the general public, as usual, but parents should have spent this money either way on feeding their children, whether they were at school or not. At least this way, it is ensured that the money is directed to the right place, where children will all definitely be fed both vital meals properly whilst at school, instead of having the money for breakfast and lunch vanish on luxury items, sweets, or cheap fast food options that some parents choose to pass to their children through the bars of the playground at dinner time.

Once children are fed properly, then it is time to ensure their learning environments are up to scratch. Even well into the 21st century, due to low budgets and broken new equipment that cannot be fixed, teachers have been observed resorting to decades-old chalkboards, overhead projectors and video cassettes in their lessons! Is it any wonder that many 21st century children are so uninspired by education? If it appears that adults fail to take school seriously, or think that it is not important enough to invest money in, then why should children be expected to take it seriously? We should be utilising technology to its fullest potential in schools. Students must sometimes feel like they are going back in time when leaving their state of the art 21st century homes and walking into their 20th century schools. So how can we bring schools into the present day? Below are just a handful of suggestions that would make a huge positive change in student attitudes to school and help to improve the next generation of human beings:

Online lessons - audio recordings of the teachers lectures/class discussions uploaded to an intra-web that only students of that class have access to, (via personal identity logins of course). It would not only help to monitor teacher performance and consistency, but would also be beneficial for absent students to catch up, and use as a tool for revisionary purposes by making it repeatable on demand.

Subject matter expert lessons from third parties – broadcasted in school auditoriums via weblink and hosted by representatives, on location, at inspirational places that many children would normally not get to see, such as NASA, NUMA, London Zoo, the Egyptian Antiquities Museum, the Large Hadron Collider CERN and any other multitude of cultural and scientific locations around the world. Where the funding, distance or practicability means it is not viable to take children to these amazing places, the places can be brought to the children via the internet.

More use of technology - tablets or touch screen laptops should be used to complete schoolwork from around age ten onwards. At the end of each lesson, the students upload what they have done to the class mainframe so it can be reviewed, backed up and added to their own electronic portfolios. Handwriting should, of course, be practised still, but let us be honest, typing is more efficient than handwriting will ever be.

Removal or at least reformation of standardised tests - when Frederick J. Kelly invented the multiple-choice test, it was to solve a national crisis at the time. The number of students attending secondary school had risen from 200,000 to 1.5 million in the space of just 25 years. Kelly, famously, was not a fan of his own creation, reportedly saying the tests were *"too crude to be used"*. Despite this, these outdated industrial age remnants remain an overrated part of school to this day in most countries. These tests are done on children as young as five years old! Are we really testing the students or is this just an easy way to monitor teacher job performance without having to observe them working? It is a waste of valuable real-life learning time repeating over and over what might come up on tests that are simply a way for governments to monitor school performance and produce leader boards. It is totally unacceptable to put primary school children under this kind of pressure for the convenience of adults.

Class sizes need to be capped - classes of thirty, forty plus students, and merging classes/year groups together is not acceptable. This is regularly done, not because schools are too small but due to a lack of funding for teachers, assistants and classroom materials. In an ideal world, class sizes need to be around fifteen to twenty students of mixed gender. The age gap between the oldest to youngest student in the same class needs to be no more than one full year maximum. If we need to build new classrooms and train more teachers, then so be it. I am sure we would find teaching a far more desirable and satisfying profession in the reformed kind of school environment we are aiming for.

More emphasis on philosophy - lessons that open up moral scenario debate, role play and group discussions can improve a child's emotional intelligence, empathy, tolerance towards others, open-mindedness and ability to cope with changes, and challenges. Philosophy should not be underestimated and it needs to be a bigger part of the curriculum from a young age.

Healthcare education - for ages eleven plus, there needs to be more attention on personal healthcare education. Including the effects on the body, and on society, that obesity, drugs, alcohol and smoking cause, accompanied with basic medical training, as a doctor or nurse would receive. The impacts people that make poor lifestyle choices have on society must be made candidly clear to children, not to traumatise them, but to warn them. This will help to reduce a massive amount of avoidable strain on healthcare and social services. Basic first aid has already been introduced into the curriculum in some countries, so this is a promising start. Reproduction, contraception and the effects of over-population on society would also fall into the category of healthcare education. As would mental health. It is very important children are taught to cope with fear and stress. A fearful society is doomed to be an angry/aggressive one, dominated and crippled by hatred and intolerance that stem from fear.

Mortality - as morbid as it may sound, we must teach more about death – we cannot ignore the basic fact of life that everything that is born will one day die. Life cycles come under the categories of science and philosophy. Death is the one thing that unifies every living creature, and it is the one thing that can therefore be used to exploit and control every member of the human race. Whilst we treat death as a taboo subject, it poses a serious risk to H-utopia and is one of the most likely reasons we will fall into dystopia. If we train our children now, with the opportunity we never had, to embrace life's natural cycle rather than fear it, then it will protect them against future malevolent powers that may otherwise exploit human fear around mortality and the unknown.

Preparation for the workplace and life in the real world - apart from work experience placements in late secondary education and higher education, there are very little opportunities in the school curriculum to prepare for life in the real world, with real workplace responsibilities. There needs to be more emphasis on career preparation, and the most important part of this is practising teamwork and collaboration. There are no exams or qualifications from primary or secondary schools that demonstrate an individual's ability to work within a team; something that is massively encouraged the day we leave school to start work, but during school, strangely, is dis-encouraged when it comes to homework, coursework, exams and classwork. To work together, confer or collaborate without express permission is deemed cheating and punishable, forming a very 'dog eat dog', socially incapable people, unprepared for building a successful working environment. As we discovered earlier on, Albert Einstein would never have been able to develop his theory of general relativity without combining the knowledge and theories of his mathematical predecessors. Ideas and inventions that can change the world for the better belong to humanity, not to any one individual. When we collaborate freely, we can achieve greater things and far more efficiently than working alone.

Rearrangement of classroom layouts - as I have already pointed out, classrooms in many schools around the world are still laid out as if our children are preparing for work on factory production lines. The layout of an ideal learning environment should be thus: students are seated at a single large joining semi-circular desk area, facing each other, as well as the teacher. Alternatively, in some younger age groups/creative subjects, it may be more practical to have several individual circular desks, with space for the teacher to sit amongst students, rather than hover over them. The desired result is to make students realise they are one team. The seating needs to be comfortable and modern. The classroom well maintained with bright and airy décor. An association with outdoors and nature; greens, blues and the presence of plants has been shown to have a calming effect. The classroom should be air quality monitored and climate-controlled. Studies have shown that students learn best in classrooms kept between 20°C and 23°C. This is common sense anyway as we know that when we are too cold or too hot, we find it harder to concentrate. No specific rule for a seating plan is required. Children of different academic ability should be mixed up, though. Trying to categorise everyone into separate table groups based on standardised testing is esteem damaging and overly competitive. Collaboration, debate and discussions between all students should be encouraged in every lesson. The children who are quicker learners should be encouraged to help their peers who are struggling, not be separated from them based on assumptions made by the teachers very early on.

A less formal relationship with teachers - there should be no requirement for children to address their teachers as Sir, Mr or Ms. Children are more likely to communicate openly with, and respect, someone who respects them in return as an equal, rather than subordinates.   There is, of course, a level of authority and professionalism that cannot be overstepped, but students are less likely to rebel against the educator when they are being treated as equal human beings.   Again, in the workplace, with the exception of megalomaniacs, most good bosses have enough self-confidence and charisma to be comfortable on first name terms with their subordinates.

Educational homework holidays – Educational holidays during the academic year should actually be encouraged as part of the curriculum, (with limits in place of course). It is crucial parents get involved in educating their children at home. Schools can only do so much if the parental figures are not bothering at home to train their children in the same way. If a parent wanted to, they should be allowed to take their child out of school for a week to admire the wonders of the Acropolis Museum in Athens, or the Uffizi Gallery in Florence, or to marvel at the Great Pyramid of Giza, or venture to Peru for a once in a lifetime pilgrimage to the monuments of Machu Picchu, or even just to visit more modest attractions on day trips, such as city museums, nature reserves and historical sites. Every child should get the opportunity to have unforgettable experiences that enhance their cultural appreciation, emotional intelligence and thirst for knowledge. It should be met with support from schools to arrange these, not truancy fines and ignorant refusals. Ask any adult to recall the most memorable week from their childhood, and it will most likely be a holiday they were taken on. Not their mathematics lessons from grade seven term two week three, on a Tuesday afternoon. Once our children start school we do not get to spend as much time with them as we should. We have school holidays, but restricted finances can prevent parents from utilising them well, due to steep price hikes on travel, accommodation and attractions for the holiday periods. Of course, there will have to be rules for this to work. For instance, holidays cannot be taken either side of an already allocated school holiday, and to compensate for lost school time that this holiday would take away, the lengthy end of academic year holiday could be shortened by a week. Then every child could be allowed their week allowance per year to book off wherever wanted, as long as requested in advance and the reason for time off involves an educational experience. Children could even document the holiday as a project. This idea has the added bonus of saving countries from coming to a holt in school holidays when all parents are attempting to squeeze in their time off work at the same time! The reason in-term holidays and absences are such a major problem for schools at the moment is because of the pressure from governing bodies, to maintain acceptable controls and statistics from standardised tests. Remove the tests, and this will not be such an issue to implement.

We have addressed the basics of enhancing the school environment, now let us take a look at some under-appreciated subjects that currently do not get enough attention, especially in primary education:

Languages and multicultural communication - there is no point leaving languages until secondary education if primary education has not focused on them. Children should start learning at least two widely spoken languages, on top of their own, from ages four onwards. It has been proven that the younger children start learning other languages, the more naturally it comes to them. Learning languages from a young age will help to combat ignorance, xenophobia and hopefully encourage more cultural interaction. European schools tend to do this, but in English speaking countries we tend to shy away from learning other languages. On top of spoken languages, we need a way to communicate globally with anyone of any language at any time, but without losing our cultural identity. Clearly, it is not humanely possible to learn every language, and the answer is not the impersonal, ignorant, sometimes inaccurate translation app on your smartphone either. It is something much simpler, personable and natural: **sign language**. A great idea would be to unify a globally understood, comprehensive sign language that could be taught in schools as part of the mandatory curriculum worldwide. Not everyone can learn every language of every culture but we can all learn the unified language of signing during our school years. This will help to bring together the species as a whole and encourage international travel to genuine culturally immersive destinations, rather than just to sunny resorts with interpreters on hand to act as a culture buffer.

Music - learning an instrument, (the triangle does not count) - young minds are like sponges, they are evolved to absorb and retain knowledge at an incredible rate compared with adults. The perfect time to learn an instrument is as soon as a child is physically able to. Music and composing it together in groups is one of the oldest forms of intelligent social interaction that humans invented. It encourages cooperation, not competition. If a child shows an interest in music, they should be supported in any training required to learn instruments, whether it be the piano, guitar, violin, or singing. It really does not matter, as long as the interest is being nurtured.

Personal, social and emotional development - this is one of the most important subjects that really prepares children for real-life after school, and for interacting better with others in society. Yet, this vital subject gets very little attention in school, and the lessons revolving around it are often quite dull and theoretical for children. There is no reason they cannot be practical. Lessons focusing on PSED can include everything from team-building exercises to basic doctoring, healthcare and first aid. PSED is a broad subject that can be merged to make it relevant to every other subject in some way. If used to its potential, not only can PSED ease burdens on healthcare and other government services but also increase understanding and tolerance of phycological and mental health disorders. Another topic that comes under PSED, and desperately needs to be covered in more detail, is migration. With immigration rising, it is important children learn about the truths and motivations behind migrating people, enshrining multi-culturalism and reducing xenophobic responses to 'outsiders'. According to the 2019 UNESCO Global Education Monitoring report, at the time of the report being made, there were more than 25 million refugees and nearly 60 million people displaced by war and natural disasters worldwide. With over half of these refugees being school-age. The report emphasises an opportunity to make something good out of a tragic situation by harnessing the potential of displaced people, using education to enhance respect for diversity. Any host country accepting refugees has a duty to carry on educating the school-aged and a responsibility to make sure their own citizens are socially and mentally prepared to welcome and accept their new peers and neighbours.

History - real history, not the tiresome, traditional and often one-sided history that has been taught in schools from a curriculum that in itself is historical, using textbooks that are antique. History is not as set in stone as many historians would have us believe. For instance, much of what we know about historical wars comes from the victor's point of view and is most likely littered with embellished detail or entirely fabricated stories that totally glorify one side and entirely demonise the other. History is one of the most influential parts of our lives. What happened in the past has made our present and continues to shape our future. We can learn a lot from real historical events; especially the ones where human actions were questionable. These should not be shied away from in education. Things are never as black and white as accounts of war would suggest. This is a perfect opportunity to open up philosophical debate in the classroom and prevent the mistakes of history repeating themselves.

Sociology - with the world suffering from so many escalating problems, sociology has never been more important, yet schools barely scratch the surface of this subject's potential. The aspiration of sociology is to find solutions to all of societies problems through methods of scientific research into matters that include human ecology, population, culture, phycology, personal interactions and social change. It is crucially important for children to begin analysing the world around them as sociologists, offering them the perspective they need to make decisions in day to day life, whilst being fully aware of all potential consequences of their decisions. The subject offers invaluable insight into how they will be able to progress in their adult lives successfully, through cooperation and positivity towards others. With such widespread subject matter, sociology can be applied to any area of learning, never missing an opportunity to set children on the right course.

Theology – studying the nature of what we call God, how human faith is expressed in all cultures, and the impact this has had, and continues to have on society. It is vitally important children are taught theology, and given the chance to debate the influence religion has on humanity. A thorough theological education will help children to understand traditions, morals, laws, wars, history and cultures of the world. The study of theology encompasses a wide range of topics, including history, sociology and philosophy. Only by studying theology can we expect children to have the knowledge and wisdom required to compare the different religions in a balanced and unbiased way, so they can make informed spiritual decisions in their lives.

Philosophical study - the study and evaluation of philosophical works from around the world such as Marcus Aurelius's Meditations, Lucretius - on the nature of things and the Chinese, Tao Te Ching. Unless philosophy is your chosen interest at university level, or you devote a large amount of your personal time to studying it, then it is unlikely you will have much knowledge or interest on the subject. It is certainly nothing you will have learnt about in traditional Western curriculum during your primary and secondary schooling. Well, I suggest philosophy should be thoroughly covered by traditional curriculum, from a young age, when children are still open-minded to ways of life other than their own. Naturally, our children's teachers would have to undergo philosophical training as part of their teacher training for this subject to be implemented successfully. It is absolutely essential to educate children philosophically.

Why is philosophy so important? Marcus Aurelius, during his time as the head of the Roman Empire, was arguably the most powerful man in the world; yet, even with all the wealth and power of the colossal Roman Empire at his disposal, he was able to be the great philosopher leader that would fit Plato's description of an ideal head of state. Marcus Aurelius was a wise man and a student of philosophy. By mentally training himself, he knew he could rule justly, whilst being less susceptible to the evil that can consume and corrupt individuals who are thrust into positions of unrivalled power. It would have been all too easy for Aurelius to rule as a tyrant dictator, manipulating his citizens into submission, for selfish reasons. The one thing tyrants tend to do is underestimate the power of the masses they rule over. When enslaved, there is only so much tyranny people will endure before they rebel, and to maintain order in such an unstable society is impossible, even for the most powerful people in the world. Marcus Aurelius was perceptive enough to realise his power would be short-lived, and his immortal memory tarnished, had he chose to rule in such a criminal way. Aurelius managed to resist the temptations that lesser men in his position succumbed to; his successors *would* become egotistical tyrants that ultimately contributed to the fall of Rome and the start of the Dark Ages - a time where civilisation had to practically start from scratch in parts of Europe.

Marcus Aurelius's wisdom was written down in his own personal journal, which was published centuries after his death in the book, *Meditations*. Now over 2000 years after Aurelius's death, it is still in print and relevant to us today. Despite being full to the brim of wisdom, it is not even a small part of mainstream education though. If the themes of classroom activities considered philosophical input of equal importance as mathematics and literacy, and every human being trained their mind in the way Aurelius did, and if philosophical works, (both contemporary and ancient), were reviewed and debated in schools, and if the students were inspired enough by philosophically minded teachers to live their lives better because of it, then it is inevitable that the world would improve significantly just with this one action alone. There are a lot of 'ifs' in that sentence and I appreciate it is a bold statement so I will give a couple of examples from the book, *Meditations,* to illustrate how relevant Aurelius's logic and wisdom still is today.

"The Universe is change, life is an opinion".

This is my favourite quote, for its simplicity and importance. By its very nature, the Universe itself *is* change. It has never been still, for its entire 13.8 billion year existence. *Progressive* change, however, is up to us. Change can be for better or worse. I already touched on earlier, how we were hindered as a species for centuries, (and still are), by technophobia, and the taboo subject of religious criticism. Heresy was a dangerous crime to commit, and it was the reason many scholars would have kept their mouths shut, saving their own lives and careers by doing so. After thousands of years of oppression, technology, science, medicine and astronomy have finally been allowed to emerge and flourish. In only a matter of decades, we have drastically changed our entire lives in almost every aspect, from communication, to entertainment, to travel, to prolonging life. We cannot stop change, but we can decide whether it is for the better and how well we accept it. On the one hand, we could be negative, fear it, becoming angry and resentful, feeding a stagnant society. Or, we could be positive, see it as a new opportunity to learn and grow both as an individual, and as a species.

"We live only in the present, in this fleet-footed moment. The rest is lost and behind us or ahead of us and may never be found."

Everyone is guilty at some point of dwelling over a past that cannot be changed and thinking about a future they will not live to see. Even Marcus Aurelius was guilty of it. That was why he had to write this in his journal - to remind himself to keep his thoughts on the present day. Yes, learn from the past and yes, have goals for the future but above all, focus on the present, enjoy what you have, and think about what you can do right now to make the lives of you and others around you better for tomorrow.

"Never regard as a benefit to yourself anything which will force you at some point to break your faith, to leave integrity behind, to hate, suspect, or curse another, to dissemble, to covet anything needing the secrecy of walls and drapes".

Quite simply, we should never allow our integrity to be compromised by our primal instincts.

"At break of day, when you are reluctant to get up, have this thought ready to mind: I am getting up for a man's work. Do I still then resent it, if I am going out to do what I was born for, the purpose for which I was brought into the world? Or was I created to wrap myself in blankets and keep warm? But this is more pleasant. Were you born for pleasure – all for feeling, not for action? Can you not see plants, birds, ants, spiders, bees all doing their own work, each helping in their own way to order the world? And then you do not want to do the work of a human being – you do not hurry to the demands of your own nature. But one needs rest too. One does indeed: I agree. But nature has set limits to this too, just as it has to eating and drinking, and yet you go beyond these limits, beyond what you need. Not in your actions, though, not any longer: here you stay below your capability. The point is that you do not love yourself – otherwise you would love both your own nature and her purpose for you. Other men love their own pursuit and absorb themselves in its performance to the exclusion of bath and food but you have less regard for your own nature than the smith has for his metal work, the dancer for his dancing, the money grubber for his money, the exhibitionist for his little moment of fame. Yet these people, when impassioned give up food and sleep for the promotion of their pursuits: and you think social action less important, less worthy of effort?"

The point is, to fulfil our potential as human beings and contribute to the greater good of the species in any way we can. I am sure we all know a few entitled or lazy individuals who could have benefitted from enlightenment absorbing wisdom from this passage in their youth. Training this kind of positive mentality will set up our young humans to succeed in their learning at school; and for their whole lives.

So far, I have made improving humanity through education sound straightforward, but there is one big problem that stands in the way of everything suggested, and it all boils down to practicability; a lack of funding, a lack of teachers, a lack of school places, a lack of motivation and a lack of room in the curriculum to encompass such variety and freedom. Does the practicability issue mean we should just not bother then? Give up on trying to change education drastically and carry on judging our children just on the ABCs and 123s? Of course not, as I said from the start, investment in the next generation is the wisest of all investments, and we cannot afford to *not* spend money on it and update it. It is up to governing bodies to realise this and provide its citizens with schools and the equipment needed. In a reformed school system with better incentives for teachers, the profession will become far more desirable and the industry much more competitive than it currently is. As for lack of time in the curriculum to freely explore all these new areas of learning, we only run out of time in the school day because we are obsessively practising repetition of core subjects to prepare students for the current focus, which is passing examinations, rather than succeeding in real life, or contributing to social progress. With a change in our philosophy and re-assessing our priorities, this problem is also voided.

Who is teaching our children?

With the school environment enhanced and school lessons improved, now we need to address the competence of school teachers. Currently, it is very much up to the ethos of individual teachers as to whether children are pushed to fulfil their potential, or if they are only taught to where they *'need'* to be according to standard government guidelines. A passive, uninspired teacher who does not appreciate the immense responsibility to society that they have, may be content in just doing their job to the minimum acceptable level in order to meet standard guidelines. These kinds of teachers do not belong in the industry. A lackadaisical and unambitious attitude, from someone who plays a vital role in forming the minds of children, is a dangerous thing indeed. Perhaps people displaying these characteristics would be better suited to working on production lines filling quotas, rather than being trusted with the complex responsibility of preparing the next generation of human beings.

There is no point in updating the school system and the curriculum if the way we select, train and motivate teachers remains unchanged. Before someone should even be allowed to start training as a teacher, they should have to undergo and successfully pass several tests, including a phycological screening, an emotional intelligence (EIQ) test and a general IQ test. The latter actually being the least important of the three tests.

Along with bigger budgets for learning, salaries for teachers need to be raised to make the sector more competitive amongst scholars and to allow for the extra expertise required to be taught. The salaries of teachers vary wildly depending on what level of education they teach at and whether the school is privately run or public, but what we are aiming for is an increased basic standard of education, and we will not achieve this whilst some teachers are being paid far less than others. We need to be setting schools up for success with genuinely intelligent, emotionally aware, and properly motivated teachers, (and teachers assistants). Currently, government employed teachers are on a modest national wage considering their immense responsibility, and the support staff employed are very often taken on as apprentices to save money. We should be providing the highest quality of education possible to the next generation of humans but sadly government funded schools are instead forced to scrimp and save like a budget motel or discount store! To reiterate, teachers have the most vital role in society, as the inspiration, knowledge and philosophies they instil on their students will determine how well they are able to contribute to society. Therefore, motivation to do their best for every student is the most important thing that a teacher should have.

Every student is different, with different talents, learning styles, weaknesses, and strengths that need to be adapted to. A teacher's job should not just be to stand in front of a group of children and lecture them on prescribed topics from within the curriculum, setting standard tasks and tests, splitting them up into ability groups to make teacher performance monitoring easier and to make test results look more impressive. Currently, a teacher's primary goal is repeating over and over until enough of what they are saying sinks in for the children to pass the standardised tests and achieve an acceptable target relative to their ability group. Whether they forget it all when they stop having it repeated to them is not important, and they likely will forget it all, because they are not learning how to do something, they are learning how to pass tests. The job of a teacher, powered by self-motivation, should be to create an enthusiastic and interesting environment conducive for learning, where everyone can be successful at every subject.   This is not an unrealistic expectation; motivation is contagious, and it will rub off on all of the students. Even if students were not interested in the subject before, a good teacher will inspire interest and get them succeeding.

Students affect the emotional processes of their teachers, and their teacher reciprocates, affecting the students back. A classroom can become a very negative learning environment very quickly if the teacher's EIQ is low.   If teachers are trained well in emotional intelligence, they will be able to work classes to their advantage instead of being emotionally overwhelmed, in which case they could end up *reacting*, rather than rationally responding, due to pre-conditioned subconscious attitudes on how to deal with certain troublesome behaviours from children. It is imperative that teachers are highly rational and emotionally intelligent for them to succeed in the classroom environment, where they will be tested to the point of emotional exhaustion by contrasting learning styles and varying student abilities. Some children have additional needs, and it is not fair on the students or the teacher if the school does not have the time, people power and resources to meet additional needs without sacrificing time from other students. Unlike most workplaces, if the teacher begins to feel stressed during work, they cannot just walk out for a twenty minute break and leave the children unsupervised, they have to deal with it and soldier on, all the time remembering they are the role model for a group of young minds, charged with setting a precedent for social and emotional behaviours and responses.

Schooling in many countries is split into two extremes. Public sector schools and private sector schools. With public sector having more relaxed targets, significantly less investment and consequently lower grade scores on average. For wealthier families, there is the option of a privately run school, where children arguably have more opportunity for success and can achieve higher scores in their standardised tests. The better results are not because children in private schools are smarter or more creative than children at public schools, but just because the financial backing going into their training is greater. It should be noted there is an opportunity for scholarships to private schools when a child excels in a certain area, such as sport or music. When it comes to training the next generation of citizens, there should be little expense spared. It is inexcusable to deny children the best education possible, just because their parents cannot afford it for them. Every child should have access to an equal, free and thorough education. It may sound financially impossible to implement everything suggested so far, but any extra costs should be regarded as the wisest of investments that will be recouped with a significant return; lowered crime, reduced strain on health and social care, greater human achievements, a more tolerant and cooperative civilisation and a reduction in population intellectual growth rates. It is vital for the positive change in humanity that society is desperately crying out for, that schooling is invested in now. I understand private schools are not going to turn free overnight and public schools are not suddenly going to be given billions of extra investment out of thin air - that is not the expectation here. I am saying we need to bridge the socio-economic gap in our society to create a basic level of education across the board that is of a high standard. I will explore funding solutions for supporting an ever-growing population in the next two parts of the essay, focusing on controlling population growth, and stabilising the world economy. Hopefully, I will earn any doubtful readers willingness to accept my dream for education is realistic and financially viable after reading the rest of the essay.

Parents continued responsibility throughout school life

Both in matters moral and academic, the role of a teacher should fall, first and foremost, to the parental figures. It has been known for a long time that the involvement of parents in education is a significant factor in a child's academic success. Thankfully there has been great progress in teacher-parent collaboration. The gap between home life and school life is being bridged with school starter home visits, homework projects from a young age, showcases/open afternoons where parents can come in during school hours, and reading afternoons where parents come in and read with their child whilst still at school. This not only makes sure children feel more comfortable in their education environment, but it also means they are more likely to keep on learning effectively at home.

Sadly, many children come from a home environment which is unsupportive or lacking interest in education. These homes are the breeding grounds for many of society's festering problems. Parents who underestimate the importance of education or have the mindset of, *"I don't need to teach them, that's what school is for"*, are not properly preparing their children for school, work, or life in general and they are making the transition between home life and independent school life harder on their children than it needs to be. If not nipped in the bud, unprepared children can respond to the frustration of sudden routine learning with misbehaviour; and it can have dire knock-on effects that dictate the rest of their lives. Furthermore, parents that have this lax attitude are not only being unfair to their own child but also to the other children in their child's teaching class, as the child from the disinterested home is more likely to have *avoidable* developmental delays caused by mental health or behavioural issues, and will require more than their fair share of attention to succeed, draining resources from their fellow students. Just to be clear, I am not talking about children with additional needs due to learning difficulties, medical conditions, or severe mental illness as these children will have one to one support in place for them anyway. I mean completely avoidable delays or mental health issues due to what I would deem as negligence on the parent's behalf.

One excuse parents may use is ignorance; they do not know what their child is supposed to be working on to get ready for school start. Even if the child does not attend a pre-school setting, as most do, there are pre-school assessments at children centres, and the teams there can offer suggestions to supplement their own work. Also, a quick online search will find the Early years foundation stage framework, (EYFS), to see what a young child should be working on for their age. Parents can educate themselves on it and do some activities centred around it to give their child a good start. If the child attends a nursery or playgroup, their activities will be focusing around the EYFS, but this still needs to continue at home and parents need to take the initiative to do it. There is only so much that nurseries can do for learning and child behaviour when it is contradicting examples set in home life. Parents are very quick to blame schools and teachers if their children are not responding well at school, but they need to consider if the effort they have been putting in at home is adequate first.

Before starting primary education, children most importantly need to work on personal care, social interaction and emotional development. In terms of pre-school homework, there is not too much pressure to teach things like the alphabet and reading because this is all taught from scratch phonically anyway in school. It is the child's behaviour, integrity, attitude and emotional responses towards learning environments that parents can help to develop during pre-school years. The following list of areas to focus on is straight from the government website gov.uk/early-years-foundation-stage (2019).

- Communication and language.
- Physical development.
- Personal, social and emotional development.
- Literacy.
- Mathematics.
- Understanding the world.
- Expressive arts and design.

The list is quite vague, and I would personally add a few extra specifics:

- Speed of thought.
- Problem-solving skills.
- Team building exercises.

One can easily find activities centred around these areas for pre-school children. All of the above can be achieved with very little formal effort, simply via everyday activities whilst parents are playing with children, building dens, reading bedtime stories, visiting museums, zoos, aquariums and galleries, etc. The goal is not to turn childhood into a military camp, obsessively pushing pre-school children into being able to recite their alphabet from memory, count to 100, recite Shakespeare's sonnets or perform symphonies to try and impress others. The aim is to excite their imagination, open up their minds to the fascinating, diverse world around them and teach them respect for learning, respect for others, and most importantly, respect for themselves. It is not school teacher responsibility to teach children respect and basic morals from scratch. By the time children reach school age, if their moral compass has not already formed, then they will be less likely to respond to discipline at school and will likely be more disruptive.

Another parental responsibility is nurturing mental strength, and it should actually be prioritised over academic preparation, to ensure children are ready to cope with the challenges independent life brings. Adults tend to underestimate the importance of children's emotions and worries because they are generally about matters adults deem as insignificant or silly things in comparison to the 'important' stresses of the adult world. All too often a child will be shouted at or even physically hit by a parent for having uncontrollable outbursts of emotion or 'tantrums'. Even if children bring concerns calmly to their parents, the adult may just brush them off casually, telling them to 'stop being silly' or 'run off and play', shying away from the chance to open up a deeper conversation and get to the bottom of the root psychological issues troubling their children. If parents take the opportunity here to talk to their children properly, they can be coached mentally to manage their emotions, make decisions and understand motives and reasoning behind their decisions.

Mental illness is a pandemic, relentlessly tormenting the human population, with 100s of millions of people suffering from conditions ranging from schizophrenia and epilepsy to anxiety and depression; and these illnesses do not discriminate with some of the richest countries in the world having the highest mortality rates from mental illness. Mental health is such a broad term, and some of the risk factors that increase a child's chance of developing a mental health condition are difficult to totally avoid in life, so we cannot always prevent children coming into contact with these. It is not wise to shield children in a bubble of non-reality to protect them from everything bad in the world. However, we can minimise trauma and mentally prepare children to cope with traumas if they do face them. The risk factors can materialise in the home, at school, or in everyday life, and these include:

- Family grievances - illness and death.
- Family breakups/divorce.
- Inconsistent or poorly implemented discipline.
- Being around substance abusers.
- Genetic disorders.
- Academic failure.
- Low intelligence.
- Bullying or discrimination.
- Peer pressure.
- Poor relationship with authority figures.

- Absent parenting.
- Poverty/malnutrition.
- Witnessing or experiencing traumatic/violent events.
- Failure of support networks.
- Parental pressure to succeed.
- Physical, emotional or sexual abuse.
- Having comparisons made against other children/siblings.
- Invasion of privacy.

We can do our best to minimise the above, but we do not live in a fairy tale, and in life sometimes bad things happen that we have no control over. The best protection against the mental health crisis affecting our children is early recognition of the warning signs of a mental health problem, and early intervention to stop it progressing. Also, to counter the risks, there are risk-reducing measures that we can do our best as adults to ensure are in place for children. These include:

- Supportive parenting.
- Good communication and reflection on positive and negative feelings.
- Celebrating achievement.
- Maintaining stability and comfort in home life as much as possible.
- Delivering consistent and fair discipline.
- Demonstrating strong integrity and values.
- Discouraging competitiveness and encouraging collaboration.
- Remaining rational and in control when dealing with misbehaviour.
- Avoiding escalating situations to dramatic levels, burdening children with adult worries, or being emotionally manipulative - all of which are easy to do without even realising sometimes.

Only with all of the above in place, can we confidently say we are doing our utmost to allow children to reach their potential, and protect them against developing mental health issues such as depression, eating disorders, anxiety, (which can range from obsessive-compulsive disorder to social phobia and selective mutism), and conduct disorders which are all too commonly found in schools. Misconduct displayed by children can include anti-social behaviour, being overly aggressive or angry, fighting, bullying, attention-seeking and deliberate defiance of authority. The potential damage to society caused by parents neglecting mental health issues, so badly that these kinds of disorders are allowed to take hold of their children unnoticed is catastrophic. The world will not change for the better in the future, and we will never attain H-utopia if the children being raised now are carrying forward problems of past generations into the future. We will always be doomed to go around in circles in an insane society of dangerous, socially inept, self-sabotaging people unless we commit to mentally strengthening our children during their most impressionable years.

The lesson learnt here cannot be overstated enough. As child developers of a highly intelligent species, that has recently acquired such a high level of responsibility, prioritising thorough education coupled with emotional development is absolutely crucial, and we should spare little expense in this wisest of all investments for the future of humankind.

Education in developing countries

In this section I have been discussing how to 'perfect' schools and iron out flaws, worrying about class sizes, having the most up to date technology available for children to use, and bridging the gaps between the quality of education in public and private schooling to create a high standard of education for all. However, all of this seems petty and insignificant when we consider the massive gulf in the quality of education in the developing world or in war-torn countries, where tens of millions of children do not even have a chance to go to school, or at best have very limited schooling with makeshift classrooms and untrained teachers. Sorting this mess out must be our focus first and foremost. As I keep stressing, H-utopia is for the whole world, not just the most developed parts. It is easy to fall into the trap of only considering our own localised society or thinking that creating H-utopia in the most socially advanced nations is challenging enough, without having to consider the whole world. But the fact is, the *only* way to maintain H-utopia is globally, by cooperating and investing as a whole species. There is no short cut to H-utopia for any individual nation by selfishly leaving others behind.

There are many complex issues hindering education in

developing countries, and they need to be addressed by the rest of the world in order to enhance the globally cooperative society we are working towards. These countries cannot do it by themselves. The problems are cyclical, spiralling ones and will continue to span generations without intervention from those who have the means to aid them, and doing so selflessly, without imposing crippling financial deficit. The reward and return is reaching H-utopia.

The number one obstacle preventing children receiving the education they need to improve their society is the same as in the developed world, (only far more severe), and it all comes down to funding, or more precisely, a severe lack of it. Developing countries rely heavily on foreign aid to support growth and sustainability. Without this investment, they cannot grow to a point where they will be able to start sustaining themselves. Currently, the percentage of foreign aid that ends up being used for education is nowhere near sufficient because it is mostly being used just for survival. The Universal Declaration of Human Rights says everyone has the right to a free, basic education, so poverty should not be a reason to miss out on schooling, but we could say the same for food, water and shelter which are even more basic human rights that should be available despite the financial situation in the part of the world a person is born into. The good intentions currently do not manifest in reality, and even basic human needs for everyone appear to be a distant dream. There is currently no such thing as a human right. Nothing is granted, nothing is guaranteed, not even water, thanks to humanity's misplaced priorities and lack of foresight. As I have already said, when people are denied the very most basic human needs, they cannot concentrate on the higher needs that involve contributing to society, such as the pursuit of knowledge and exercising creativity. What is more, being severely malnourished in childhood impacts brain development and affects concentration. A child cannot learn efficiently on an empty stomach, as the animalistic, biological need takes precedent over higher human desires.

Even when there *are* schools, in many cases they are distant and far apart, leaving those attending travelling miles by foot, fearing potential violent attacks on their journey. Some families in developing countries are so poor that they cannot afford for their children to go to school even if there is one nearby; they need them to work and provide for the family as soon as they are old enough to physically do so. This is especially true with girls, if a family has to choose, they will generally send the boys to school over the girls, as the girls have an opportunity to marry out of poverty at a very young age and so apparently are not as reliant on education as much as boys are. This sad fact is observed in much of the developing world, and as a result, families remain locked in a cycle of poverty and gender discrimination for generations, feeding an oppressive, stagnant society. Sometimes the only way to break the cycle is for parents to sacrifice their own lives, leaving themselves destitute, in order to send all of their children to school, therefore enabling them to develop the skills required to build their own lives somewhere wealthier than where they were born. However, this is not beneficial for growing communities. The skills learnt need to be retained in the poor areas to help them get out of poverty.

It is apparent that education in developing countries needs to be tailored to what is going to be useful in helping a specific community and their localised society. The raw potential is there for the children to change their lives for the better, with just as many budding entrepreneurs, doctors, builders, skilled tradespeople and teachers as there are in the developed world, they just are not currently being recognised and nurtured. Developing relevant skills and tailoring appropriate training to each student is not just something for helping the developing world to help itself out of poverty; we should be doing this in schools around the globe. Instead, we are churning out robotic exam masters who can pass tests when they have been repeatedly fed the answers but are not capable of contributing to society with ingenuity or creativity. In life there are no standard tests, the variables and possibilities are infinite, and the individual human potential is far beyond what schools would have their leavers believe when they finish with average or lower test scores.

There are instances in the developing world where even intelligent graduates with good degrees in traditional studies remain unemployed and unable to contribute in their local communities, being forced to abandon their home countries because there is no practical application for their training there. Attaining knowledge is useless, merely a hobby, without the opportunities to apply it somewhere for practical benefits in society. Skills massively outweigh knowledge when it comes to developing countries, and so this should be the focus of education; to start building the pyramid from the bottom up. This is a natural progression stage in education that cannot be skipped over during social development. To put it another way, there is no point training a generation of accountants, if there are not enough tradespeople and local entrepreneurs in need of their services. Or, what is the point in producing a class of rocket scientists if the country they live in does not even have the means for a space program, or engineers with the skills to build rockets? One of the most basic rules of learning is, we all learn to walk before we can run.

In the most underdeveloped parts of the world, the education needs to start with personal social and emotional development, encompassing health, hygiene, team building and real-life situations. Lessons need to be centred around first aid, sex education, problem-solving, taking initiative, recognising symptoms and understanding progression of diseases, (as well as learning the source of them), identifying business potential in local areas and carrying out projects in the community that require collaboration, delegation and planning, to develop organisational skills. Of course, literacy is important, as an illiterate society, no matter how skilled, can only progress a minimal amount. Once literate, students can carry on teaching themselves.

There are a lack of teachers in the developing world which presents another problem, but as always there is a solution if we try hard enough and if the investment is made in the technological aids that we sometimes shy away from utilising even in the developed world, especially when primary education is involved. Virtual lessons, virtual teachers, or real teachers, perhaps semi-retired ones, from the developed world via video link would be a real benefit to developing countries if made available via the internet. But without reliable electricity in many schools, let alone broadband, this is a long way off. The so-called 'world wide web' is not worldwide by any means. Despite being implemented over 30 years ago and something many of us could not imagine being without, it is estimated not even half of the world's population is online. The internet gives everyone the opportunity to learn and communicate on a global level. As long as a person is literate, they can use the internet as a tool to gain access to information on any subject without needing the physical textbook, which many schools in developing countries lack, having only a handful of outdated textbooks to share between a whole class of 100 students in extreme cases. As I have already discussed, the lack of real teachers is a big problem globally, not just in developing countries. Children from war-stricken countries stuck in refugee camps are missing out on vital education too. The casualties of war go much deeper than those killed in battle. Social development is decimated, and it can take a battered nation decades to fully recover, with education not being a priority or even a possibility in some instances.

The situation is indeed desperate, but it is not hopeless. Many organisations around the world are taking on the challenge of educating the developing world and disaster zones with the use of technology: instant network schools have been provided by the United Nations Refugee Agency in partnership with the Vodafone Foundation. The makeshift schools receive a laptop with a hotspot modem, a speaker, a projector and 25 tablets pre-loaded with educational software. There is no requirement for the presence of a physical, trained teacher, but it requires volunteers to organise the classes at least.

There have also been multiple philanthropic efforts by Google, which launched a 50 million dollar global program to support organisations that help children who do not have basic numeracy and literacy skills. They have developed their Rumie educational tablet, for children who are literate enough to educate themselves with this pocket-sized 'library'. The content can be updated from the internet but does not rely on the internet to access the reading material. They have also developed Storyweaver, an open-source platform to share and translate books. This has been particularly useful for educating millions of children in India via the organisation, Pratham. The platform combines Google Translate, transliteration tools, and human volunteers to make the translations as accurate as possible.

A partnership between Amazon and Worldreader has successfully distributed thousands of pre-loaded kindles to people in sub-Saharan African countries. Many of the schools in these countries lack even basic supplies such as books, writing materials, and desks. So, this kind of technology is the answer to opening up the world of literacy to those without access to libraries. eBooks are cheaper than the paper book and far easier to deliver than physical copies to remote areas. This is a great way to launch underdeveloped areas into the 21st century and get the children there fascinated by education. Without education, these countries will always remain in poverty, unable to help themselves progress beyond a basic level of social development.

All of this philanthropy is very magnanimous, but we should not have to rely on the willingness of philanthropic organisations, or even charities, to help those less fortunate. These are government responsibilities. A sustainable solution requires a complete overhaul of the world's economic structure, which could take decades, simply because people cannot agree. In the meantime at least an overhaul on taxation could be achieved in the short-term, in order to collect a fair share of taxes from the world's richest who are not contributing a relative fair amount. The answer is obvious, tax rates should be agreed globally to close tax-dodging loopholes, but this still involves global cooperation. It is more complicated than it sounds because of political reasons, and financial rules, not practical problems. In theory, it is simple, but the problem boils down to people motivated by personal greed. Therefore, in conjunction with tax overhaul, we need a crackdown on corruption. It is public knowledge that there are whole networks of corruption and bribery, involving government officials, politicians, solicitors, accountants and in fact, anyone who holds any kind of power. The fundamental issue is a lack of financial clarity allows people to get away with it. It is unfair and immoral for 1 per cent of the population to hold 90 plus per cent of the world's wealth, whilst children are dying of hunger and poor sanitation every minute of every day.

I have digressed to a point now where it has become necessary to move on to identifying the risks of population growth/world economics. I will discuss what we can do to negate the risks, in order to make our goals for education and H-utopia realistic and achievable for everyone, no matter where they are born in the world.

Managing human population growth effectively

"Animals can be driven crazy by placing too many in too small a pen. Homo sapiens is the only animal that voluntarily does this to himself."

- Robert A. Heinlein, Time Enough for Love, 1973.

...The exchange from nomad to the farmer was arguably the time in our history where we left our carefree utopia in the Garden of Eden behind, ate from the metaphorical tree of knowledge, and completed the transition from animality to humanity, acquiring a greater responsibility beyond our own selfish existence...

Let us begin by putting the human race into perspective: somewhere deep in history, human beings became influencers of the Earth, no longer content existing as mere figures of the landscape. Our ancestors made a conscious decision to leave their natural environment. Unlike their unambitious animal cousins, humans sought adventure, invention and exploration, driving them to make a habitat in every corner of the Earth. Using their ingenuity, they moulded even the most seemingly inhospitable places into a home. The human legacy became something greater than simply passing on genes. Discoveries, inventions, language, plans for the future, science and art pushed each generation forward, building on the retained cultural knowledge of the previous one. However, the biological evolution that delivered the human race to this pivotal point of higher consciousness was thousands of times longer than the cultural evolution that followed, and therefore remains a significant part of the animalistic driving force in an urge to reproduce and survive at all costs. Humans are no different from any other life on Earth, in that respect.

The Earth is 4.6 billion years old and amazingly has been home to life for most of its history. The oldest known fossils showing life on Earth are approximately 4.2 billion years old. The ancestor species of all primates first appeared in the fossil record around 65-66 million years ago; survivors of an extinction event that eliminated about three-quarters of plant and animal species on Earth, including the dinosaurs, who before their untimely demise lived on Earth successfully for around 165 million years, in a variety of forms. It was around 15-18 million years ago that something resembling our modern human brain evolved, hosting the precursor to prefrontal lobes and the neocortex. Our ape-like ancestors at the time would have begun experiencing something akin to human consciousness and the strong self-awareness, that all other creatures on Earth previously lacked, and still do.

The most widely accepted view is that humans, in our current distinguishable form, have only existed for between 40,000-200,000 years, (although new fossil discoveries may very well challenge this). The oldest confirmed 'humanlike' fossil has been dated at 4.4 million years old, discovered in Africa. It is estimated our hominid line diverged from the rest of the modern-day ape lineage between 5 and 8 million years ago. We are probably looking at around 6 million years ago that an African ape species evolved features that differentiated it from other apes; having smaller canine teeth and the ability to walk upright on two legs for reasonable distances. Again, this theory may be challenged by future discoveries. It would be arrogant to boast we know everything that happened millions of years ago based on an incomplete fossil record. Sadly, distinct transitions of hominid species between 7 and 5 million years ago are poorly documented in the fossil record. This is something that anti-evolutionists have clung to, ignorantly demanding to see the 'missing link' that science fails to deliver. Of course, there is no 'missing link', only endless adaptations, random mutations and unnoticeable changes in the short-term, that turned into big changes over the mind-boggling course of millions of years.

We are fortunate to have any fossils at all, as the conditions required for fossilisation to take place are quite special. In order to fossilise, the remains of a creature must be in an oxygen-deprived environment and need to be covered quickly, by particles of sediment deposited by wind or water, before scavengers can consume them or the environment can decompose them. The physical remains, once safely entombed in sedimentary rock are then slowly replaced by other minerals that seep out of the surrounding ground, forming a rocky replica of the organism's original form. The fossil is then discovered by humans after millions of years of erosion have brought it back close to the surface. On rare occasions, something even better than a fossil is given to us by nature: perfectly preserved specimens complete with skin and hair. Bodies of ancient animals and humans have been discovered in peat bogs having undergone a process known as peat bog mummification.

Rocky fossilised remains of very early hominids discovered include Sahelanthropus and Orrorin, both examples of the Australopithecine genus. These have been found in the Great Rift Valley in eastern Africa, as well as parts of the continent that now fall in modern-day Kenya, Ethiopia and Tanzania. The famous 3.2 million-year-old female Australopithecus specimen, known as Lucy, was from a species known as Australopithecus Afarensis which lived in eastern Africa for nearly 1 million years. There is irrefutable evidence that Lucy's kind walked upright, including hardened hominid footprints in the geological record from 3 million years ago. Australopithecus was not a particularly tough creature in comparison to the many predators it shared its environment with; it was slow, weak and particularly vulnerable to accidental death from injury. Furthermore, as their brains were developing into more complex organs, childhood was longer than competing animals, including other primates. Our ancestors overcame their weaknesses with two crucial inventions. The first was social - only by staying in groups would Australopithecus have stood a chance of survival. As many would have perished from injury, infection or being eaten before reaching old age, most children would find themselves orphaned before old enough to care for themselves. This meant in order for the young to survive, there must have been a sense of community and organisation in which the young were 'adopted' and raised by the surviving elders. As sad as it is, orphans started our ancestors off on a 2 million year biological journey of change towards cultural evolution.

The other crucial invention came once our ancestors became bipedal as a primary mode of movement, freeing up their hands entirely. The distinct genus, 'Homo', evolved around 2.5 million years ago. An early hominid, Homo habilis, had dexterity enough to fashion and use crude tools, but more importantly, after use, these tools were not simply discarded but were stored to re-use at a future time. It was during this revolution that our ancestors began developing a more complex foresight, bestowing upon their descendants the symbolic gift of the future. By 'discovering' the future, our ancestors no longer lived only in the present as all other animals tend to do but began to ponder beyond their own selfish existence and this is perhaps the most vital discovery of all. It took nearly 2 million years from the invention of crude tools by early hominids to reach a point where their descendants' biological evolution transformed them into something we would recognise today as a human being.

Groups of our part animal, part human ancestors, migrated out of Africa on several different occasions after becoming primarily bipedal. It was not just our ancestors, but also their cousins who migrated out of Africa over the aeons. Another distinct transition in the fossil record is the Homo erectus, which evolved around 2 million years ago. Similar to modern humans in body but nothing like us in mind; their brains were significantly smaller than ours. Despite their small brains, we know Homo erectus was one of the earliest explorers, as examples of their fossils have been found in parts of Africa, Europe, and Asia. The latest big migrations out of Africa were modern Homo sapiens around 300,000 years ago, and again 70,000 years ago. They met and interbred with the descendants of earlier hominid migrations who had already colonised Europe, the Neanderthals and the Denisovans. The ancestors of these now extinct distant cousins had left Africa hundreds of thousands of years earlier than the ancestors of Homo sapiens, who were left behind to carry on evolving differently on the plains of the Savannah. Around 100,000 years ago there were a variety of hominids living on different parts of the planet. Had they all been gathered in one place, it might have looked like a scene from J. R. R. Tolkien's, The Lord of the Rings. There were even 'hobbit' sized hominids, Homo floresiensis, who stood at about a meter in height and lived on the island of Flores in Indonesia. Their small stature, but large feet were likely due to what is known as 'Island Dwarfism', where limited resources in an isolated environment for a long time will consequently reduce a species size over the course of many generations, as nature favours the small who need less food to survive. Neanderthals, Denisovans and Homo floresiensis were the most recent to go extinct out of at least a dozen different hominids that had evolved. All were ultimately outcompeted by modern humans who were better adapted for surviving the dramatically changing climate tens of thousands of years ago.

Evidence suggests that all hominids, even Homo sapiens, almost became extinct around 70,000 years ago, as many species went through a genetic 'bottleneck'. Although the cause is disputed, one explanation is the Toba supervolcano erupting in Sumatra, Indonesia. It may have caused a ten-year long volcanic winter and been responsible for deforestation in large parts of the world, which would have been a key factor in the eventual extinction of all remaining hominids apart from

Homo sapiens. Estimates vary for how close we came to extinction. Some researchers suggest there were as few as a thousand human beings left on Earth at one time, making us a seriously endangered species. Luckily, some of our ancestors must have been particularly hardy, resourceful and determined to have prevailed through this terrible time. Bottleneck events in the animal kingdom have happened throughout history, and whatever the cause may be, they are ultimately beneficial for a species' genes; the fittest and the smartest would have survived these incredibly trying periods in history, earning the right to become ancestors.

For the 60,000 years of nomadic life that followed the bottleneck event 70,000 years ago, the human population probably never rose above 5 or 6 million worldwide. The innovation that opened the door to exponential population growth came at the end of the last ice age, with the emergence of new vegetation, including a fertile hybrid wheat in the Middle East known as Emmer, which humans cultivated. An even more improbable hybrid later occurred between Emmer and another grass plant. The result was large bread wheat, too strong to easily break up and scatter its seed naturally in the wind. The relationship between humans and this wheat became symbiotic as the hybrid relied on the human speciality of exploitation to have its seed manually transported to a new location for planting. The domestication of grains and animals began around 10,000 years ago and has provided humans with a predictable food supply ever since. Furthermore, the farm environment provided a stable, safe home to rear children, allowing women in farming tribes to rear more children than hunter-gatherers could. Before too long, farmers outnumbered foragers, and the nomadic way of life almost completely died out, except in a few isolated pockets of the world. The exciting discovery of farming, and the monumental effect it had on early human society echoed from pre-history all the way down through the ages, until the sentiments could be recorded in written legends. We can observe the transition from nomad to the farmer in, amongst other sources, the Old Testament of the Bible. Jericho was an envied oasis on the edge of a desert, ideal for agriculture as water and wheat combined in geographic perfection. Joshua brought the tribes of Israel to Jericho on their way to the promised land. A teeming city fortified to protect its settlers from attack whilst promising prosperity, food, water and knowledge to all dwelling within its high walls and tall towers. Knowledge shared by the people who built Jericho certainly delivered on a promise for a better and stronger future, as did many other early cities long lost to time no doubt.

We know from the legends and archaeological evidence that Jericho's walls fell; on more than one occasion in pre-history, perhaps not from attack, but from nature itself. Jericho did have one fatal drawback to its location, the true nature of which would have been beyond its settlers understanding at the time. The Red Sea and The Dead Sea lie along a continuation from where two of the plates that carry the continents on the Earth's mantle ride side by side. As they thrust past one another, the surface all along this continuation feels the effects of the shockwaves. As a result, earthquakes have always plagued the axis on which The Dead Sea lies. This could offer some insight into why so many haunting memories of God's miracles/punishments surround this part of the ancient world, including flooding, The Red Sea running dry and of course, the walls of Jericho falling.

Humans taming, and selectively breeding animals to use to their advantage has had a similar effect on folklore and legend. In Greek mythology, we can observe the reaction to the domestication and selective breeding of horses for warfare in very ancient times. For a people who had never witnessed warriors riding on horseback, the survivors of these attacks would have passed down embellished stories to their descendants, distorted over a thousand years to confidently claim the 'centaur', a powerful part man, part horse beast, once really existed.

So, farming changed the course of human history, but how exactly did our ancestors get to that point of exchange? They did not just stop hunting and start harvesting grain overnight. There had to be a pre-curser that influenced early farmers to explore this avenue. Based on anthropological studies of modern humans that still live today in isolated societies, practising hunting and gathering alongside simple agriculture, it is almost certain that ultimately, we owe civilisation to women and not men. It is a logical assumption that women were the first to plant gardens, to fulfil potential food options for their nomadic tribe. Whilst the ancient men were occupied with hunting animals for perhaps days at a time, the women of the group would have gathered fruits and seeds. They would have discovered seeds could yield more food, when the spilt or discarded ones germinated in convenient locations near to their camps. This inadvertent discovery would fit nicely with the biblical story of Eve persuading Adam to 'eat' from the tree of knowledge, resulting in their casting out from Eden, the animal haven, and becoming something more human and ambitious, walking the arduous road to civilisation.

What is more, farming knowledge was perhaps lost and re-discovered many times. There is evidence that humans living in tropical forest regions of Asia and South America altered their environments to grow food at least 45,000 years ago. This foresight to plan for times of food shortage is likely why Homo sapiens became the last remaining hominid species, able to occupy every habitat on the planet. So, it seems farming may not have been a sudden revelation, but a long practised part of human life passed down for thousands of years until there became a greater widespread opportunity for it following the end of the last ice age. Carefully tended to proto-farms or gardens meant the size of a tribe would not be limited to how many could be sustained in one place, as with hunting and gathering alone. Planted clearings would have attracted herds of grazing animals such as goats and sheep which would then have been captured and their potential exploited also. As the gardens grew into farms, the responsibilities of farming became greater, the need for hunting became less, and some of the men would have been roped into the farming instead. Tribes would have been less inclined to move around, not wanting to abandon the hard work they had put into developing their farms and herding their livestock. As crops became more successful, to a point where there were surplus amounts of food, there would have been a requirement for a kind of governmental administration to take charge of storing the spare food and saving it from spoiling, so it could be distributed as needed, and fairly, during times of poor crop growth.

Over the generations, as tribes of perhaps 100 people grew into societies of thousands, etchings, (which evolved into writing), would be required to keep track of distribution. The first governments were born, learning how to govern in proto-cities such as Çatalhöyük, which existed between 9,400 and 7,700 years ago in modern-day Turkey. The apparent equality of the structures excavated at Çatalhöyük strongly suggest early attempts at government began with good egalitarian intentions. Naturally, some tribe's farming capabilities developed faster than others and those lagging behind, rather than put in the extra hard work, may have opted to attack and usurp competitors' farming towns and so, premeditated warfare was born. These opportunists likely forced the development of more complex societies, with a unified language, which would have made it easier to communicate innovation from town to town, and by creating a need for specialised professions. For instance, guards or soldiers would have been needed to protect the land. Warring invaders would also have driven a need for building; walls got bigger, fortifications stronger and armies of guards grew larger. We now see the earliest human professions inevitably forming because of the choices our ancestors made. Farmers to tend to the land and animals, governmental administrative workers to organise the food stores, soldiers to protect the settlements and builders to provide protection and shelter to growing communities. Everyone would have had their place in this communist-like state, and in this kind of society, there became more room for protection of the vulnerable. It was no longer survival of the fittest; the weaklings or 'runts' would be more likely to survive in farming communities than hunting communities, and so their genes would be passed on. Those who would have died young as nomadic hunter-gatherers now had a chance to live and reproduce in a more comfortable environment, driving population growth.

With growing populations to sustain, and some physically unable to contribute fairly, there would have been a need for taxation, powering social development. Searching for new materials to build and craft with, humans realised the financial potential of mining. With the invention of mining, the opportunity arose for towns and individuals to gain wealth through trading, and so ended the brief reign of egalitarianism. Those who controlled the resources of a mine, along with the greatest accomplished warriors would have worked their way to the top of establishing hierarchies in society, and so we had the humble beginnings of what we now call 'royalty'. All of this social development was not an intentional plan when our ancestors began farming; it was merely an inevitable outcome of our ancestors having made decisions which increased their survival chances during times of extreme environmental stress. They likely had no concept of the long-term consequences they would impose on future generations when they intervened in, until this point in time, entirely natural course of evolution on Earth. During times of food shortages, faced with life or death, humans would not have had the luxury to ponder if agriculture was really a step forward for our species socially and genetically, or just a step sideways, to a different, not necessarily better or healthier way of life. Going against nature, exchanging hunting animals and gathering food, for rearing livestock, breeding it against nature to their advantage, and growing food from scratch, was the most monumental decision in early human history. Relative to the million years spent as hunter-gatherers, everything quite suddenly became more complicated and sophisticated - economics, social structure, inventing, family life, architecture and complex building. The exchange from nomad to the farmer was the time in our history where we left our carefree utopia in the Garden of Eden behind, ate from the metaphorical tree of knowledge, and completed the transition from animality to humanity, acquiring a greater responsibility beyond our own selfish existence.

Humans modified plants and animals on the genetic level, and it resulted in a population boom for our species. However, the modified nature changed us genetically in return. Farming humans developed some nutrition-related health problems that did not as badly affect their hunter-gatherer cousins. A less varied diet and an over-dependency on grains meant vitamin deficiency and dental decay was more prominent in farmers due to increased consumption of starchy foods. Their growth was stunted, with average male height falling from 5 foot 10 inches in the Palaeolithic to 5 foot 3 inches in the late Neolithic, brain development was also delayed and fitness levels reduced. Hunter-gatherers were rarely afflicted with disease; their primary cause of death was accidental injury, and subsequent wound infection, whereas farming brought with it a tsunami of illness. Working in close proximity with livestock, using the milk to make dairy products, as well as harvesting and storing meat, meant an increase in human exposure to bacteria, parasites and infectious illnesses, either caught directly from the animals, from rodent pests, (in the case of plague caused by Yersinia pestis), or contracted from consuming the animal products. We even suffer the effects now with inherited, lifestyle illnesses, such as diabetes, a rare condition amongst the remaining tribes of hunter-gatherers who tend not to consume more calories than they burn, but common in the developed world. The adverse effects of the society we have created go beyond the physical body; there is a mental health pandemic, afflicting millions of people across the world with depression and anxiety due to an ever more overwhelming day to day life, in a world our species is not evolved for.

A world of impending deadlines, economic constraints, the monotony of specialised occupations that leave us unfulfilled, but we must endure anyway to pay bills, and the relentless bombardment of external stimuli, including media, advertisements, background electronic appliance noise, traffic noise, sirens and artificial lights. Overpopulation in cities and urban living force us into close contact with thousands of strangers in a single day, (more than our small groups of hunter-gatherer ancestors would have encountered in a year of roaming and exploring). This modern life we have created against nature is enough to test the sanity of humanity to its limits, and it is not surprising that so many people are struggling mentally to adapt to this relatively new human environment.

So, what is the answer? To renounce our technology and return to the nomadic way of life? Of course not, but the lesson here is that we must consider the actions we take and the choices we make now, to survive and prosper, may have unforeseen consequences for future generations. We have a responsibility to set the next generation up for success by mentally and physically preparing children for the world they are born into.

Despite the drawbacks, known at the time, and unforeseen for future generations, farmers had a higher frequency of children than hunter-gatherers and so farming, and civilisation prevailed as the dominant way of life. Mothers would not have needed to breast-feed their offspring for as long, as there would have been readily available, calorie-rich food stores suitable for nourishing babies and toddlers. With more children surviving into adulthood and having children of their own, tribes grew into communities, splitting into family units as several generations of a family now survived to live simultaneously. Larger workforces allowed for the expansion of farms into towns and so farming became the centre of human civilisation and development. Driven by competition for resources and the invention of economics, civilisation, which relies upon cooperation and government, gave the human race spare capacity to invest time in non-subsistence activities such as the arts and sciences. This same spare capacity has sustained population growth.

The environmental effects farming had on human health did not affect reproduction too badly, because individuals generally inherit characteristics that make them more successful at surviving infancy and therefore humans lived long enough to rear offspring before succumbing to illness. That is all that is required to produce a very successful species. Longevity is nice to have but not required. Advantageous characteristics tend to appear more frequently in the population simply because those individuals that did not have the necessary genes for survival were more likely to die before reproducing and rearing children. This is what drives evolution and usually in a positive way. However, it is not always the case that only good genes get passed on, of course. Health issues that do not kill the afflicted in their youth do not stop an individual reproducing and passing on the defective genes. The adverse health effects farming had on the human body did not necessarily prevent reproduction, as they did not start to affect health too badly until later on in life and so the genes of farmers were passed on, flaws and all. After thousands of years of procreation, humans were becoming drastically more self-domesticated, less suited to living outside. The changes were slow but sure and are still going on. We are constantly evolving, changing into a slightly different species from what we previously were, and we will continue to do so for as long as we are around.

Physically, the variety evolution produces is astounding; yet, on a genetic level, all life on Earth is basically the same. Fundamentally the only real-life on Earth is the complex molecule, deoxyribonucleic acid, (DNA). 'Genes' that use our bodies as hosts to survive and reproduce indefinitely. Everything else is an elaborate outcome of physical form running away with itself over billions of years, where thanks to a combination of environmental stresses, selective mating and complete chance, genes have produced a wide variety of hosts, including pretty complex hosts like human beings. Actually, in reproductive terms, we have become unnecessarily complicated and inefficient. The time it takes us now to reach sexual maturity is nearly twice as long as our early ape-like ancestors. The increasing size of the modern human brain means childbirth has become an excruciating and traumatic event for mother and baby, that often requires medical intervention to avoid injury or death, followed by a very long childhood, where any offspring are totally dependent on their parents for many years.

Since we developed the science to decode the human genome and compare it against other species, we have learnt that the genes in humans and the genes in our closest living cousins, chimpanzees, (although separated by at least 5 million years), are rounded to 98 per cent identical, and amusingly we are around 60 per cent identical to bananas. What all of this proves, is that humans are not the pinnacle of evolution as some arrogantly believe. Instead, it shows we are just one exotic variant that happens to have survived extinction by the skin of its teeth long enough to become more intelligent than any other creature on Earth. This does not make us better vessels for genes, though. In fact, the most successful hosts on Earth are brainless bacteria. They were here before any other creature or plant, they have survived every extinction event, and will be the last things alive on Earth long after every other creature has perished, making them better-suited candidates for the pinnacle of biological evolution if there is such a thing. In terms of cultural evolution, there is no competition, though. No other species on Earth has undergone cultural evolution. It has taken our species to an era of body-altering science and technology, and consequently, we are no longer at the mercy of biological evolution.

Dominion over nature, environment, and powering the population cleanly

It was God of the Old Testament that appointed human beings as keepers of the natural world, granting our species dominion over the Earth, and its other inhabitants, as the long-awaited saviours of Earth. It makes one wonder, how Earth and its creatures managed for billions of years before we got here to 'save them'.

Our ancestors organised their spiritual feelings into religion to help explain the existence of human consciousness and to create rules for societies increasing in complexity. Ironically, there is really nothing in Judaism, Christianity, or Islam that tells us to look after the natural world and to treat all creatures equally. The opposite if anything; unlike Taoism, Buddhism and earlier spirituality that taught us respect for the Earth and nature, the newer, monotheistic religious organisations drew a dangerous line between divinely elevated humans and the natural world they occupied.

In modern monotheistic religions, there is a strong suggestion that every other living thing is here for human benefit, to exploit, devour or sacrifice as we see fit. Even in religions that promote re-incarnation, to be reincarnated as anything other than human is widely viewed as a punishment. This egotistical attitude has been strengthened over the centuries by religions that arrogantly touted mankind as the ultimate life-form in a Universe that revolved around humans. Although, it should be noted that some animals are considered 'sacred' by certain religions and are elevated to a higher place in society than other creatures, based off of ancient ideas that these animals possess certain admirable characteristics that humans should endeavour to attain, such as strength, serenity and wisdom. For instance, the elephant is considered a very important creature in Hinduism for these attributes.

The circle of life is subconsciously appreciated by all other creatures on Earth, including isolated hunter-gatherer human societies that still exist. Predators demonstrate respect for their prey as they know their survival depends on them. Exploitation is a modern human speciality; we often take more than what we need from the supply we have 'been given', to make our existence more pleasurable, even if it is at the fatal expense of others; driving animals to extinction by deforestation and relentless hunting for sport or fun. The only other creatures that regularly hunt for fun, (not for food, territory or protection), are carnivorous mammals that have been manipulated by humans, such as domestic cats that are fed enough by human owners but their instincts to hunt are so strong they do it even when not hungry. Whether this would really be considered 'fun', or just uncontrollable survival instinct, it is difficult to say.

To be fair to modern religion, humans began exploiting nature's resources long before we were 'granted' dominion over nature by The Bible. One of the earliest known instances of mass human deforestation was the Cedars of Lebanon, a vast forest decimated over time to build, amongst other things, King Solomon's temple, and it continued to supply countries such as Egypt for centuries with timber and paper.

The products of progress that the Earth provides to humans are not always towering in plain sight. Over hundreds of millions of years, enormous quantities of plant and animal life died, sank to the bottom of muddy swamps or to the ocean floor, where over the aeons the remains transformed into what humans discovered as coal, oil and gas - the fossil fuels that made the industrial revolution possible. Humans realised the potential for these fuel types that were hundreds of times more efficient than anything previously at human disposal. They could be used for powering machinery, heating homes, generating electricity on a mass scale, building and powering cars, boats and planes. For over

150 years, billions of us have taken advantage of fossil fuels, taking them for granted in our daily lives, to generate the power for the lifestyles we have become accustomed to. Coal, oil and gas formed the economic structure we have today and continue to dominate the economy. The political and financial power that the wielder of these resources attained is nothing short of monstrous. Not only bringing unmeasurable wealth to the fuel companies themselves but also the auto-transport companies that could surf the black oil tidal wave with them.

With the population of Earth reaching the level it has, the consumption of these fossil fuels is beyond ridiculous. We are all very aware fossil fuels are not a renewable energy source and will eventually run out, yet we still predominantly rely on them as if they were going to last forever. How do the companies and conglomerates that 'own' nature's resources deal with apparently dwindling supplies? They raise prices faster than normal inflationary rates. As if the price hike is going to make some consumers stop living in lit and warm homes or driving their vehicles to work anymore. With extreme dependence comes unavoidable corruption. The lengths that nations will go to in order to defend, or steal, a share of gas and oil reserves is frightening. Before coal, oil and gas even get refined to power our machines, first and foremost they fuel immoral and inhumane behaviour. The technologically advanced society we have developed so quickly over the last 150 years is thanks to the power these fossil fuels provided us with, but they have not come without a cost. The by-product of these fuels, carbon dioxide, warms the atmosphere more than usual by trapping heat on Earth and contributes to the 'greenhouse effect' more than any other greenhouse gas. It also pollutes our urban areas with carcinogenic fumes. It is time we let these aeons old organism's remains rest in peace. Our journey to H-utopia will be delayed indefinitely, unless we stop relying on these types of primitive fuel for our primary energy use. There are other options now, that could be properly invested in if they were not being totally or partially suppressed because the financial return is much lower than fossil fuels, due to them being from a renewable or potentially infinite source. The power and wealth fossil fuels granted to those in possession of them is godlike, and now we are relying on those who have elevated themselves above humanity to choose to be benevolent gods and show wisdom enough to use their power to relinquish the hold they have over humanity, for the sake of the future.

The industrial revolution cannot be credited to one genius, rather a collaboration of human ingenuity. Unlike those solitary historic geniuses who advanced science for thousands of years, in honourable pursuit of truth, the industrial revolution advanced science in the pursuit of social enterprise. Inevitably, due to human personality flaws, the greed became too much for some to resist and we now find ourselves on the verge of dystopia with 1 per cent of the human population dangling dependency over the remaining 99 per cent. There are other options that will remove this dependency and give the power back to the individual if we can be allowed to pursue them financially unhindered. Apart from the well-known wind energy and solar power, which have flaws that have undermined the viability of alternative energy in general, let us explore some more reliable fuel options to see if they have the potential to power the whole population in H-utopia:

Tidal energy – as the name suggests, this form of energy production harnesses the movement of ocean water to power turbines and produce electricity, just as wind energy uses the wind to power turbines. However, tides are significantly more reliable and predictable than wind. It is estimated, even with today's technology, a fifth of the world's power demands could be met by tidal power alone if energy companies and governments committed to building the facilities. Just by exploiting the natural ebb and flow of coastal tidal waters, France, Canada, Russia, South Korea, China, the Netherlands and the UK are amongst those to have produced power with tidal energy plants, but they are not yet producing enough energy to allow for any reduction in carbon fuel burning, with just one or two facilities each. For instance, France's Rance Tidal Power Station, at the time of writing, reportedly only supplies around 0.12 per cent of the country's energy needs. One problem is, engineering projects to construct such power plants are immense, so it can take years, and billions of investment to complete just one facility. There is also an ongoing debate over the negative effects these invasive sites have on ocean habitats. Nevertheless, if constructed to their full potential, this form of renewable energy could provide countries with a large percentage of their power demands, and with virtually no waste, no fuel needed to operate, and relatively low running costs long-term. This is a definite candidate to be considered for more widespread use in countries that are not landlocked.

Geothermal power – geothermal power plants draw energy from the internal heat of the Earth itself; generating electricity using steam produced from naturally occurring reservoirs of boiling hot liquid, miles below the Earth's surface. The steam produced rotates a turbine that powers a generator to produce electricity. There is massive potential for this kind of energy source to produce a sizeable share of the population's rapidly growing energy demands. For as long as the Earth exists as a habitable planet, there will be geothermal energy available to exploit. Like solar and wind energy, it has a minimal environmental impact, but it has the bonus of being far more reliable than these sources; we do not have to worry about fluctuating power levels and potential shortages if there is not enough sun and wind, as geothermal power plants have a power output that produces 24/7. It also means that we need not be concerned about activities such as drilling under the ocean and transporting fuel via tankers, which comes at a heavy cost/risk of pollution to the environment. As with most forms of energy production, there are downsides though. Geothermal energy is location-specific, so we cannot construct geothermal power plants where it is most convenient for us; only where the zones of energy happen to be strongest, which may be many miles from any urban areas. Most developed countries have geothermal power plants in use, with the biggest users being the USA and the Philippines. The optimistic potential is only estimated to be 10 per cent of global energy needs by the end of the century, and with the deep subterranean highly expensive digging involved in building these power plants, (that can trigger earthquakes and release natural greenhouse gasses into the atmosphere), there is a significant expenditure and associated risk to consider before pushing this form of energy production to its potential.

Nuclear energy - perhaps the most efficient form of alternative energy, already providing countries with up to a quarter of all their energy needs, whilst releasing no carbon dioxide from the power plants, (although mining for uranium can mean using fossil fuel powered machinery). It works by a process called fission, where the nuclear energy is generated from the splitting of uranium atoms. This produces heat, and in turn, steam that powers turbines to generate electricity. It is so efficient, a piece of uranium the size of a ping pong ball would provide a lifetime supply of energy for a person. To put this into perspective, the equivalent amount of fossil fuel a person burns through in their lifetime would be a mountain of coal approximately 5km high and 2km wide. However, there is a nasty by-product of nuclear energy production, and it is lethal to life. Barrels full of radioactive waste must be buried deep underground for thousands of years until it becomes safe to even approach without protective clothing. This lethal waste is not the only problem with nuclear power. It is also not renewable as uranium is limited. It may take decades or centuries, depending on how much more we start to use, but it will run out one day. At current rates, we probably have around 200 years before it runs out on Earth. There is also a fear surrounding nuclear power, and the fear is warranted. The consequences of human error have never been more severe than where nuclear energy production is concerned. The worst-case scenario being millennia of radioactive contamination in the air, land and water for thousands of square miles around a nuclear power plant that has experienced a 'meltdown'. Chernobyl and Fukushima are grave reminders of how quickly nuclear disasters can escalate and how horrific the effects can be on our environment and our lives. Aside from leaving radioactive nuclear contaminants in the air, there is another lousy legacy. To decommission an old nuclear power plant can cost billions but it takes up to 60 years to fully decommission one, so we do not pay for this right away, we are effectively borrowing from our grandchildren to save money for this generation, and this is not good future planning.

Hydrogen gas - unlike other forms of natural gas, hydrogen is a completely clean-burning fuel. Once produced, hydrogen gas only emits water vapour as a by-product, which is technically a greenhouse gas too, but nothing like as potent as carbon dioxide or methane. Sounds ideal, but there is a flaw. Extracting hydrogen from water does mean the use of fossil fuels again or at least using another form of renewable fuel. Hydrogen gas produced via electrolysis is a real possibility for powering the planet, but it depends on what is producing the electricity. The electricity must be produced somehow, and it would be needed in great quantities. Currently, we burn fossil fuels to produce a lot of our electricity. So when considering this form of alternative energy, we must consider the cost, both environmentally and economically. The only way I could see it working long-term is by combining it with renewable energy to extract the hydrogen, and this would result in an energy source that could power the population with practically zero greenhouse gas emissions. There are times of excess electricity production from wind farms, and this is restricted. Instead of wasting it, this excess electricity could be used to produce hydrogen gas through electrolysers built into wind farms.

Biofuel – we can assume, this is the oldest form of energy production used deliberately by humans. When humans first discovered fire, they would burn the organic materials around them to keep the heat energy releasing. This also released trapped carbon into the atmosphere that the plants and trees had absorbed during their lifetimes. Biofuel is maybe not the most efficient or environmentally friendly form of energy production and as the most primitive energy source, may not make an appearance in a typical futurist's vision. However, it can still be of use to us, for instance, in the form of waste-to-energy power plants. Instead of just burning crop leftovers and wood, we can burn our rubbish and benefit from it. As a species, we generate hundreds of millions of tonnes of landfill waste each year. Rather than leaving this to rot in a landfill for decades, whilst contributing to the greenhouse effect with the release of methane gas anyway, anything that cannot be re-cycled can be sent to facilities that incinerate the rubbish, turning the waste into power. This is a renewable and sustainable form of energy production, as we will always have waste to dispose of, and incinerating rubbish reduces the volume of mass down to one-tenth of its size. It is also worth considering that in the short-term, methane is a far more potent greenhouse gas than carbon dioxide. If we can make power whilst preventing methane release and reducing landfill, this solves several problems at once. The public perception of burning rubbish is not good as people assume the toxins would be horrendous, and they can be, if burnt in uncontrolled environments, such as on a garden bonfire. Just as burning fossil fuels produces gases, the gases produced by burning waste can be very harmful. However, we have the technology to render the gases safe and harmless before releasing into the environment, such as catalytic converters, which can be incorporated into to car exhaust systems.

Before reviewing, I think it necessary to briefly look at how our confidence in alternative energies can be undermined when there are failures in production. Domestic failure of solar power is a perfect example. Solar power is one of the first that springs to mind when we think 'renewable energy'. However, despite being long-established, it is currently not used to anywhere near its potential. Perhaps partly to blame are misleading government incentives and poorly constructed panels. These failures have seriously undermined the domestic potential of this alternative energy and furthermore, fuelled a mistrust in the motivations surrounding green energy. For instance, in the UK in 2010, the government launched a feed-in-tariff that was meant to encourage homeowners to create their own renewable energy by allowing the installations of solar panels on the rooftops of their homes. It was a huge incentive for anyone toying with the idea of spending thousands to put solar panels on their houses, and it helped to get nearly a million homes around the UK fitted with solar panels. The scheme promised to pay the homeowners for 25 years. However, by 2019 the installations had dropped 94 per cent, and the industry of installing them suffered thousands of job losses after the government announced it was planning to stop the feed-in tariff scheme. Those with solar panels already installed, even faulty ones that are not generating power efficiently, will continue to collect pay-outs, but households getting new panels installed will not receive the incentive as before. The renewable energy industry is supposed to be something that is growing, but with domestic solar power, it achieved the opposite because of quality control and financial failures. A cynic would tell you many companies involved in the domestic solar panel boom were in it for a short-term moneymaker and had no intention of creating a resilient and durable product to help fuel the future. With our current economic systems, it may be too much to expect of the human race to do something truly selfless and great for future generations with no immediate financial reward. I will suggest what we can do about this in the next section on 'Preparing an economy for H-utopia'.

The practical application of solar energy could rival that of fossil fuels if pushed to its potential. For example, building enormous offshore solar islands in parts of the ocean that receive a lot of sunlight, such as off the north coast of Australia and in the Arabian Gulf. It is speculated that just one solar 'island' half a mile wide could generate enough energy to power a commercial passenger plane for a year, by solar energy being used to generate electricity for splitting seawater molecules to isolate hydrogen, which would then react with absorbed carbon dioxide to produce usable methanol. This is just one example of alternative energy not fulfilling its potential.

Not keeping all of our eggs in one basket

By combining and pushing to their potential all of the alternative energy sources described above, including solar and wind energy, it is feasible we could produce 100 per cent of our energy needs cleanly. Perhaps not as convenient or lucrative as fossil fuels, but the renewable, clean and less susceptible to corruption are the best choices for H-utopia. It is obvious that we cannot rely on just one type of fuel and should invest in a multitude of different energy productions that are renewable and pollutant-free, in order to provide a sustainable, resilient, long-term plan for powering our way to H-utopia, with a reduced environmental impact being a priority. Despite the initial high investment, tidal power should be something we invest in perfecting, as well as hydrogen gas energy, but combined with renewable sources instead of fossil fuels for the electrolysis process.

There are other interesting energy solutions that will be possible in the not too distant future for our descendants to utilise, such as fusion power. Harnessing the power of the sun itself in outer space, where the energy is higher than on Earth is something that has been hypothesised for a long time. The so-called Dyson Sphere or Dyson Swarm was first described in 1937 by Olaf Stapledon in his science-fiction novel, Star Maker. The theoretical energy source works like so: a spherical megastructure is built to surround a planet's host star, absorbing all of its otherwise wasted energy output. Looking to the biggest energy output in the solar system is logical for an advancing civilisation needing fuel for powering its technology and growing population, without compromising its home environment. There is even the potential to produce our own fusion reactors, (mini stars), right here on Earth. This would be on of the most ambitious projects ever undertaken by mankind, but sadly it could be decades before being perfected and put to practical use, and we cannot wait decades to stop using fossil fuels. I will review the viability, potential and breakthroughs of fusion energy, and other futuristic forms of energy in more detail during the final part of this essay. In the meantime, we cannot keep on burning fossil fuels as if there is no tomorrow, waiting for a future of fusion power that may never have a chance to arrive if we fail to look after our resources now and create contingency.

A duty of care to the entire population

The number one cause of human death is not cancer or heart disease as some may guess. In fact, the greatest cause of ill-health, suffering and death across the world is poverty. People who die preventable deaths because they do not have access to clean water, medicine, adequate shelter and sanitation. The following are some figures published by the World Health Organisation, UNICEF and other organisations that deal with poverty-related illness. These statistics are all from research that was carried out between 2010 and 2016 so may have changed slightly, but not drastically. The results of this report are public knowledge, as are up to date estimates, but one has to make an effort to go looking for these numbers, they are rarely reported on TV or by mainstream media outlets which generally focus on more trivial human affairs and short term controversies to grab the attention of their audience. However, to neglect a duty of care and ignore this is an international disgrace:

- Starvation kills 9 million people per year - more than the death toll for malaria, AIDs and tuberculosis combined in 2012.
- Over 800 million people globally are malnourished.
- Ninety-eight per cent of those who suffer from hunger live in developing countries. Five hundred and fifty-three million live in the Asian and Pacific regions, whilst 227 million live in Sub-Saharan Africa. Latin America and the Caribbean account for 47 million.
- Over 60 per cent of the world's hungry are women, who have limited access to resources because of the patriarchal societies in which they live. Because of the prevalence of hunger in women in developing countries, malnutrition is a leading cause of death for children. Approximately 3.1 million children die of hunger each year, accounting for nearly half of all deaths in children under 5.
- Forty per cent of pre-school aged children are estimated to be anaemic because of iron deficiency, and anaemia causes 20 per cent of all maternal deaths.
- It is estimated that between a quarter to half a million children go blind from Vitamin A deficiency every year.

- Malnutrition causes stunting amongst children, a condition characterised by low height for a child's age. In 2013, it was estimated that 161 million children under five were stunted worldwide. Malnutrition also causes wasting, a condition characterised by low weight for a child's age. In 2013, it was estimated that the bodies of 51 million children under five were wasted.

Great strides have been made towards ending world hunger, and thankfully there have been improvements in the 21st century. Many of these figures are down compared with figures coming out of the end of the 20th century. The Food and Agricultural Organisation of the United Nations estimates that: the total number of hungry people worldwide has been reduced by 216 million people since 1992. It is evident some regions have developed quicker than others; Latin America reduced its hunger rate from 14.7 per cent in 1990-1992 to 5.5 per cent in 2012-2014, and South-East Asia reduced its hunger rate from 30.6 per cent to 9.6 per cent in the same timeframe. Sadly, one region that has shown little reduction in hunger has been Sub-Saharan Africa. Whilst the hunger rate in this region fell 10 per cent from 1992-2014, the number of hungry people actually rose during this time period, from 175 million to 220 million.

Research has shown that the world produces enough food to feed everyone; food availability per capita has increased from approximately 2220 kcal per person per day in the 1960s to 2790 kcals per person per day in 2006. Poverty, (the financial means to get food distributed to you), NOT food shortage, is the number one cause of world hunger. The World Bank estimated that 10.7 per cent of the human population lived on less than $1.90 per day in 2013 and as of 2020 there are over a billion people live on less than a dollar a day.

Another problem is that three-quarters of the world's poorest have to rely on growing their own food. This leads to widespread food insecurity as drought, and natural disasters cut off the food supply for entire towns and villages. Many people in the developing world do not even produce sufficient income to purchase land to grow enough nutritious food. This is an issue of 'food access'. The Food and Agriculture Organisation (FAO) defines four dimensions of food security, all of which must be fulfilled simultaneously for food security to exist. The four dimensions are:

1. Physical availability of food.
2. Economic and physical access to food.
3. Food utilisation.
4. The stability of the first three dimensions over time.

World hunger has proven to be a difficult problem to solve, despite the efforts of many nations and organisations working to eradicate it. As mentioned, world hunger statistics show that great progress has been made, particularly in East Asia, South-East Asia and Latin America, but it is not just access to food that poses a problem. There is a more fundamental issue, and that is a lack of access to clean water - something that should be the most basic of rights for every living thing.

- Six hundred and sixty-three million human beings do not have clean water to drink.
- (WHO/UNICEF Joint Monitoring Programme (JMP) Report 2015)
- Around 289,000 children under five die every year from intestinal illness caused by poor water and sanitation. That is almost 800 children per day, or one child every two minutes.
- (WASHWatch.org)
- Every minute a newborn baby dies from infection caused by a lack of safe water/being in an unclean environment.
- (WHO, 2015)
- Forty-two per cent of healthcare facilities in African countries do not have access to safe water.
- (WHO/UNICEF, 2015)
- Nearly half of all people using dirty water live in sub-Saharan Africa, and one-fifth lives in Southern Asia.
- (WHO/UNICEF Joint Monitoring Programme (JMP) Report 2015)
- Globally, 19 per cent of the urban population and 49 per cent of the rural population lack an adequate toilet.
- (WHO/UNICEF Joint Monitoring Programme (JMP) Report 2015)
- At current rates of progress, everyone in low and middle-income countries will not have clean water until the year 2057 – 27 years behind schedule.
- (WHO/UNICEF Joint Monitoring Programme (JMP) Report 2015

and WASHwatch)

- At current rates of progress, everyone in low and middle-income countries will not have adequate toilets until the year 2135 – 105 years behind schedule.
- (WHO/UNICEF Joint Monitoring Programme (JMP) Report 2015 and WASHwatch)
- Globally, 31 per cent of schools do not have clean water, and 34 per cent lack adequate toilets.
- (UNICEF, Advancing WASH in Schools Monitoring, 2015)

Despite the best efforts of charities and organisations over the years to support poverty-stricken parts of the world, the predictions just to provide adequate toilets to everyone is over one hundred years away! We are talking about H-utopia, but we cannot even confidently say everyone will have access to plumbing by the year 2100! H-utopia is for everyone, not just the rich half of the world. Sorting this disgraceful poverty out once and for all has to take priority, and it should not be reliant on rich philanthropic individuals taking on additional responsibility to sort out government issues with their own plans. There is a growing inhumane response to charity in a world where, even in the developed parts, people are slipping back into poverty. This has led to some people treating charities with resentment, frustration and even suspicion, after decades of campaigning for the same thing have not solved the problems. The attitude of some is that people in developing countries should stop having so many children. However, people suggesting this solution need to realise that only 100 years ago in the developed world, before access to sanitation and antibiotics, it was common for families to comprise of more than ten children, some of which were not expected to live out their childhood. We cannot tell or force people to go against every instinct to reproduce in the hope that at least one of their offspring will survive. There is no simple fix solution, rather a combination of all of the following, but it will require support and cooperation from the whole of humanity:

- Food supplements in a drink form that contain all of the vitamins and minerals humans need.
- Genetic modification of food, and the production of cultivated meat.

- Better population control measures through education and access to contraceptive choices.
- A reformation of the socio-economic structure of the world to allow any funds necessary to be found without having to rely on charity and philanthropy.
- Addressing political failures in the afflicted countries.
- Global investment in sanitation projects for developing countries to ensure water supplies remain uncontaminated.
- Protein farms that take advantage of the high protein content of insects.
- Seaweed farms/edible algae for protein.
- High rise farms using mirror systems to get sunlight to every level. Utilising wasted space to get ten acres of farm for every one acre of land.
- Converting failing farms into government facilities, purchased from the private owners, who are then employed.
- Desalination plants for parts of the world that suffer with draught.

The suggestions on this list could be beneficial for the whole world, not just poverty-stricken parts. For instance, we could really bring farming into the 21st century with global, government investment into improving the efficiency of the industry. With brilliant initiatives, such as constructing indoor, multi-storey farms, perfectly climate controlled for yielding crops all year round, growing more efficiently than nature ever could, and with a reduced need for pesticides. With future farms like this, there comes the potential for a new wave of employment in what has been becoming a very automated industry. We no longer live in a world where we can afford wasted space when it comes to food production. We need to be as efficient as possible, and using around one-third of all land on Earth just to feed and rear animals to kill for our food is far from efficient. Building farms upwards when we cannot build outwards, on the other hand, is an ultra-efficient use of space.

Another incredibly efficient use of space is farming insects on protein farms. To breed insects requires a far lower utilisation of land, water, fertiliser, pesticide, feeding, and has a far smaller impact on the environment than breeding large methane-producing mammals. With over a million species of insects on Earth and over 2000 eaten by humans in various parts of the world, the potential from this diverse resource has until recently been overlooked as a potential emergency solution to preventing starvation deaths. With the recent realisation of this potential, an entirely new insect-based food industry has emerged, already making substantial progress developing products from the world's most diverse and plentiful group of edible organisms. The thought of eating bugs may make some readers squeamish, but this is not literally eating bugs, this is providing a protein source in products that can take the form of powders, pills, oils, etc. This will save lives in parts of the world that are currently malnourished.

Another major breakthrough that is already being heavily invested in is cultivated meat (lab-grown meat). This is not an idea for the distant future but is already a reality now, and this has the potential to change the world more than any invention of the 21st century so far. It is sustainable, environmentally friendly and animal friendly. Producing meat in this way, we will not have to use crop harvests to feed and fatten up millions of animals that are being raised for slaughter, and as a bonus, we will not have to cause unnecessary suffering to animals. There are already meat-free meat substitute products, made with plants, fungi or soya, widely available that contain the protein we need and can be produced to appear and taste similar to the real thing, but they will never be the only solution as they are not to everyone's taste. Many people just cannot seem to live contently without meat, so this new breakthrough of growing actual cuts of meat from animal cells without them ever being part of a living, feeling, polluting, potentially infectious and resource-draining animal, is a great alternative. Let us examine the advantages and disadvantages of lab-produced meat.

Advantages:

Animal welfare - the endless suffering and exploitation of animals should be the number one reason on our list for stopping, or at least severely reducing, real meat consumption worldwide. Animal farming rarely has animals' interests in mind, with their comfort being an afterthought at best. Efforts are made to make ourselves feel better about what we know deep down is unethical, telling ourselves it is nature - the food-chain. As a hypocritical society, we have felt almost unanimous rage at hunters killing wild animals, whilst we are chomping down a beef burger for our lunch, made with the combined meat from dozens of minced up cow parts. We have a hatred for hunters who kill one animal which is considered beautiful by society, but we turn a blind eye to millions of farm animals being butchered every year because they are not appreciated in the same way. We have decided their purpose is not to be admired; it is just to be eaten. When you think about it rationally, farming animals is worse than hunting them, because at least animals have a chance to run away in the wild. Many people will argue that it is just nature; if you came face to face with a hungry lion, it would not think twice about eating you. But this argument is flawed. Are we really willing to judge a lion by the same standards as we judge ourselves? They do not have the mental capacity or understanding we do, to realise that there are ingenious alternatives to real meat that would give them more efficient and healthier vitamin and protein intake that chomping down potentially diseased raw meat and blood. Furthermore, before eating us, a lion would not spend three years fattening us up whilst keeping us in a filthy cage then transporting us in cramped lorries to be cut up into unrecognisable shapes and neatly packaged, which leads onto my next point.

Improved efficiency - the efficiency of growing meat products in a lab is 99 per cent better than rearing the real animals from scratch, having to feed them, (overfeed them in some cases), find the land to keep them on, deal with their waste and methane pollution, then have to kill them when the time is right, transporting their bodies to be butchered, prepared and packaged and then transported again to various shops for sale. The amount of space we need to produce meat in a lab compared to real live animal meat is a tiny fraction, it does not have to be fed, and it only has to be transported once if the production facilities are used efficiently.

Health benefits - lab-grown meat would be much healthier than the real thing. Animal meat is a source of many food-borne illnesses, such as salmonella and e-coli that cause food poisoning. The closure of slaughterhouses would reduce this, and reduction in farming for meat would also help reduce transmission of disease from animals to humans. In addition, lab-grown meat will have all the best bits and none of the bad. It could be supplemented with vitamins and have none of the excess fat, gristle and carcinogens that can cause cancers of the bowel.

Sustainability - consumers get through tens of millions of tons of meat each year. This demand creates a massive need for livestock supply on an industrial scale. The negative effects on the planet are immense. Apart from the needless suffering of the farm animals, natural habitats of other creatures are disturbed by the massive amount of deforestation to provide land to house the farm animals, and fields to farm so extra food can be grown to feed them. There are also the greenhouse gas emissions that all of these extra livestock produce. It is estimated that livestock may be the cause of 15 per cent of all greenhouse gas emissions. The cycle of the meat industry is thus: they are given life by us, they pollute us, they are killed by us in their prime, and they poison us slowly in their deaths.

Combatting antibiotic resistance - the living conditions of animals raised for meat, particularly pigs, are often so filthy that the animals are given regular antibiotics as a precaution to prevent loss of life and therefore loss of profits. However, this overuse of antibiotics as a preventive measure in farming is unethical as the medicine works its way into the human food supply and is partly responsible for growing antibiotic resistance in human bacterial disease. If we carry on casually using antibiotics as preventive medicine in farming, (or in general for that matter), then in the future they will not be effective anymore as a medical treatment and death from serious bacterial infections could return as one of the biggest human killers - bigger even than cancer, heart disease or starvation.

Disadvantages:

Consumer complaints - the taste of lab-grown meat will undoubtedly be distinguishable from the real thing and may prove wholly unsatisfying to some consumers. Over time I am sure better results would come from improvements in synthetic flavouring and the cultivating process. Even if the process can be perfected, so it is indistinguishable from the real thing, there is a paranoia surrounding food sources that are deemed unnatural, such as genetically modified (GM) foods. Some people would simply refuse to accept any unnatural foods out of mistrust. Proper education of the next generation can help to combat this phobia.

The financial impact on the farming industry - understandably farmers and slaughterhouses are going to be against this significant threat to their livelihood's for the financial implications. The transition from eating animals to eating synthetic animal meat is not something that will happen overnight. It may take decades and several generations for the transition to be complete, and during this transition period, the meat farmers must have a fair chance to evolve their businesses and transform their facilities with government funding. I do appreciate the implications for the animal farmers but going back to what I have already said, this is a pill we have to swallow if we want to progress. We cannot let nostalgia for outdated professions and greed come before advancements for the good of humanity and life on Earth. The biggest inconvenience we have to endure in order to solve world hunger, and many environmental issues all in one go is meat farmers having to convert their farms and slaughterhouse facilities into cultivating labs. Farmers could even be given a chance to sell their land, for a fair price, in a government scheme to buy land for building multi-storey, automated crop farms that can produce food regardless of extreme weather such as droughts, floods, snow and ice.

Despite the drawbacks, I conclude that another action for our future H-utopia should be to begin preparing for a move away from consuming real animal meat on an industrial scale like it is today. Killing animals for our consumption is an outdated, inefficient and frankly barbaric practice, that will almost certainly be looked back on by future generations as a dark time in human history. There are alternatives that we now know, due to our scientific capabilities, have the same nutritional value as real animal meat and can even be given the same flavour and texture synthetically.

    This is our generation's chance to bring the light and be remembered for ushering in a new era of humanity and compassion. Obviously, the expectation is not for the change in billions of people's eating habits to occur overnight, but we should begin to think about this as a long-term goal. The change will come naturally as people's eating preferences transform, and the demand for real meat gradually reduces over the coming years. It is essential that traditional farmers, who have supported humanity for generations with their tireless labour, do not suffer, and are given fair opportunity to convert their facilities with government grants when the time comes, enabling them to continue providing for humanity.

For environmental reasons alone, the future diet of our species will have to be predominantly vegetarian and synthetic. This much is clear. However, it is going to take time, perhaps several generations, for people to adjust to this drastic change in lifestyle.

Water, water everywhere, but not a drop to drink

Even with an estimated 350 quintillion gallons of water in Earth's oceans, we have regional scarcity of this most basic human right. Seawater makes up roughly 97 per cent of the water on Earth, yet it goes to waste because it is unfit for human consumption. The utilisation of this plentiful resource could be a solution to regional scarcity of freshwater. It is not beyond our capabilities to desalinate and decontaminate seawater even now - there are thousands of facilities around the world that have been doing it for decades. So why are there so many people without water to drink? Well, the desalination process uses an enormous amount of energy that currently requires burning fossil fuels to generate. Because salt dissolves so easily in water, the chemical bond is not easy to break without a powerful energy source to power the thermal distillation or membrane separation. Thermal distillation of seawater on a large scale is the equivalent to boiling billions of kettles a day. Membrane separation is the modern choice as it is far more cost-effective and works via filtration and a process called reverse osmosis to separate the salt from the water. Either way, the technology and power needed to run a desalination facility are expensive, and not something developing nations have the means for. The desalination facilities are predominantly in rich countries such as Saudi Arabia, where oil power is cheap, but freshwater is scarce. The facilities are also terrible for sea life that can get sucked in and killed. Then there is the dilemma of what to do with all of the leftover super concentrated brine, which usually just gets pumped back out into the ocean, upsetting the local environment. The whole process is inefficient, bad for the environment and costly. However, despite the economic and environmental drawbacks, desalination will continue to be a necessity as we run low on natural freshwater. Perhaps with a renewable energy source to run the facilities with, (tidal energy springs to mind as a logical choice), it will become more sustainable as time goes on. There are also several ways to reduce the environmental impact of brine wastewater:

- Purpose-built evaporation ponds - the brine can be accumulated in shallow surface ponds allowing the brine to further concentrate as freshwater evaporates.
- Deep well injection - brine can be channelled into subsurface rock layers to keep it from re-entering the oceans. This is a costly option though that requires a lot of potentially dangerous drilling.
- Public uses - brine can even be put to use as a de-icer for roads in winter months and to control dust in dryer climates in the summer months by spraying.

As usual, there are solutions to every problem. It just comes down to a lack of investment. With 350 quintillion gallons of water floating around the Earth, there is no excuse to not have running toilets for everyone until the 22nd century as is ludicrously predicted.

Humane solutions to slowing down population growth

Stabilising our population growth is the most difficult challenge we are facing in the near future, and it will force us to make some serious, responsible decisions that we may not want to make, but with nearly 8 billion people on Earth and with a growth of around 200,000 every single day, either we choose to make the decisions or nature will make them for us.

Over the last couple of centuries, due to advancements in medicine, and public health/hygiene, human population growth has become exponential, doubling in size roughly every four decades. You do not need to be a mathematician to realise this is clearly not sustainable. Something has to give sooner or later; otherwise, by the second half of this millennium, there would be so many humans on Earth that we would all have to be touching to fit on it! We can imagine this in theory, but in practical terms, this could obviously never occur as nature intervenes; the environmental implications alone would be catastrophic a long time before getting to the stage of filling all of the landmass on Earth with human beings.

When we make the irresponsible decision to have too many children, there is no excuse in the form of ignorance, as we all know it to be a mathematical certainty that if we carry on breeding at the rate, we currently are, as a species, then nature will intercede with disastrous consequences within the next couple of centuries; yet we casually carry on ignoring our responsibility to avert this disaster, hiding behind "our right" to have 5, 10, 15, 20 children or more in some cases. The thing about rights is, they are subject to change and can be revoked if we abuse them. This should be an absolute last resort by an authority, and something that we must avoid at all costs, as forceful removal of a freedom we have always had will only take us to dystopia ultimately.

Any advanced civilisation growing up in the Universe will inevitably come up against the 'sustainability problem' at the same point of sudden scientific and medical advancement that we reached in the 20th century. The sad truth may be that a good percentage of any civilisations in the Universe at this point in their development may lack the will power and wisdom to surpass this challenging stage and will end up stubbornly destroying themselves instead of cooperating with global lifestyle changes. As time marches on and we happily accept modern conveniences, including technology, medicine, sanitation, all of which make our lives better, we must realise we cannot have everything. There are humane solutions to every problem, but it will take a cooperative, openminded, responsible, judicious and worthy species indeed to overcome the many practical and ethical issues population control raises.

Brace yourselves, for we are about to dive headlong into controversy to find answers. We already have humane solutions to maintaining equilibrium between birth and death that we are all very aware of. Many of us have just been too afraid to use them for fear of persecution or of stumbling onto a 'slippery slope'.

Birth control and abortion

Until the 20th century, the greatest birth/population control was mother nature herself. Nature is cruel and relentless, picking off the easy targets in babies and infants. Only one hundred years ago, even in the most developed parts of the world, the chance of parents losing their baby between birth and one year old was around 10-15 per cent on average. Some poorer families would have experienced much higher rates. When you consider stillbirths and child deaths, it was not unusual for a couple to have ten children and only have two or three of them survive long enough to have children of their own. If you look into your own family history, you will realise this tragic fact and appreciate how lucky you are to be here.

The significant improvements came in the 1940s onwards, and by the 1990s, the infant mortality rate had dropped from 15 per cent to 0.5 per cent. Thanks to better sanitation, antibiotics, pregnancy monitoring, hospital births and vaccinations, it was not just more babies surviving; the health of older children also improved. Diseases that once purged the adolescent population such as pertussis, diphtheria and measles were practically eliminated during the latter half of the 20th century. The horrific population purgers of history, including bubonic plague and smallpox, have long been banished and some serious illnesses that affect children and adults alike that remain but are now treatable include tuberculosis, gastrointestinal infections from contaminated food and drink, bacterial infections of the gut/urinary tract, and infections of the throat and respiratory system. These problems are caused initially by viruses as common as rhinovirus or strains of influenza, and bacteria such as streptococcus or e-coli. The illnesses often start mild but left untreated the germs can kill their hosts when bacteria spreads to the heart and brain via the blood. All of the above diseases and countless others have either been eradicated or have become easily treatable in modern times, saving billions of vulnerable lives, which has had a dramatic effect on human population growth.

Average life expectancy decades and centuries ago may have seemed ridiculously low, but this is not to say that many people did not live to a grand age. The average lifespan was significantly reduced in the past, because of infant mortality dragging it down. For example, if we did a survey of ten new-borns in the year 1850, and five of those individuals died not long after being born, and the other five lived to be one hundred years old, then the average life expectancy of the people of 1850 would misleadingly be calculated at fifty years old. The dramatic decline in infant mortality in the twentieth century correlated with dramatic increases in life expectancy. It was not as clear-cut as the elderly necessarily living longer, but also children who were given a chance to overcome the childhood illnesses and live their lives to the full potential nature was robbing them of previously. Advancements in medical science, better living standards, better nutrition, environmental interventions, properly constructed houses - with heating, improvements in sanitation and plumbing, and warm water on tap for washing away pathogens are all factors that helped overcome infant mortality.

The only downside is, the above has now left us with a dilemma in the 21st century, there are soon going to be too many of us for the amount of resources we each use. So what is the solution? We cannot stop treating illness, we cannot let our vulnerable die when they can be saved, we cannot stop medical advancements, and we should not stop progress in general. We also, should not have to watch our loved ones dying slowly and in pain from horrible diseases, when a cure is possible. So how can we keep our humanity/ethics intact, whilst maintaining sustainability at the same time? We find the solution by asking a simple question. To control population do we:

A) Allow loving and living conscious men, women and children to die from preventable illness?

B) Prevent too many, as yet not conceived humans from being conceived and born?

Most would hopefully agree, the latter is the humane and logical option, but it does not resolve the stalemate between, wanting to delay death and the psychological discomfort that comes with the unnatural act of preventing birth. Allowing death to occur provides less effort and seems altogether more natural to us, but this is not the choice our civilisation has made. We want to advance medically, we want to save all of those who can be saved and extend our lives as long as humanely possible, and so we should if we want to create a great civilisation. Therefore, the bottom line is, we have a responsibility, nay, an obligation, to control birth far better than we currently do.

Stricter birth control is a controversial subject, but it is the lesser of two controversies, and a stride that we must take on our way to H-utopia. With infant mortality rates at practically zero in the developed world. Allowing couples to go on to breed four, five, six, seven or more children is just not sustainable. Higher amounts of children per family are especially witnessed in the extremes of society, the very poor and the very rich/famous.

Even having three children is unsustainable when they are all surviving and all having their own children. Ideally, the number needs to be indefinitely capped at one child per person, equalling two per couple. An heir for yourself, and another heir for your partner, equalling two heirs between you. This is just about sustainable, (when taking into account some people do not have any children), but is it in any way enforceable?

We have to tread carefully here as dystopia eagerly awaits for us to fall into its trap. It is important to realise that the world does not have a population problem. Only certain countries do. Therefore there is no one size fits all solution. We have to tailor our approach to tackling population problems where they are most severe. China and India, for instance, have a combined approximate three billion people alone.

Then there are developing countries where the majority of parents still reproduce as families in the developed world used to one hundred plus years ago because they know that tragically many of their offspring stand a high chance of dying from illness and disease before reaching adulthood. Needless to say, infant mortality is not an acceptable form of population control. Parents in developing countries need confidence their children will survive before birth rates will drop, and no amount of contraceptive education will stop the desire to keep having children until they know the ones they have will survive. This transition happened in the developed parts of the world decades ago after the rollout of vaccines and as antibiotics became more easily available. There is no way to skip over this step in development, but it can be sped up. Population in developing countries will increase faster before stabilising. The more support they get from the developed world who have already been through this stage of social and medical revolution, the more efficient it will be.

Even in the most developed parts of the world, we are not even close to reaching Hans Rosling's famously called 'age of peak child', the pre-emptive moment when the human population stops increasing due to a combination of environmental barriers and social wisdom. Although it is certain the population cannot increase forever, and there is a finite limit to what the Earth can sustain, there is no guarantee humanity will survive to see the age of peak child or maintain the equilibrium once there, without significant intervention.

So what can we do to avert social calamities caused by

overpopulation? The world can learn from China's successes and mistakes. China currently has the largest population on Earth, closely followed by India (which will likely overtake them in the near future). In 2018 China announced it would be relaxing its one child per family law that dates back to 1979. The law, although very responsible and desperately needed, has been the subject of controversy over the years, for its alleged use of forced abortions, forced sterilisation, and fines in an attempt to strictly limit births.

It was realised in 1950 the rate of population change in China was not sustainable. 1.9 per cent each year. To put this in perspective, a growth rate of 3 per cent will cause the population of a country to double every 25 years. The extreme measure was necessary, and it worked. The birth rate in China has since fallen, and the rate of population growth has stabilised at around 0.7 per cent. However, there have been negative impacts that we need to acknowledge. Knowing they could only ever have a single child, parents had a preference for boys. As a result, large numbers of females ended up homeless or even killed, and up to 90 per cent of abortions were female foetuses. The long-term negative effects were becoming apparent. Therefore, in recent years couples have been allowed to have a second child if their first child was a girl, or if both parents are themselves from single-child families. Another long-term side effect of suddenly only allowing a single child per every two people means a rise in the number of elderly people in comparison with young. If not carefully managed now, China's elderly population in the future could struggle to be sustained by decreased numbers of working-age citizens.

Just a handful of nations setting rules to control their population is not going to work, as there will be resentment if there are different sets of rules for different people. One child per person, (two per couple), needs to be agreed as a guideline across the whole world. However, this should not be imposed in a dictatorial law like it was in China. It is important the 'Two-child guide' is implemented with benefits rather than punishments. For instance, the first two children could receive free education to university level, as a kind of scholarship for humanity. A further benefit could be free childcare and free health care. Any subsequent children would receive only part of these benefits with parents having to support childcare and contribute to education in the form of population tax. For the extremely rich end of the spectrum, the multi-millionaires of our society, this kind of benefits system will not be appropriate as they would be financially able to support as many children as was humanely possible to produce. So in the case of overbreeding millionaires, there may have to be some kind of large lump sum charge for any extra children being planned in families that hold over a certain threshold of wealth. The two-child guide has to apply to everyone regardless of wealth, or it will not work. No one can be exempt from the responsibility, even royalty.

A further measure is to offer financial incentives for men and women who have already had children, to have vasectomies or tubal ligations to prevent further unwanted pregnancies. The cost of these sterilisation procedures are several thousand, but even with this cost plus the incentives paid to the patients, society would profit massively in the long run from this initiative if it were successful at reducing the rate at which the population is growing. It is not ideal that we should have to do this, but in an ideal world, everyone would be wise enough and selfless enough to realise the implications of their own actions and control their breeding just for the ethical reasons alone. If hitting over breeders in the pocket and incentivising those toying with the idea of sterilisation are the only things going to work for now, then that is what we will have to do.

With reduced additional pregnancies being planned, it should encourage parents to dedicate more time and attention to be spent with the children they already have. This not only saves us from overpopulation but also produces a generation of better nurtured and cared for human beings, making our journey to H-utopia so much easier. In the past, we needed to produce quantity, purely because of the high infant mortality rate. Doing anything but that would have gone against our primal instincts. But we have overcome infant mortality now and should be wise enough to see that we should focus on the quality, not the quantity of our children.

This plan may sound extreme from our point of view today, after what we have been used to, but for the next generation of supremely educated, openminded, ethically raised humans living at the brink of H-utopia, this practice of breeding will become the norm. I know this because if it has not, then there will likely not be any future to speak of at all. We have to be selfless enough to think of the bigger picture, beyond our own lives and do our best to comply with what must be done. The alternatives are far worse. I acknowledge the plan has the potential to become complicated as there are some flaws that cannot be ignored. In the interest of being thorough, I shall do my best to address the following obvious loopholes:

1) Accidents happen

Some estimates have suggested that perhaps 40-50 per cent of all pregnancies, in the developed world, are unplanned. Generally, these 'accidents' will be the first and/or second child though. After the second child, the number of third babies conceived completely unplanned drops. Couples become more cautious, due to increased financial burden and practicability of housing more offspring, even being more likely to undergo sterilisation procedures, (and incentivising these as suggested will mean even more people will opt for them). Research shows the average number of children per family in the UK, for example, has already fallen to less than two. So actually, for those who may have thought it not possible for a nation to control its reproduction willingly, some densely populated countries are already well on target to achieving this part of the H-utopian action plan just due to initiative alone. Obviously, it is not just the UK we have to consider though. The whole world needs to commit to reducing the average number of children per family to two or below. We know that in China it had dropped to less than one child per family, with the extreme family planning law that was in place for several decades.

At the opposite end of the spectrum, the African countries Niger, Mali and Somalia have some of the highest birth rates, between six and seven children per woman, born on average. However, these countries are also in the top ten globally for infant mortality, roughly on par with where the now most developed countries were 120 years ago. Most of the countries in the top 25 list for fertility rate and infant mortality rate are African countries. H-utopia is for all of humanity to share, not just the most developed countries. However, cooperation to get there is equally everybody's responsibility. As infant mortality rate globally decreases, it will mean more women than ever before will be living to reach reproductive age, so the population growth rate will increase initially, but allowing preventable deaths of babies and infants is not an acceptable form of contraception in our H-utopia, or indeed any civilised society. We absolutely need to keep investing in saving the children's lives who are born in undeveloped countries as a matter of international urgency, but as more children survive infancy, we need to equally invest in preventing unwanted pregnancies there too. Decades of effort to bring contraception and sex education to developing countries has been slow, but sure. There has been a global drop in fertility. The average number of children born per woman worldwide was estimated at 2.69 in 2017, compared with 4.97 in the1960s. So, we can see that globally the trend is in the right direction, we just have to keep on top of this, supporting any countries that are above 2.0, in providing better education, combined with more attractive benefits, where applicable, for those following international breeding guidelines. However, even if all the targets for the use of contraception were met, there would still be many millions of unwanted pregnancies, sometimes the contraception fails, and this leads us onto the next problem to be addressed.

2) Stigma around abortion

It is unacceptable that shame and social oppression can affect a pregnant woman's ability to seek and receive proper medical care and support when it comes to terminating an unwanted pregnancy. The stigma that shrouds abortion can make a woman feel inferior for even considering it. The level of shame can depend on the circumstances of the individual, such as religious beliefs, (or parents' religious beliefs), cultural values, social status, or age.

Stigma has grown due to many factors. For one, the personification of the foetus, due to improvements in scanning technology. Another cause is indecision over legal restrictions, which reinforces the idea that abortion is morally wrong, amongst law-abiding people. So, the woman considering abortion is well aware she could be doing something legal today that is considered homicide after the next vote on the matter. The legal limit varies around the world. In the Republic of Ireland, abortion is illegal at any time during pregnancy, unless there is a serious threat to the life of the mother. In most countries, abortions up to 14 weeks into the pregnancy are legal, increasing to 24 weeks in cases of rape victims or foetal abnormalities. In the UK the legal limit was lowered from 28 to 24 weeks in 1990. Abortions after 24 weeks are now only allowed if there are severe foetal abnormalities or there is a serious risk to the mother.

The 24-week limit is not random; there are many factors that are taken into account, including, at what stage it is thought the brain develops enough to feel pain. Although, since the limit was set, there has been increasing evidence than unborn babies can feel pain much earlier than this, at around 20 weeks, but we cannot know for sure. Some research suggests as early as five weeks, but this is unlikely. When a person is in pain, say, for example, you stub your toe, a signal travels from the toe up through the nerves in the leg, to the spinal cord, and from there to the brain. In the brain, the information sent is transmitted through a web of neurons to the cortex, where it is translated as a pain response. It is not evolutionarily necessary for a foetus to have this kind of response until its body is developed enough to survive outside of the womb if born. The evolutionary reason for pain is to quickly stop a creature from doing whatever is causing the pain. Often, pain is a warning sign that you are doing something that could be potentially endangering your survival if you carry on. Even if a foetus at this early stage did have a fully functioning nervous system, (which it does not), campaigners against abortion, (who often have strong religious backgrounds), claim to be against unnecessary pain and suffering. What they may not realise, is they are hypocritical, for the same religiously motivated pro-life attitude towards end of life seems to encourage suffering, on people who do have a functioning nervous system, and can fully experience a slow and painful death.

At the time of writing, some estimates suggest there are around 210 million pregnancies occurring each year, and approximately 46 million of these end in induced abortion. Research suggests that two-thirds of those that have abortions anticipate society's stigma and feel that they have to keep it secret, even from close friends and family. Some are even apprehensive about going through with the procedure because of what their healthcare professionals will think of them after. All of this puts an unfair amount of pressure and shame on the woman, with some even opting for potentially dangerous self-induced or underhand abortions, rather than telling anyone they know. Of the 46 million abortions per year worldwide, studies have claimed roughly 40 per cent are not performed under safe conditions. The pregnant woman should be able to make the decision to seek proper medical care confidently without fear of persecution; and to be able to make the decision quickly, avoiding unneeded, upsetting delay.

The earliest known surviving premature baby was born at 21 weeks. For this reason, many think the legal limit for abortion should be kept lower than this. Enforcing perhaps 18 weeks as a worldwide maximum, coupled with better education on the subject, and maybe even the compulsory use of anaesthetic for the foetus during the procedure to eliminate any chance of suffering, the stigma could be significantly reduced. Most women know by week 18 that they are pregnant. It is arguably, enough time to make the decision if the guilt and stress society currently imposes is removed, making the whole process more efficient. We need to work on changing the perception that abortion is a 'necessary evil', but instead acknowledge the experience of abortion as a normal and beneficial procedure for (wo)mankind, and all of humanity.

A maximum limit needs to be agreed internationally. If it is legal in some countries but not others, then the stigma will never be removed. In the countries where it is illegal, it only means more women opt for risky 'underground' abortions anyway, and authorities who ignore this, or put little effort into stopping the practice, are incredibly irresponsible and clearly not fit to set such laws. At the same time, though, we do have to be careful abortion does not become used too casually, as a form of contraception. It is, after all, an expensive procedure that costs from hundreds to thousands, depending on how far along the pregnancy is, and with an estimated 46 million abortions annually worldwide that is a lot of money, for forward-thinking countries that offer the service for free, to foot the bill for. More thorough education at school and free, easier access to contraception, and emergency contraception such as the 'morning-after pill', should help to combat this. Even during sex education at schools, abortion is not really covered in any detail, and it certainly does not do the job of removing the stigma. That is because schools, (particularly religious schools), are scared to promote or even normalise the abortion procedure for fear of backlash from parents who oppose it on religious grounds. Once again religious organisations, shrouding themselves with misplaced divine infallibility setting themselves beyond criticism, are found at the root as a cause for damaging society, and mentally impairing our children.

3) Wanting a specific gender

With the aid of revolutionary genetic techniques, choosing the gender of a child, (also known as sex selection), is no longer science-fiction but a real possibility. The best method is Preimplantation Genetic Diagnosis, which is close 100 per cent accurate in predicting the gender of an embryo. The process uses DNA 'probes' to determine what the gender will be. The embryo of the desired gender can then be implanted into the mother. The only problem is, the world is not accepting it. This advanced genetic technique is highly controversial and is even illegal in some countries, including the UK and Australia. However, some people are so desperate to have a girl or a boy they will do the alternative, which is to keep trying, ending up having more children than they wanted, or can really cope with, just to get one of the gender they wanted. This is burdensome on society and not fair on the children that were not really wanted.

The controversy stems from an ethical issue. Some argue that it is 'playing God' or that we do not have the right to interfere with natural processes. Other people may believe it is a slippery slope to eugenics, which is a highly controversial subject due to some immoral attempts in the past where people have tried to impose their own eugenic agenda forcefully. With this science, there is the potential to influence hair colour, eye colour, height, intelligence, etc. Are we really going to be able to exercise the restraint to stop at just choosing the gender? But the fact is, we already do interfere with nature on almost every level. The impact we have on this planet to generate power for our lifestyles, breeding dogs for our pets, racehorses for our amusement and financial gain, beefy cows for our food, dairy cows for our milk, prolonging life with medical science, organ transplants, blood transfusions, IVF to help conceive for those with fertility problems, plastic surgery to change our appearance, and surgery to change our gender, the list goes on. So if it is a possibility within human capability, and we are fine with doing all of this, then why should we not utilise the science to increase the chances of our children having healthy genes, and to be the desired gender of the parents, therefore reducing population growth? I think the technology should absolutely be used, however clearly there is potential for evil, and so it should be regulated carefully, so not to be abused.

The moral questions raised here would fill a book on their own. I am not going to debate it in too much depth, but improving human health and longevity as far as science will allow, is an interesting subject, and I will come back to it towards the end of this essay during my examination of Human potential in H-utopia. For now, I bring it up only to demonstrate that the technology is here and available to the public, in certain countries such as the USA and Italy, where it is legal to choose a child's gender.

4) Children with severe disabilities/limited life

There will be situations where parents have their one or two recommended offspring, and one or both of them have severe mental and/or physical disabilities, that will prevent them from living a normal, long life and from reproducing. The above actions that we have already discussed could significantly reduce the number of children in the future who are born with severe/painful genetic birth defects. No civilised society would have any issue whatsoever in making an exception to the rules in these kinds of circumstances, and the parents should be eligible for full support to have additional children, should they wish.

5) Changing partners and wanting to start a new family

Changing partners and wanting to start a new family is not a rare occurrence. This will be the thing that may complicate matters most. It is not an issue that can be improved with better education or more advanced science. It is just one of those things that can happen in life. I suppose if the generations of the children are spread apart significantly enough, then technically it will not cause too much of an issue. Having four children spaced over 25 years is not like having four children over the course of only eight years. The question of whether this second new family should be given the same benefits as the original family could be dependent on mitigating circumstances, such as timescales involved, how many children there were from the previous marriage and if both or just one of the partners had children already from a previous partnership or not.

Time will tell whether we will be wise enough as a species to manage our own population, but it cannot be overstated enough, that if we cannot do it on our own, it will be done for us, either by nature, or authority as it was in China.

Euthanasia

Whilst on the subject of controversy, I am going to delve straight into another taboo subject. Merely the title alone will already have some readers flinching furiously. But let us take a mature approach and review with an open mind the practice of ending life medically.

The first documented evidence of euthanasia, as a medical

practice in human society, is from ancient Roman and Greek times, where the euthanised person would take an oral toxin to end their own life. The practice was even supported by the renowned philosopher, Plato. A more contemporary advocate, German philosopher, and sociologist, Karl Marx, who adopted the idea from Francis Bacon's philosophical work, Euthanasia medica, pointed out that doctors have a moral duty to ease the suffering of the dying, when death is inevitable and imminent, by assisting with administering lethal, but painless, medication. In the time of Plato, Francis Bacon, and even Karl Marx, uncontrollable population growth was not an issue in the slightest, so this was not the motivation for their support of the practice. For thousands of years amongst society's free thinkers, it was purely seen as the humane thing to do.

There is a stigma nowadays around suicide, assisted for medical reasons or otherwise. We cannot bear to let any other creature suffer prolonged pain when faced with inevitable death, yet we suffer it ourselves out of some apparent sense of martyrdom. Why is this? There must be an underlying reason for such objection to euthanasia. Is it because we arrogantly consider ourselves too important as 'highly evolved' beings to end our lives early? Or maybe it is because we object on religious grounds; we think only God has the power to end human life, even though we assume the power to end all other animal life when we see fit? The Catholic church is one of the biggest opposers to euthanasia, and they are not alone in their objections; most religions will class suicide, assisted or otherwise, as a sin against the creator.

It may even be because we have a paranoid fear that euthanasia is going to be introduced to kill us all off when we get old. All of these arguments against euthanasia are of course complete nonsense. As already pointed out, it is a practice that has been used for thousands of years long before human population growth was an issue. The practice was not invented for depopulation, but rather for compassion and humanity in the face of indefinite suffering.

I believe we do need to make efforts to remove the stigma surrounding euthanasia and that a person should absolutely be allowed to make the free decision to end their life early for medical reasons when suffering from incurable/fatal illnesses. Euthanasia is already legal in certain forward-thinking countries, such as the Netherlands and Belgium. The rest of the world should follow their example. Not only does euthanasia offer a dignified release for those who do not want to suffer anymore or wait through the pain, whilst their bodies get to the point where their organs slowly shut down. But it would also ease the human population growth rate and reduce massive strain on the healthcare industry, caring for the terminally ill who do not want to be here anymore and cannot possibly survive their illnesses.

If we do go down this road, there is an obvious pothole that we must be careful to avoid: that euthanasia becomes too casual and gets forced upon patients. Of course, it can never just be up to a doctor to take on the decision to euthanise someone after a diagnosis! No matter what the circumstances, it must remain entirely within the patient's own hands, and there should be rigorous phycological testing and counselling before it is agreed with the patient. The case could then be submitted to a legal council to approve. It should also be noted that this should never be a service available for those who are not physically nearing death either -for instance, someone who is suicidal as a result of mental illness.

Applying some rational friction to the slippery slope

The 'slippery slope' argument put forward by absolutists, who have limited vision and judge others by their own ignorance, is the only hindrance preventing us from making the mature decisions worthy of a civilised society. So-called 'hard' ethical decisions, such as euthanasia or abortion, are only hard from an absolutist's point of view. Someone with limited vision who cannot see an intermediate or mitigation, only seeing black or white; "it's murder, it's a sin, simple as that". With thorough sociological and philosophical training from early childhood, as I have suggested already, the next generation of human beings will accept ideas such as euthanasia as the right thing to do, and we will be seen as the barbaric ones in our generation for allowing suffering, misery and martyrdom to continue all around us, in the name of preserving God's divinity, or whatever excuse we wish to attempt to justify ourselves with to the future generations. Would we tolerate any excuses from witch hunters of Salem, or from those who were a part of the Spanish Inquisition? People who devoutly believed they were doing the right thing by God and that their horrific means justified the end?

I am going to wrap this up and make it as simple as possible. I know that the above will be met with misunderstanding by some, but the suggestions made really are the least painful/least extreme options for a civilisation at the stage in its development that ours is. Surely, we all wish to progress beyond this stage successfully to provide a great future for our offspring, not to leave them with an overpopulated, undernourished, apocalyptic hell, or a totalitarian authority for a government?

Are there alternatives to abortion and contraception? Sure there are. But they do not bear thinking about. The alternative we are currently using, (inadvertently), is keeping large parts of the world in perpetual suffering, with high infant mortality, allowing the rest freedom to live in excess. Another awful alternative, that wreaks of dystopia, is to have an authority control breeding entirely, as had to be done in China. Or even next-level control, by making natural birth illegal without state permission, perhaps even growing humans in a laboratory instead of a womb, only allowing one child per couple upon a successful request to reproduce. Another option, the most disastrous of all, is to just carry on as we are and breed ourselves into oblivion. When we think about it rationally, it becomes obvious what we must do. We cannot be so childish that we really think we can carry on breeding uncontrollably as well as postponing death until the last possible moment in dying people, often against their will. We are allowing our genetic urge to produce and sustain as much life as possible takeover our impartial rationale, but by doing so we are putting immense mental and physical strain on our entire species, and it will all be in vain as our descendants will suffer the consequences in a terrible legacy of burden and disaster.

Maybe in the distant future, if we are wise enough to survive long enough, we will be able to breed freely again, leave Earth, to become an interplanetary species, colonising the galaxy. Or maybe our descendants will decide to be the 'last generation' and choose to live forever as immortals indistinguishable from gods. Either way, to allow our descendants the privilege of choice and freedom, as we have, first we must overcome the problematic stage we are currently at by making some rational and responsible decisions.

It will require determination and cooperation on a global scale to combat the psychological discomfort that comes from preventing birth when for our entire evolutionary history we have been programmed to make babies for the sake of our survival. We no longer need to do this as we once did, and at last, we are slowly coming to terms with this fact. I hope.

Preparing an economy for H-utopia

"When I give food to the poor, they call me a saint. When I ask why the poor have no food, they call me a communist".

- Dom Helder Camara, 1909-1999.

...People that have no apparent conscience if the source of their wealth is suffering of people below them in the socio-economic hierarchy are dangerous ego-maniacs, as detrimental to society as natural disasters...

Throughout the history of civilisation, we find that attaining wealth, (and the power attributed to it), has nearly always taken priority over what was best for advancing society as a whole. Money and social progress have a complicated relationship; sometimes, they remain in equilibrium and help each other to grow exponentially, as they did during the industrial revolution. Mass production removed scarcity and allowed the poorer classes to purchase goods previously out of their financial grasp. Significant improvements in living standards for the poor came in the 20th century, as great medical advancements were made and booming industry allowed the drugs for preventing prolonged illness and death from curable disease to be mass-produced and distributed. On the other hand, however, money can really tread on the toes of social progress and even reverse it, or at least stall it, as it did for hundreds of years in Europe with the feudal system.

Money and social progress fall out of equilibrium when a minority of individual's wealth and power are selfishly grown exponentially and indefinitely, whilst a majority of others are left behind, fluctuating in and out of poverty.   In most of the world's societies, it is now not possible to live without money, and the common perception is, the more wealth you have, the more important you are and the better you are able to live. Certainly, a human's basic survival needs become threatened when money runs low, and this can continually stretch a person's integrity, motivating them to do things more and more unethical to secure their survival and to guarantee their family's survival, even if that means other families must perish. People cannot be blamed for adapting to their environment to survive; this is not just human nature, but the nature of every living thing. However, as an intelligent species, we have the capability to rationalise, foresee events far into the future and adapt to our environment, changing our situation for the better whilst steering clear of any looming social disasters.

Money is a critical tool at our disposal that allows civilisation to cooperate and trade. Without a means of trade, everybody would be preoccupied only with a subsistence living and progress would only ever be minimal. There would be no doctors, engineers, astronauts, inventors, retailers or authors.

Money only becomes detrimental to society when greedy people disregard foresight and elevate themselves above their fellow humans, to a phycological state where ego, one's sense of self-worth, is left uncapped. Someone who is greedy, accumulating more wealth than they know they need, may consider themselves to be succeeding in modern-day life, but this mindset actually stems from something very primitive and animalistic. Over millennia we have evolved to hunt and gather resources to ensure the survival of our offspring, to ensure our genes are amongst those passed on to the next generation. But it seems as if nature, not anticipating 'civilisation', did not evolve a natural cap to this wealth accumulation drive. One's ego is often judged by accumulated wealth, and we gather tokens of this wealth to show off our excess worth. 'Curb appeal' houses and mansions, private jets, flashy cars and sparkling jewellery. The marketing industry understands and exploits this with certain brands such as Rolex being a statement of wealth rather than something of great additional function or value for money.

During our short lives, every action we take and every decision we make shapes the future in infinite ways, and this is our only true legacy. Most people alive today descend from royalty somewhere in their family history, but consider this: do we all get to live like royalty now, just because some of our ancestors did? Money and possessions are lost to time, through disputes, wars, theft, usurping, addictions, lawsuits, etc. No matter how much we accumulate in an attempt to pass down to our children, by the time it gets to our great great great-grandchildren, it is unlikely they will all get an equal share. For instance, a millionaire could end up with 100 great great great grandchildren as descendants, and all but one of them could live in poverty, (maybe even all of them if the money is squandered). Even current royal families, with ancient heritage, do not inherit their wealth from centuries ago. Depending on how closely related to the monarch they are, members of royal families may inherit property and heirlooms, but actual *'new'* money constantly has to be earned or collected using long-established power to continue taking a percentage of wealth from the kingdom as a whole. So even for the descendants of royalty, there is no guarantee of wealth.

The only legacy guaranteed is the future itself, and our actions to shape the future will determine how priceless or worthless that legacy is. The world is different because each and every one of us is in it. Had any one individual out of the 100 billion people that lived on this Earth before us not had lived, then the present would be different from what it is right now. This impact on the universe as a whole is the part of us that is immortal, along with the memory of us that remains in the consciousness of those we have impacted during our lifetimes. A rational human being would step back and realise that at the end of their short time on Earth, the epitaph on their gravestone does not say 'here lies a fabulously rich individual'. On the contrary, when all the seconds of your life clock are over, the judgement on your epitaph is only whether you were beloved and by whom.

The only brakes on the urge to accumulate wealth are laziness, fear and physical time available when the functional tasks of eating and sleeping are complete. As hunter-gatherers, or even early farmers, we could only accumulate so much without spoiling and wastage. However, in our modern society, our wealth can grow limitlessly even as we sleep, as 'debit' in our bank accounts. So, in the absence of a natural evolutionary cap on the instinctive drive to accumulate wealth, a very conscious rational human decision is required. People that have no apparent conscience if the source of their wealth is suffering of people below them in the socio-economic hierarchy are dangerous ego-maniacs, as detrimental to society as natural disasters. Survival of the fittest in a future society could be translated as survival of the richest, but the people of a ruthless 'dog eat dog' world like this would never reach H-utopia, and the only immortal part of people from this type of society would be irreversibly tarnished forever.

So, what should we do to ensure our legacy is a positive one? There are countless paths available to us and almost all will lead to dystopia with our current socio-economic structures, and ego-centric mindsets. The following are five examples of futures where greed overpowers social progress, and the relationship society has with money remains out of equilibrium for too long:

1) A totalitarian world government that has been forced into formation by an oligarchy. This could be justified by the leaders as the only way to prevent war, crime, disease and starvation.
2) A barbaric future where a nuclear war has reversed social progress by thousands of years.
3) A future where most humans have been replaced by either cloned slaves or artificial intelligence and only the wealthiest humans are left living freely, as immortal masters of Earth.
4) A total extinction of the human race because we proved incapable of collaborating effectively to prevent natural disasters.
5) A virtual reality world where the human mind no longer exists in actual reality and the body is maintained by bio-mechanics. Everyone interacts synthetically and peacefully because crime, war, wrongdoing, suffering and death are not programmed into the VR and therefore cannot occur. Although this risk and misery free world may sound pleasant, it would not be real, and free will would not be an option. Furthermore, there is risk; the risk that the VR could be hacked by terrorist organisations or preoccupy us to the point where we become ignorant to potential threats from the outside universe, such as asteroid impacts. To live forever in VR, our real planet would either have to defend and maintain itself entirely automated or another option would be for people to take turns in reality, performing a kind of custodian duty as 'watchers'.

These futures may sound like plots for science-fiction, but they are all real potential futures that have been predicted to unfold, (perhaps all of them one after the other), if we continue to follow unrighteous paths and stubbornly refuse to acknowledge and negate the risks we pose to ourselves. Clearly, none of these futures resemble anything like the humanist utopia I have described. So, what is the right financial path? How can we guarantee to steer clear of leaving our grandchildren doomed to suffer the consequences of these potential dystopian futures? Let us begin by reviewing some socio-economic systems to see if we can gain wisdom and find a potential strategy that suits everyone, and is also effective at managing risks to society indefinitely.

Capitalism versus communism

Capitalism is an economic system that pursues financial self-interest without limits. It allows individuals to freely enhance their collection of private possessions, and increase their personal control of resources, (including people), and money. Capitalism is fundamentally the accumulation of wealth, where individuals can save, or hoard, large amounts of the world's economy for themselves, sometimes to an obscene level, in the case of multi-billionaires. With capitalism, anyone has a shot at becoming extremely wealthy, and numerous individuals from humble beginnings have proved this, surpassing wealth far beyond royalty.

It was as recently as the 18th century that capitalism really came to the forefront as the main economic structure in many parts of Europe, America and Australia; made possible by the modern banking system, combined with technological advancements which enabled global communication and more efficient/automated machinery capable of exponential production. One of the precursors to capitalism was mercantilism, which was based on controlling resources, land and buildings. Mercantilism was not so much about monitory profit, but rather, controlling the most resources. The profits you could make from each resource had a relatively low, finite limit in comparison to today. Today you do not need access to anything more than a laptop computer to generate millions in profit, making a fortune without needing to personally control any resources or have any people power whatsoever. Due to the revolutionary era of the 'dot com' millionaires and billionaires, online video sensations, and advertising potential with social media, capitalism has run away with itself to a new extreme, and it has highlighted some serious flaws with the system. Mainly that profits became more important than people and that 1 per cent of people can control more money than the rest of the 99 per cent put together. Before the 18th century, people were the power. To make any kind of a living, employers needed a lot of people, and they needed to look after those people, or they would have a revolution on their hands, causing their income to grind to a halt. A monarch is only a monarch because of their subjects. Without loyal worshippers and admirers, a monarch is just a normal person who has delusions of grandeur.

It is tempting to think capitalism is the only way to run a 'free' society and most of us in the developed world have adapted to live our lives as capitalists, accepting it as the best type of society, because we feel free. But is there something better? Can booming industry, technological advancement, farming and worldwide trade be possible without *unlimited* financial reward as an incentive? Prior to capitalism, it was already a requirement to provide workers with equal shared resources and representation. In fact, many of the modern-day freedoms such as democracy, republicanism and social contracts all pre-date the reign of capitalism. They are not the products of a capitalist society, so we do not owe our freedoms to capitalism. Modern-day capitalism is not about freedom; it is about decreasing resources whilst increasing profits. In this kind of society, people are a burdensome expenditure that must be tightly managed by business owners. Labour force is kept to an absolute minimum, and jobs that can be automated, generally are. This even applies to organisations like schools and hospitals, which ludicrously have to be operated as businesses with tight budgets in a capitalist world, meaning they either have to resort to charging for their services, or rely heavily on government distribution of taxpayer money for their funding.

Another flaw of capitalism, is repeated recession and instability. Booms and busts caused by cycles of overproduction and under-consumption were predicted by economist and sociologist, Karl Marx. Although capitalists would insist otherwise, we have proved that we are not wise enough to manage this problem because even now this still happens with relative predictability. Unbelievably it has actually become an accepted part of our economic structure and something we just have to deal with as best as we can. Every time there is a recession, the un-savvy's lives are turned upside down, but for the shrewd opportunist, a recession can be a chance to prosper at the expense of other's misfortunes, whilst buying up their cheap repossessed homes for instance, ready to rent back to them or sell for a profit when the market recovers.

Capitalism has been dominant for around 200-300 years and during this time, there is no denying it has driven progress forward fast by rewarding the entrepreneurial mindset, but its potential has limits, and it has proven to be incredibly flawed: encouraging short-term thinking and opportunist mindsets, accompanied by an 'every man for himself' attitude, which is completely contradictory to the principles in our united H-utopian society. Those with greater integrity tend to suffer in a capitalist world, in comparison to the unscrupulous, who prosper whilst overlooking consequences to others, even if the 'others' are 99 per cent of other humans on Earth, including their own descendants. With this kind of attitude, we will never achieve truly great ventures, such as the exploration of space or creating an unlimited renewable energy supply, because there would be nothing in it, at least in the short-term, for capitalist investors who require quick and guaranteed returns on investment. Capitalism, as it is today, does not fit hand in hand nicely with humanism and therefore at first glance, does not appear to be the economic structure that aligns with the values in our future H-utopia. However, I am not disregarding it. I do believe it is possible that capitalism could be adapted to be made more sustainable and attractive for all. The problem we have to overcome is, the people benefitting most from it currently, will not want to change what is working for them, and they are the ones holding all the power, of course. For capitalism to suit H-utopia, we would need to find some kind of a compromise that promotes and rewards integrity.

The only true economic system is capitalism; the rest are more social/political experiments. We will briefly explore some of the other ways people around the world run their societies, (or have run them in the past), that do not advocate everyone trying to make as much money as possible from as little time, resources and financial investment as possible.

At the other end of the spectrum, stemming from a dissatisfaction with capitalism, we have the equally flawed communism. A social/political movement from the mid-19th century. It was the brainchild of Karl Marx and Friedrich Engels, who both wanted an end to capitalism. Observing the exploitation of workers by opportunist employers, they recognised the potential catastrophes of a future under the control of capitalists. The principles of their joint idea were published in 1848 in *The Communist Manifesto*.

In Engels's and Marx's ideal world, all private ownership would be forbidden. Instead, the needs of society would be put above individuals, much like a bee colony working for the good of the hive. The production of goods and food would belong to everyone equally. The philosophy was put simply: "Everyone gives according to their abilities and receives according to their needs".

The movement was surprisingly successful at finding advocates across the world; adopted as the political structure by countries in Africa, Asia, South America and Eastern Europe. One big flaw with communism is, the leaders of communist states can easily become corrupted by power. In every successful colony, the workers need a 'queen bee' to control them and impose the agenda. For a colony to prosper, there is no room for non-compliance, (freedom). As Plato realised in *Republic,* (which describes something similar to communism), that no ordinary person would be able to run this kind of society successfully. Furthermore, how do we elect who would be the chosen one to rule as 'queen bee'? The answer is, we do not. Communist states are not famous for being democratic, and the leaders are not normally voted in by the masses; they tend to elect themselves.

In November 1917, (falling in October on the Julian calendar), the Bolsheviks, led by Vladimir Lenin, launched a coup d'état against the Duma's provisional government, seizing power in the 'October Revolution'. They remained in power, with Joseph Stalin succeeding Lenin as leader in 1924. They changed their name to the Communist Party. They nationalised public services such as railways so that they were all controlled by governing planners. The communist party continued their growth becoming the Union of Soviet Socialist Republics, (USSR), which stayed in power until 1991. This example of communism has been followed by other financially successful and globally influential countries since then, including China. Lenin truly believed that the ultimate goal of a stateless, egalitarian global society, where everyone was in charge of their own destiny, would be attained for all of humanity through communism. Although a stateless, global society where everyone is equal and in charge of their own destiny sounds good on paper. In practice, communism did not turn out to be the ultimate perfection Marx, Engels, or Lenin envisioned. During the decades of the USSR, there were some serious failures in quality control and in the coordination of the production planners in charge of running the Soviet Union. It proved impossible for the planners to efficiently coordinate all of the financial decisions about production, food consumption, investment and trade throughout the participating countries. The Soviet economy was plagued for decades with production issues at both extremes, with shortages of some supplies, and too many of others. For example, there were shortages in production of basic supplies such as toilet paper, and wasted harvests rotting away on farms, not necessarily because the food would not have been consumed, but because of logistical failures; there was a lack of storage facilities and a there was a lack of ready transportation. Issues like these were happening right up until the end of the USSR and the collapse of communism in Eastern Europe.

Failures in quality control manifested because the factory managers had enormous pressure from the governing planners to meet their quotas. Because they focused on quantity, not quality, substandard products were inevitably the outcome. Unlike in a capitalist society, communist workers usually have complete job security regardless of performance, (as long as quotas are met), and there are limits to rewards, with no big financial incentives for those who excel beyond requirement. Even when job loss does occur, new jobs are readily available. Although job security will sound good to many people, tired of an overly competitive capitalist job market, it does not provide sufficient incentive to work hard and efficiently, or with any real ingenuity. It discourages the entrepreneurial mindset. A harmonised global society living like this would be less inclined to push their limits and invest in major ventures. The fundamental issue being, that more intelligent, resourceful, hardworking people gain little or no extra reward beyond their fellow less hardworking 'comrades' so are faced with the choice of being de-incentivised or to cheat the system. Disincentivised people lead to the quality control failures that were witnessed in many communist countries. In communist states where our genetic urge to accumulate wealth is capped so harshly, the advancement of sciences and applied technologies are inherently weakened, as the pursuit of knowledge relies on philanthropy alone. This naturally leads to state funded espionage as a means to keep up technologically with the envied capitalist countries who greatly reward innovation and initiative.

Following the collapse of communism, the ex-communist and undeveloped African countries looked to Western developed world and to capitalism for an example of how to run a financially viable society. The obstacle was never a lack of resources or ingenuity in these nations but a lack of clarity when it came to legal ownership over property and resources; who would benefit financially from utilising them, a conflict of written laws, and a difficulty networking with the rest of the world. It was challenging conducting business with the ultra-capitalist West who were now lightyears ahead of the ex-communist and developing countries thanks to capital incentive driving production and efficiency, with advanced laws to protect inventions such as intellectual property rights and trademarks, irrelevant to communism but essential to capitalism.

Developing nations have just as many entrepreneurial, ambitious and talented individuals as the developed world, but there is only so far their talents can take them in politically suppressed environments lacking sufficient economic infrastructure. Even the wealthiest entrepreneurial geniuses of the richest countries in the world, would not have succeeded in their ventures without patents to protect their ideas from being ripped off, enforceable and legally tight contracts, limited liability protection, insurance policies, and fungible property representations for pooling resources. Ex-communist or underdeveloped countries, that have suffered from political failures, host one third of the world's population. Even today, roughly one out of every three people live in poverty because of these historic socio-economic failures, and many individuals have had no choice but to adopt extralegal activity in order to access their human rights, to build a home, or to grow a business with the desire and intention to be able to contribute to society legitimately. Sadly, this illegality only delays recovery of the afflicted countries and fuels a xenophobic attitude from the developed nations towards minorities attempting to better their lives, and the lives of their families back home, by migrating for legitimate work or education. We observe this inhumane response from capitalists all over the world when there is a supposed threat that they may have to share a tiny amount of their accumulated wealth: North Americans towards South/Latin Americans, Western Europeans towards Eastern Europeans, South Africans towards North Africans. As if the humans who were born in the poorer ends of the continents are not as deserving of the same lifestyle people have in the richer ends. As a consequence of all this, any system that does not promote capitalism to the extreme is deemed dangerous, and no responsible nation dares to consider anything else for fear of being left behind financially, as countries in the developing world have been. However, as we have seen, the failure is with the written laws in these countries, not necessarily the socio-economic structure. Exactly the same dilemma occurred in the developed world hundreds of years ago, and it was overcome. Before the boom of the industrial revolution, the suburbs of European countries were teeming with extralegal organisations that were outproducing and outcompeting the official guilds and mills that were manufacturing in the cities. Governments eventually realised the entrepreneurial potential they were missing out on. So the world leaders gave their blessings and governments changed laws, which allowed production to take off.

Feudalism

A system that was dominant in Europe for around 800 years. Fundamentally, it worked on the age-old philosophy of, "you scratch my back, and I'll scratch yours". Land was originally granted to barons for services and loyalty to the Crown. The barons would then divide up their land which would be given to lords, who would act as middlemen between the nobility and the peasants. In return for being given the estates, the lords would provide taxes for the monarch, or provide men to be trained as soldiers for the kingdom. The British Army can trace its roots back to feudalism. Lots of small communities formed around the local lords, who would support the peasants in return for their services in the upkeep of the land and the manor. This was more than an economic system; it was a social way of life. The lord's manor or castle was the centre of the community, where peasants would gather in celebration for festivals or retreat to in fear, for protection against invaders. Farms, villages and eventually, towns, would develop around estates.

Although the system technically worked, with little economic turmoil, it was a massively progress hindering system. Enabled by acquiescence and religious allegiance to the monarchs, who vainly believed they were given divine right to rule; a belief that was encouraged by the Catholic Church. After building churches in most peasant villages, bishops could cash in on their dioceses. Feudalism is a prime example of the few controlling the many, the rich controlling the poor, exploiting them for financial gain. In the middle ages, when feudalism was most prominent, the vast majority of the people living in the UK were peasants. Although officially 'free', peasants were practically slaves and were obliged to the lords. They owned nothing of value themselves and relied entirely on their local lord for their very survival, and survival is all they received. They worked every day except the sabbath and received only what they needed to stay alive, to a modest average age of 40-50 years thanks to disease, malnutrition and poor living conditions.

Socialism

A system where everybody shares an equal ownership/responsibility of society's production. Including labour, goods, and natural resources. There is a percentage taken for the good of the nation, which goes towards education, social care, foreign aid and military amongst other things, but after expenses, the profits are spread between the workers as guaranteed incomes. Socialism's aim is to eliminate poverty, and it tries to do this by preventing conglomerates from taking control and profiting off of a country's natural resources, whilst exploiting workers. With socialism, everyone has equal free access to health care and education. Some countries, including the UK and New Zealand, have adopted this aspect from socialism, providing a state education and national health service to everyone, regardless of their work efforts, tax contributions, or financial situation. However, a private healthcare and education option is still available, if one is able/willing to pay for it. When it comes to providing human rights, making them available for free is absolutely the only right thing to do. Having a sick, improperly educated population is massively financially burdensome. The greatest nations invest in their people, and this is the most inspired and admirable part of socialism.

Although socialism promises prosperity and comfort for a time, it can seriously compromise longer-term financial stability and growth. For instance, a socialist government that decides to massively increase the minimum wage for workers may sound like a good thing, especially to those who have low paid jobs, but the economy of a country that does this too often is doomed to fail. This is because socialism, ironically, does not consider the cost to everyone in society. An individual who earns minimum wage could be influenced by the promises of a socialist government but in order to call themselves a true socialist they need to consider first that the cost of their wage being increased could be that their colleagues are made redundant so that their higher wage can afford to be paid by their employer. Furthermore, in an absolute socialist country, our employers and biggest tax contributors may even choose to take their operations out of the country, to set up in a country that appreciates capitalism more, or worse, go completely bankrupt, causing massive job losses, resulting in unpaid debts, especially from small businesses which would suffer the most from sudden and drastic wage increases. This then compromises the lenders who reduce lending and/or increase their interest rates, and recession is the outcome. As small businesses close, the wealthiest companies expand, and so ironically, conglomerates begin to naturally form, in a socialist state that was supposed to be against them! As a result, socialism has been demonised alongside communism.

Another problem with socialism is, it is against human nature. It counts on the fact that everyone will happily cooperate for the greater good whilst relinquishing personal wealth. But of course, we humans can be highly competitive people, and our selfishness would overthrow this kind of a society every time there was a window of opportunity for personal gain above others. This problematic trait cannot be cured entirely, but it can be treated from the roots in childhood. By changing the way children are put against each other from very early on in school and in the home. Currently, it is beneficial to bring out competitiveness in children, so they are able to compete in the predominantly capitalist world. Whereas in a socialist world, cooperation is the key. Socialism would be more likely to succeed accompanied by the reformation of the school system we discussed earlier, to play down competitiveness and build on cooperative working. This is something that should be done anyway, regardless of our economic structure. As with communism, we risk losing innovation because entrepreneurial thinking is not rewarded enough like it is in a purely capitalist society, and so progress would be slower, production quality would be lower and incentive to work may be reduced. Just as it has done with communism, this can lead to state-sponsored espionage to keep up technologically with the capitalist countries, fuelling worldwide tension and conflict.

For any nation that adopts aspects of socialism, it is absolutely vital to educate people from a young age to appreciate the costs of socialism, urging everyone to take more responsibility for their own lives and wellbeing to prevent society becoming overly dependent and ungrateful. Some ways to reduce strain on socialist services, keeping them viable, could include first aid and basic medical training as part of the school curriculum. Also, improved and simplified disease home testing kits being made available to save doctor and hospital time. As an example, the most commonly used tests for diagnosing prostate cancer currently include blood tests, a physical examination known as a digital rectal examination (DRE), an MRI scan or a biopsy. All of this expensive and inefficient testing could be negated if men can confirm a negative result just by taking regular home tests using nothing more than urine samples that are sent via postal service directly to a laboratory. Men may also be put off by invasive physical examinations so having this service available would also mean fewer men would die from this disease, or allow it to progress to the point of requiring expensive, drawn-out treatments and surgeries. A free healthcare service is of course not free, it is paid for by taxes, and we all pay these in some way. Socialist services such as this fail when greedy, selfish or ignorant people take advantage of the state provided services, putting unnecessary strain on them with overuse, or even taking legal action against the organisations, employing the services of 'no win, no fee' solicitors in unwarranted scenarios to make a quick buck. This, in turn, drives insurance premiums higher and renders the free services less viable and less reliable as costs have to be recouped from somewhere. People who consider taking legal action against free services first need to stop and consider if it is really warranted, as their small gain today could mean a loss forever of free services for everyone. This again highlights the biggest flaw with socialism: that it wrongly assumes everyone will cooperate and consider the greater good, resisting opportunities to scramble up the ladder whilst trampling others below.

Before moving on, I need to digress slightly here, as it is relevant to review further the insidious effects 'claim culture' can have on society.

Seeking compensation at every opportunity is something that has been escalating out of control since the invention of the internet, which has allowed everyone easy access to 'have a go' with no win, no fee personal injury lawyers. The negative effects go beyond just insurance premiums driving up the cost of living for everyone. Compensation culture actually influences the way we think and act in society. It has made us less responsible for our own lives because there is always the chance to accuse someone else of being at least a tiny bit responsible too, and unless the defendant can prove without a doubt to the contrary then they will be forced to take responsibility and pay for someone else's misfortune. Consequently, we have been reduced to risk assessors first and foremost, having to consider if there is any financial risk to ourselves before we help others. This is most true in the case of public service givers: medical carers, police and teachers who are forced to constantly treat patients, potential criminals, or students as potential walking lawsuits.

The decline in an ethos of care in the public sector is directly linked to litigation concerns. Even if people do not follow through with legal action, just the threat of legal action as blackmail alone is enough to scare businesses and organisations into settling quietly. The corrosive effect of this attitude has the potential to destroy humanism and never allow us to reach a united society. Some genuine cases will require legal action for justice, and a percentage of those will warrant financial compensation if irreversible damage is done. But the cases and settlements need to be regulated better than they currently are to deter people, who are motivated only by greed, from trying it on, exaggerating injuries or fabricating mental health problems that an incident has caused them, to increase or prolong pay-outs. It is currently even possible to make a regular living from compensation claims, this is a very anti-social life choice, and it is a failure of society that this is possible. The lesson here is simple: to take responsibility for our own lives and if compensation is genuinely warranted, take only what we *need*, not what we want for our greed.

The threat posed by oligarchies and plutocracies

From the Greek, oligarkhes, meaning *few governing*. With absolute capitalism, this potentially dangerous power structure lurks in the shadows, enabling a handful of individuals/companies/families, to assume unsolicited responsibility for the rest of society because of their extreme power and influence. Most oligarchies are plutocratic, meaning the members are rich, and their almost limitless wealth allows them to control the economy on a global scale. Oligarchy members are not necessarily extremely rich; they may have some other reason for being so politically influential, such as scaremongering or blackmail. Whether oligarchy or plutocracy, these few at the top of society ruling over the many are able to stay in power by working with each other and combining their political and/or financial influence across the world.

The scary thing about this power structure is, it can hi-jack any of our socio-economic systems to fulfil an agenda. It can even be hidden in the guise of democracy. The people in charge of an oligarchy or plutocracy are not elected by the public. However, if they desired, it is theoretically within their means to use their immense power and wealth to influence the elected democratic leaders to carry out an agenda for them discreetly. In some instances, an oligarchy may even have enough power to influence a monarch, ruling an entire kingdom or empire from the shadows. Although the risk of this occurring is present in any society, it is only in a capitalist society without limits where it is an inevitable outcome. If we allow it to manifest, a society under plutocratic influence has the potential to tiptoe into totalitarianism, where governing powers have absolute control over their citizens, removing most or all freedoms. Potentially even the freedom of critical thinking or innovation.

A plutocracy's power comes from a small group of people, all of whom will have expertise in each area of society. Decisions are made with relatively little disruption to the rest of us, allowing 99 per cent of the population to focus on their own lives without having to take on the burden of society as a whole. We can spend our time selfishly and know that someone else is making all the important, (some may say boring or difficult), political decisions for us. So, we can just go about our lives climbing the ladders in our careers, upgrading our homes and trying to reach our own personal goals. Whether that be inventing a new technology, buying a bigger house or a faster car, or winning a sporting event. We will be left alone to do these things that we feel we need to make us happy and be able to live our lives pretty much how we want, so long as we are not impeding the oligarchy's interests. An oligarchy depends on the disinterest or distraction of the masses to maintain its power. Because of its discreet nature, this has become a topic of fictional dystopian works, associated with paranoia and conspiracy. Consequently, potential threats from this very real and well documented political structure have been repetitively downplayed by mainstream sources, meaning many of us naively ignore the threat to humanity from oligarchies and plutocracies.

The comforts provided for the general population can be appealing, and it is tempting to trust it, allowing an oligarchy to take the full burden of society, so the rest of us can absolve ourselves of any responsibility. But we should not be fooled by this wolf in sheep's clothing. There are dire consequences of allowing the few to control the many. Plutocratic oligarchies are sociopathic and selfish by nature; they do not mind if some of the human population is poor, hungry and suffering, in fact, they desire it, as global financial inequality helps them to maintain power and balance. They bleed nations dry to fill their own pockets and do not leave enough for everyone else when, actually, there should be plenty of wealth for everyone in theory. They can create monopolies, stage economic booms and busts, influence media outlets, and manipulate supply and demand to benefit themselves. Such an example of this manipulation was the De Beers diamond empire that controlled up to 90 per cent of the world's diamond supply for a lengthy part of the 20th century, by stockpiling the gems and effectively drip feeding them to the world to make them appear rarer than they actually were. Combined with clever advertising, they were then able to charge obscene amounts of money for their product. The social pressure to buy diamonds as a sign of affection continues to trend to this day even though the truth of the immoral scheme is now public knowledge.

An alternative: capital incentivised socialism

We have experienced first-hand the flaws of capitalism, communism and socialism. All of these economic systems, in their extreme forms, are vulnerable to exploitation that will leave us tumbling mercilessly into dystopia. Capitalism has become the most dominant of the three, with the most attractive feature being that it allows us to exercise our primal greed without limits. There are no doubts that capitalism has served us well in terms of sudden technological advancements, but it is not sustainable forever. Capital**ism** is a type of extrem**ism,** and the problems include regular financial turmoil, constant war for profit and an 'every man for himself' attitude. Commun**ism**, also a form of extrem**ism**, endeavours to do the best for everyone, but it is hopelessly flawed because people are not incentivised enough to excel in performance, and therefore communist nations resort to spying on capitalist ones to avoid being left behind technologically. Due to this lack of incentive and a reduced interest in personal property, they suffer from logistical failures and political failures that, ironically, increase the very poverty they were trying to reduce. Because of the extremist nature of these systems, neither of them appear to be viable systems for H-utopia, especially when they compete against one another as they have done historically, causing international tension between extremist nations who each advocate their extreme as the ultimate one whilst demonising the other. Continuing with the anti-extremist theme for H-utopia, logic suggests that we create a hybrid socio-economic system, a mixture of capitalism, socialism, communism, sanity, humanity and common sense called: **capital incentivised socialism.** With this hybrid system, the best aspects from all other ways of running a society can be combined to offer a humane solution that looks after the population, preparing it for greatness, without destroying entrepreneurial progress. This mash-up of all socio-economic systems would open the door to many exciting opportunities that would simply not be achievable in a world where humanity chooses to live by extremist laws. Why should we confine ourselves to a box when we have unlimited potential if only we are brave enough to break down the four walls and work together to overcome the rigidity and divide imposed for centuries on our species?

We have learned how socialism has its benefits to society but equally has drawbacks. For instance, the free healthcare and education that helps to maintain a strong, healthy and intelligent workforce, also makes it very easy for people to have more children and overwhelm these provided services. Therefore, it is crucial people are made to understand the long-term consequences of abusing and overusing free public services. One idea proposed to help people understand the cost of a 'free' health service, is to present patients with a bill after treatment, as an eye-opener to show how much the treatment they received has cost the country. Combining ideas like this with a more thorough education in schools, centred around first aid, self healthcare, basic doctoring, and nutrition will slowly begin to ease the burden of socialist gestures to humanity. I have already covered in enough detail, birth control incentives and how crucial the role of education is if we want to be allowed access to the great things H-utopia will bring. If we change our approach towards birth control and utilise education to its potential, as already suggested, then capital incentivised socialism can work in theory and free services can remain viable, rebuilding an ethos of care in H-utopia that has been declining in our current society.

So how would money work in a society that practices capital incentivised socialism?

Keep in mind that the primary objective is to remove the risk of plutocracies taking control of 99 per cent of the world's wealth and hi-jacking society. It is vital that wealth be redistributed more evenly to ensure power remains with the world's masses. Once this has been achieved, there are so many great things that can be safely introduced to benefit humanity, that would be too risky to attempt in a world of financial extremes, obscurity and corruption.

One way we could implement capital incentivised socialism in the workplace is to make it a legal requirement that no CEO or highest-paid employee in a company could earn more than ten times the amount of the lowest-paid employee within the company. There is a risk that this could force the formation of conglomerates because the incentive to work for small businesses would be diminished. Smaller businesses whose directors, or owners, are paid modestly, would not be able to offer their cashiers, receptionists or delivery drivers high enough incentives to be able to compete in the employment market. However, it is evident, even with pure capitalism, we are already heading for a more technological and scientific-based future workplace, as centralisation and automation make laborious jobs obsolete. Companies such as Amazon have been systematically killing off high street department stores and niche shops alike for years now. Amazon employs a lot of people, but equally, they take advantage of automation wherever possible to reduce the need for unnecessary labour force; and this is the same with all big business. In many of the stores that do remain on the high street, and in hotels, self-service points replace the need for employing as many cashiers and receptionists. This change to our future workplace could be unavoidable no matter what we do on the way to H-utopia. After all, H-utopia is destined to be a great and wise future forged with change and progress, by people working together for something better. It is not supposed to be a stagnated, museum of a future, made simple or quaint, steeped in nostalgia and desperate preservation of old ways whilst its people desperately try to delay technological progress by force.

There may be a practical way to rescue the small business model from disappearing in the future, with an even more ambitious initiative that could work in conjunction with the redistribution of wealth within individual companies. If we were to impose a limit on how much wealth one person or organisation is allowed to hold onto at any one point in their private bank accounts, this could redistribute wealth out evenly across the entire world. Before outrightly rejecting such a scary, radical idea, please open your mind for a moment and indulge me whilst I hypothesise how this could work, and provide a positive financial impact for 99 per cent of people. Even the leftover 1 per cent would not suffer any hardship.

Here is the theory: any extra earnings over the set limit could be automatically channelled into a government-controlled trust fund, aimed at providing funds for domestic lending with ultra-low interest residential mortgages, as well as funding assigned projects for the good of humanity worldwide; directing funds to areas all over the world that desperately need investment, such as healthcare, education and scientific/medical research. Although we have a lot to thank charity and philanthropy for, it is not wise or sustainable to become reliant, as a species, on ultra-rich individuals, allowing them to take extra responsibility for humanity, making decisions and carrying out agendas that affect everyone. Because governments of the world are so grateful that someone else is sorting out the mess they cannot afford to, the philanthropic individuals can carry out their agendas with little or no democratic regulation into their affairs, and the day we forfeit democracy for an easy life, will be the day we truly find ourselves stepping into dystopia. It is not for charity to sort out where government has failed in their responsibility.

Hypothetically, for the sake of this example, I will set a limit the equivalent of 500 million pounds sterling for an individual, and 5 billion for an organisation. Before proceeding, I want to make clear I am not saying the very rich have not earned their money and are not entitled to spend it how they see fit, and to keep earning it. They absolutely are, of course. A social dilemma occurs when not enough money is spent in the right places, and trillions remain hoarded by the world's mega-rich in order to maintain power as well as wealth. This renders the economy susceptible to manipulation, (deliberately or inadvertently), by a tiny percentage of the population. As banks invest their billionaire customer's money, lending to their other clients, they do not do this out of the goodness of their hearts. Private banks scrutinise applications for loans and mortgages, picking and choosing who they lend to, not necessarily who really needs the money just to stay alive or purchase a modest home for their family. Any money lent by traditional banks often comes with crippling amounts of interest, liable to wild fluctuations. The profits do not fund global projects for the good of humanity as a whole. They only grow that specific bank's wealth and control, whilst empowering the nation they operate from. Banks in their current form are the number one tool of manipulation for any plutocracy.

So this is how a limit on wealth could hypothetically work: an individual has 500 million debit in their account. If they spend some of it, assuming they are still earning, then their account would start filling up again, back to the 500 million limit, maintaining their wealth but never exceeding the limit. If they are not spending it but keep earning, then the overspill will not be sent into their own private bank account, for the bank to pick and choose where to invest, but instead will automatically be channelled into a central, global, government-operated trust fund for humanity. I know I will have lost many readers here as there is an inherent distrust or lack of confidence in government, particularly a global one being put in charge of dishing out wealth. I will address this mistrust shortly and offer the solution. This money accumulating in the trust fund would not be for making spreadsheets look good or growing any individual's ego, or accumulating an individual nation's power. Every penny would be reinvested in projects for the good of humanity globally. To try and keep money within their companies, and prevent it going to the trust fund, an imposed limit would likely force the redistribution of wealth anyway within companies by making CEOs re-think how much they pay their lowest paid workers, meaning even a menial job would be a very lucrative and desirable one in a wealthy company. What would be considered cheating the system is if the very rich tried to give away their money to all of their extended family and friends, (forming a potential oligarchy), instead of letting the money and its associated power go to the government controlled trust fund. This loophole could be closed with improved financial clarity. By stopping the flow of the world's economy being controlled by a few companies, families, and banks, operating out of a handful of the richest nations, it will put a stop to dangerous political oligarchies forming, who have their own selfish agendas. Fundamentally, what a limit on personal wealth does, is limit the power individuals can wield over the rest of humanity, instead offering a fair and democratic redistribution of wealth globally, which is crucial to ensure everyone has access to H-utopia and philanthropy does not exemplify itself from democracy. Just because someone is very rich, it does not mean they should have the power of a dictator; to decide what is best for humanity, with no debate to challenge their decisions tolerated.

I am aware the suggestions so far are unenforceable by today's regulatory standards and will be met with much rejection and outrage, mainly from the very rich no doubt, but we need to think outside of our own ignorant bubble. We should not be so stubborn that we force ourselves into a tiny box where we must choose between two extremes to leave the box, just because it is easier and clearer to deal in absolutes. We should be rational enough to want to find a compromise that makes our society better, even if it is more complex. All of the suggestions above could be possible in a future with tighter financial controls than we have today, improved political clarity, simplification of lenders, and with a crackdown on tax evaders using multiple accounts.

Sometimes companies bank in a different country to where they are primarily conducting their business, which is not good for building a circular economy in the country that is predominantly buying the products or services because the same country is not benefitting from the multiplier effect by having all of their spent money reinvested locally. This enables conglomerates to save money in tax havens elsewhere in the world, whilst undercutting all of their smaller competitors back home, driving small businesses into the ground. The easiest way to close these loopholes would be to introduce a world electronic currency and agree fixed global tax brackets to make banking overseas pointless. Another innovation that would be required for this personal capital limit idea to work, is simplifying how people save and spend money.   To further improve financial clarity, it could be necessary to allow only one personal bank account per person that is assigned at birth, much like everyone is assigned one national insurance/social security number that is kept for life.

Admittedly, this kind of compromise to capitalism is not ideal and has the potential to be overly complicated, but then none of the social or economic structures are ideal - far from it. We are not trying to attain ideal though, just something that is better than we have now, and I believe absolute capitalist or absolute anti-capitalist economic structures are not sustainable and do not suit the values of H-utopia as they are extremes.

It is ironic that there are many people who hate capitalism, campaigning that it is not fair for everyone and promoting total anti-capitalism as the change we need, but these complaining campaigners clearly have not considered that it is only capitalism that offers a fair, free chance for everyone to create wealth for themselves and to use that wealth to express themselves with individuality and ingenuity. Communism does not allow for this kind of freedom. Thus, the logical answer is to combine the two extremes, allowing accumulation of wealth still, but with safeguards and limits to prevent it from becoming monstrous. Only with a compromising system such as capital incentivised socialism can we maintain the freedoms personal wealth secures, whilst simultaneously redistributing wealth more evenly across the global population. The inevitable dark place absolute capitalism has brought us to is 1 per cent of people having more wealth, and therefore power, than the rest of the 99 per cent combined.

We should be focusing on cooperative investment into the human population as a whole, where every continent is looked after. We cannot continue to rely on philanthropy from the one per cent, taking it for granted as part of an action plan for H-utopia, or indeed any future society. When applying for a business loan, or applying for a mortgage, a lender would not take into consideration irregular financial gifts in your application. It is not smart business planning to rely on such things. We need regular, indefinite, guaranteed support for the weaker areas of society, to efficiently bring them into equilibrium with the rest of the world. The hybrid system proposed to redistribute wealth can do this very effectively.

Furthermore, there would be better opportunity to ensure foreign aid is spent wisely. Currently, in many wealthy countries, a proportion of tax collected goes on foreign aid. However, many people in the countries foreign aid is coming from resent this, likening it to throwing cash at a person who is begging in the street; a lot of the time, money given will be misspent rather than being invested wisely in improving their situation. There is a lot of negativity about tax money being given away in foreign aid as it is not always ending up benefitting those who need it most, instead going straight into the pockets of corrupt officials in the recipient countries, or just being poorly invested. Many would argue that it is better and more caring to actually make an effort to purchase food or clothing for a homeless person than to just throw money at them. Just as it is better to commission a hospital or school to be built in a developing country, instead of opting for the lazy option, throwing the money in their direction and saying "do what you will with it, we have done our bit for society". This simplistic approach to foreign aid is significantly prolonging the development process and fuelling further frustration that tax money is being wasted.

What is more, with capital incentivised socialism and a global electronic currency in place, there would then be a possibility that all of the various other tax funded government benefits and allowances could be overhauled, and something truly inspired and great could be done for humanity: a standard global allowance for everyone, with the purpose of fulfilling the most basic biological, selfish needs for all humans; to ensure everyone has access to adequate food and shelter. This is an investment that must be made if we wish to reach H-utopia. If a human is preoccupied with the very real prospect of starvation or homelessness, they are reduced to animalistic motives and are not planning ahead, considering others, (present generation or future), or thinking about fulfilling higher human needs, such as love, respect, knowledge, morality and expression. Therefore, the humane and socially beneficial thing to do would be to allow everyone a basic amount of credits as a rock bottom income, (for instance 1000 credits per month per person, regardless of marital status). This is the right thing to do, but before we get carried away, there are some pitfalls to avoid with this kind of benefit:

1) Dependency on authority means less independence and potentially reduced liberty.
2) Extra inflation caused by the benefit could undermine it.
3) The money could be misspent, fuelling illicit substance addiction or further personal debt.

To avoid the pitfalls there would need to be rules and regulations. The H-utopian global allowance would have to be set at a sensible level and crucially, would have to be distinguishable from normal money and restricted to certain items. As I have already suggested, every human being could be assigned one, and *only* one, bank/credit account at birth that they would be able to use to start saving into from birth. However, upon turning 18 years old, an individual would be assigned a second credit account which would be paid into only by government. The minimum credits required to pay for enough food, water and shelter to a give basic quality of life could be paid to every adult's government credit account at regular intervals, thus removing all financial stress and re-directing human attention once and for all away from mere survival and onto a higher plane of existence. The credits in this second account would have to be distinguishable from regular credits in an individual's primary account, to ensure the money is not misspent by people who are helplessly addicted to non-essential items. These credits would have to be restricted to food items, prescription medicine, utilities, rent, repayments to a certified mortgage lender, etc. A registered business, lender or utility provider being paid in these credits would have to register with the government scheme to exchange them. As another rule, the credits in this account could not be accumulated by an individual person. For example, if someone has 300 unspent credits from the previous month's 1000 paid in, when this month's pay day came, they would only have 700 credits paid in to top them back up to the limit.

Of course, additional benefits would still have to be paid to those who are genuinely unable to contribute in any way due to severe health problems, as they are anyway with our current welfare systems.

For those who may presume this level of socialism to be financially impossible, remember, 'credits' are just electronic figures. In a cashless society with no physical gold or silver ever needing to exist, the 'H-utopian Global Allowance' could, in theory, be produced from thin air, exempt from any economic strife that the rest of the economy may ever fall victim to. In other words, there would always be credits available for every adult on Earth to get their basic human rights and essentials. These government credits could also be available to withdraw in limited amounts of paper cash, to satisfy anxiety surrounding cards being declined, but the paper cash would have to be very limited, time-restricted, or person-specific to avoid counterfeiting and criminal activity re-emerging.

By working, extra credits could be earned on top of this, up to the hypothetical limit of, let's say, 500 million. The amount that the credit limit is set at must have strict safeguarding in place that cannot be changed without referendum. To avoid losing financial incentive and slipping into communism, and to avoid becoming dependent on authority and slipping into totalitarianism, I would suggest the amount must never be allowed to drop any lower than the equivalent of today's 250 million pounds sterling. It could start at 500 million initially but then be reduced by half over the course of several decades as humanity adjusts to the new system.

Anyone who argues that having a spare 500 million pounds,

dollars or 'credits' is not enough for one person to have influence over at any one point is beyond greedy and I would regard them as having a suspicious or selfish agenda. What makes one single human being so important that they must have billions of credits whilst millions of others do not even have water to drink?

Before continuing, there are a couple of points to clarify: firstly, with so much money collected from the richest parts of society, income tax thresholds could be significantly heightened, meaning people on low to medium incomes would not need to sacrifice any earnings to taxation. Secondly, if an economic system such as this were to be implemented, those who already have wealth saved above the limit should not have to pay it back, as they may have financial obligations already in place, (many of them charitable), that could be undermined. The only sacrifice with this system would be when it came to inheritance. Anyone who had more money saved than the imposed limit would not be able to pass on more than that amount of credits from their fortune to any individual beneficiary. Otherwise, this system would not be effective in redistributing wealth in a future society, and we would never be able to flatten the human hierarchy.

If we want a system like this implemented and want it to be viable, the responsibility is not just with government. As already discussed, we all need to appreciate the consequences of having too many children and accept our responsibility to slow down population growth. For only then will we prove wise enough to handle capital incentivised socialism and the benefits that come with it. The goal is to sustain our global population in a more humane way than we do currently, which is keeping a large amount of the world's population in extreme poverty. This is the most unacceptable, sickening part of human society and capital incentivised socialism, with the financial changes suggested to accompany it, has the potential to fix this efficiently with practical and rational changes to the world's economic structure.

Moneyless society, a possibility?

Education, healthcare, food and water. All are basic human rights essential to us; yet, in some parts of the world, these are viewed as privileged luxuries by millions of people who have to do without. As we have discovered already, there is enough food and water in the world for everyone, so that is not the issue. The problem, we are told, is that there is not enough money in the world for everyone to live comfortably. But says who exactly?

Money is not a physical thing, as it once was. When we get paid into our bank accounts electronically or when we pay in a cheque, the bank does not go out and find the equivalent value in gold and silver to put in our personal 'vaults'. They do not even print the extra paper cash notes. All they do is type the numbers on their computer screen and you are suddenly worth a bit more than before, showing as 'debit' in your account. You can in turn transfer this debit as you wish, to any other individual's account in exchange for goods or services that would otherwise have been unavailable to you. If everyone in the world went to their banks at the same time in an attempt to claim all of their electronic debit back as actual gold and silver coins, the banks would be in serious trouble as they do not have it, no one really does. They would not even have enough paper notes, which are just another form of 'I owe you' anyway, which have no real value. This is why there are rules in place, restricting us from claiming our real money all at once like this. So if money does not really exist, apart from electronically, can we not just give humanity more of it so we can feed all the starving? Or better yet, can we just get rid of it entirely?

From our perspective and what we are used to, living in the 21st century, the idea of going back to a moneyless society seems like a laughable impossibility - childish and primitive. But actually, it is far from impossible and far from primitive. It is actually pretty easy and could, in theory, be done overnight. Whether it would be beneficial or not is another matter. Would the benefits of a moneyless society outweigh the negatives? Just to be clear, I do not mean an alternative to money such as a barter system, I am talking about what a completely money/trade free, egalitarian global society would look like and how it would function.

On the plus side, it would put an end to poverty and world hunger, and it would reduce crimes related to stealing and greed. In a moneyless society, production of goods and services as well as technological, scientific and medical advancements would have no hindrance and would be free to fulfil their potential, as they would no longer be restricted by overhead costs. Unemployment would no longer be an issue as all of that extra production would need a larger workforce, and because there would be no need for competitiveness anymore, the inventing and manufacturing processes would be much easier. Without budget constraints on schools, everybody would get an equal and full education. Hospitals would be able to provide all the free healthcare needed, and there would be no profit in war so we would likely live more peacefully.

Before we get carried away, clearly there would have to be restrictions to replace the limit money imposed over consumerism. Otherwise, demand would massively outweigh supply because everything would become disposable. For example, replacing a new car with another brand new one, because it had a small dent, or because we all want to drive supercars rather than our sensible cars. There would have to be rations and regulations in place, or we would go quite mad within a matter of hours in a moneyless world. For it to work, the rationing would have to be enforced by a complex computerised system, and we would likely have to convert our society to an extreme version of technocracy, with facial recognition everywhere and human microchip monitoring, which is something many people are highly suspicious of because of the potential for authoritarian abuse. We would still all have to do our jobs, or the world would cease to function and without money there as the enabler that forces us to work, we would need another incentive to replace it. For example, if you do not go to work, you have rations reduced to basics with just a minimum amount of food, water and energy supplied.

There would need to be maximum allowances too, in order to stop individuals taking way more than they need. This means the way we live and work would have to stay pretty much the same; except we would not have the stress and anxiety that unemployment and money can cause us.

It seems the biggest issue with the removal of money is the removal of scarcity. In the real world, there is a finite supply of land and natural resources that would soon be overwhelmed if not restricted. What I mean is, we could not all have massive mansions, surrounded by hundreds of acres of land, and we would have to have strict birth control laws enforced. There is another problem, without increased wages for incentive, who would want to work longer hours or work in the more challenging, stressful job roles? Would we all have to be assigned job roles based on aptitude tests and forced to work the careers we are told, or have restrictions on purchases heightened for those willing to do the harder jobs? Clearly, this would not work and certainly does not sound like a utopia. Any attempt to switch to a completely moneyless society is a form of extremism, and there are far too many complications and risks to even attempt this drastic change to human society. Assuming we still live in the real world and have not decided to live in the kind of virtual reality future I briefly described earlier, then personally, I cannot see it ever working out, even in the longer-term. Maybe one day, if we can develop an unlimited, renewable source for our energy needs, and have become an immortal spacefaring civilisation, focusing on colonising other worlds as our primary objective, then we would be able to phase out the use of money. It is impossible to know for sure how perception and priorities will change as society evolves. Just as we regard the feudal system of the middle ages as primitive, our descendants in the 30th century may regard our current form of trade as primitive and anti-social, but for now, this is getting into the realms of science-fiction. We need to work with the less extreme options to improve upon what we have already built, just as I have suggested with the introduction of capital incentivised socialism and the benefits attributed to it.

For the time being at least, money is the simplest way for the world to achieve equilibrium between supply and demand, whilst allowing us the freedom to be self-reliant, dignified individuals. If money is gone, then supply and demand have to be balanced some other way. The alternative is letting an authority regulate it artificially, and this is not a wise thing to do. It could easily lead to totalitarianism if corrupt individuals in charge decided to go mad with power. The rationing amounts could be reduced, for whatever reason the authority sees fit and with money worthless and gone, we would be at the complete mercy of the authority for our survival. For this reason, more than any, I will never be an advocate of a moneyless society. But is our H-utopian future sustainable in a society obsessed with money? The biggest problem with money is the corruption it causes. Sadly, two of the biggest profit makers in the world are:

1) **Human illness** - in the form of pharmaceutical companies.

2) **War** - in the form of arms dealing and resource grabbing for the winning side.

An unimaginative individual may assume that if our society makes a determined break away from these two biggest earners, the world economy will collapse. War is good for business, no doubt about it, but only for the winners. It is obviously not good for the losing side who have their cities decimated and their own nation's economy destroyed. In a similar way that illnesses are not good for the families of those afflicted.

If the world economy is dependent on the infinite, intentional suffering of our species, then is this really a good enough reason to allow it to continue; with companies profiteering from preventable war and preventable curable illness? Is it because we cannot imagine there is any other way in which we can have a successful economic climate and stable population than to maintain perpetual suffering in some parts of the world or allow the suffering of people that are towards the bottom of the socio-economic hierarchy? A sad point of view indeed and not one worthy of a species, with our capacity for problem-solving. When it is not affecting you personally, it is easy to ignore, but there are no guarantees that you or your family will not be affected at some point in the future if things escalate.

What if the trillions we 'invest' in war each year could be saved? Imagine what exciting ventures that money could be injected into. To name a handful: deep space mining, artificial intelligence, genetic advancements, artificial meat, research into producing unlimited environmentally friendly energy and fixing sanitation problems in the developing world, so developing nations can begin contributing to the world's economy.

Money is not the problem. Capitalism without limits, poor investment, misplaced priorities, lack of financial clarity and an uncooperative, overly competitive society are the problems. We do not have to completely remove money and healthy competition from society to reach H-utopia. The compromise of capital incentivised socialism is far better than the extreme options. The only difficult part is cooperating globally to agree on how it could work best and then implementing it globally. It would not work if some nations retained unlimited capitalism.

The end of private ownership and reduction in planned obsolescence

In the developed parts of the world at least, people have become obsessed with, and accustomed to, personal ownership. We already discussed the importance many wealthy people place on status symbols, such as wearing a Rolex watch or driving a golden Lamborghini, for example. Both of these products do the same basic job as thousands of other cheaper variations of the same product. A watch tells the time, and a car drives from A to B. When a variation becomes too elaborate and expensive, it becomes poor value for money, making it an irrational purchase. I believe the phrase is 'more money than sense'.

In a completely rational world, no one would own their own car. Pay per journey driverless vehicles could get us all wherever we needed to go. Pulling up at our homes and taking us to our destinations. When we are ready to go home, we simply call another one to pick us up. If they break down, a replacement would be sent straight away. There would be no road tax, no MOTs, no maintenance and repair bills, no road traffic accidents and all vehicles could be powered with renewable energy. According to many futurists, this is the inevitable destiny of cars one day.

If this happens with cars, we can expect the simplification of other elaborate things that we currently insist on privately owning, such as our homes which come in all sorts of shapes and sizes. From caravans, to tower blocks, to mansions, to bungalows, but perhaps the future of housing may be simplified to building energy, space, and cost efficient pods that are provided for us to cheaply occupy for our lives, as an alternative to big expensive brick houses that take months to build and use an enormous amount of resources to construct. Public provided driverless transport pods, and pod living accommodation may sound undesirable to us, but for our descendants, this could be the norm and a far more rational, clean and efficient alternative to how their grandparents stubbornly insisted on living; in their big dusty old energy leaking brick houses heated with fossil fuels and driving around in their polluting, oily old internal combustion motors responsible for around 3000 deaths a day globally from accidents.

Capitalist society has created an unwritten list of things we must achieve to be considered succeeding at life, and right at the top of the list is to purchase our own homes, and to upgrade these homes when possible. Of course, most of us never really *own* our homes for the majority of the time we spend living in them. We spend a lifetime working to pay back lenders for the privilege of being allowed to remain dwelling in the buildings we call our homes, as we move from small to bigger and better properties, whilst remaining debt slaves.   The social pressure that drives the obsession with private ownership leaves people taking irrational financial risks just to keep up with the Jones's. If we stay alive long enough, the entire amount of the purchase price, plus interest will eventually be paid on the buildings we live in. During this long period of repayment, there is always the risk property values may fall below the price we originally dealt at, leaving us in negative equity and financially unable to sell and move on, putting even more pressure on to continually meet payments. During times of recession, private owners still repaying are hit worst, as property price crashes can postpone profiting off of investments for potentially decades.

Mortgages, along with running vehicles, are probably two of the biggest monthly outgoings for average families, and many will take out further loans to afford vitals such as food and clothing on top of these. We may dream of winning the lottery, so we can outright purchase a supercar, but this still will only take us from A to B as any car would. We may dream of living in a mansion with fifty rooms, but at the end of the day, the only rooms we really need and use every day are a kitchen/diner, bathroom, one bedroom per occupant and a reasonably sized daytime living/entertainment space. These four room types are where most people will spend the majority of their lives in the home, no matter how big it is. We may stubbornly insist that living in modest pod-style housing will rob us of our individuality because we design and decorate our homes to reflect our personality, individuality and character, but generally, the larger the house, the less of our personality shines through it. Mansions tend to become show homes, filled with meaningless, decorative items that serve no real purpose but to show off excessive wealth.

When we shop online, we can spend hours browsing through thousands of the same product in different variations to decorate and furnish our homes. Thanks to mass production techniques, the same basic item is available over and over again in slightly varying décor, shape, size, colour and degree of quality. Take, for example, an item as simple as a vase. What is the purpose of a vase if not to display with some flowers in? The cost of purchasing a vase could be as low as a few cents from a charity store or yard sale. On the other hand, it could cost tens of millions of dollars for a Ming or Qing dynasty Chinese porcelain vase. Then we have everything in between, the thousands of replicas, trying to mimic these rare and famous antiques in design - available for a fraction of the price but because mass-produced the sales total the same amount of money eventually.

Imagine a world where humanity had done away with many of the replicas, copies, variants and for want of a better word 'tat' that people are overwhelmed with when choosing. Tat is produced in excess because it is cheap; the quality is not important because when it breaks, it is cheap to replace. The cost is to the environment when the item is inevitably disposed of because it is too worthless or broken to sell or repair. Mobile/cell phones are a prime example of disposable products terrible for the environment, because of how quickly and thoughtlessly they are replaced. The practise of planned obsolescence makes sure of this. Only in a future not driven by capitalism without limits can we begin to combat the environmentally damaging, wasteful and unethical practice of planned obsolescence. Although we have argued capitalism is good for driving forward technological advancement, this is not the case with planned obsolescence, as this is not about producing genuinely better quality products in great strides. Planned obsolescence actually caps potential, slowing down technological advancements. If anything, it is more comparable to the communist state production ethos of filling quotas with quantity and not quality; and actually, does not allow for uncapped brilliance to design and build with integrity.

We all remember those household items from our grandparent's homes that have been there since we were young and remain there today in solid working order, seemingly miraculous by nature as they last a lifetime. Yet we are lucky if we get a couple of years use out of our modern-day appliances before it is time to upgrade or replace broken, outdated or faulty items. This is because of the increasing practice of planned obsolescence and its a crime responsible for millions of tonnes of waste every year ending up in landfills, much of which gets sent overseas as 'second-hand merchandise' to electronic wastelands in developing countries, who accept it as a way for them to generate revenue. There is a constant stream of electronic waste from the gluttonous developed world, and much of it ends up being burnt or being handled by child labourers in developing nations, exposing them to carcinogenic substances such as lead, cadmium, chlorinated dioxins and other harmful toxins. The mobile phone industry is one of the worst offenders for committing blatant planned obsolescence. Before the manufacturers have even released the latest model, they already have the replacements for that one lined up ready to go. Fundamentally the same, the most important difference usually being cosmetic, and often more prone to accidental damage because of the deliberate design flaws built-in. They even have the cheek to sell insurance to cover their faulty products, profiting further from the unethical practice.

So, what can we do about planned obsolescence to support the change in our socio-economic structure of the world, and to help reduce environmental damage? The unimaginative option is for governments to do what they do best and place a 'green tax' on poorly produced items. However, a better and more effective idea is to offer an incentive for manufacturers to consider the environment more in its production ethics. Instead of just taxing the offenders, the government needs to use that money to reward with credits those who recycle and manufacture genuine quality whilst keeping their products affordable.

For the environmental impact alone, in some countries, it is actually becoming a criminal offence to blatantly build-in planned obsolescence in manufacturing. Enforcing this law is not easy, though. There will always be loopholes around the system for companies to carry on doing it more covertly. There is a better enforcement than the law, and that is the power of us as consumers, and where we choose to spend our money. We can make the right choices, educate ourselves into this immoral practice and boycott the worst offenders. Choose the companies with the most integrity, which produce higher quality. Instead of just moaning about delivery times, or superficial things, we can use our rights as consumers in our feedback and reviews to demand better products built with fewer toxic components and better longevity.

We can also recycle responsibly and always try to maintain and repair our items before we just replace them. We have become lazy as a species because it is much easier with our disposable incomes and online ordering to just replace something rather than put up with the inconvenience and effort of routine, preventive maintenance or repairing it once broken. So I cannot be accused of not practising what I preach at this point: the laptop computer I own, and the very one I wrote this essay on, is currently around nine years old. I chose a durable model from a reputable brand that was slightly more expensive than other options in the first place but is standing the test of time so has saved me money in the long run. I have updated it and maintained it myself, the hardware is all original, and it performs as fast, and reliably as any brand new equivalent I have tested it against, I have no plans to replace it any time soon for any shiny new 'upgrades' because there is no *need* for me to do so.

One of the oldest examples of planned obsolescence was, and still is, the light bulb. Dating back to the very beginnings of the practice, nearly a hundred years ago, and with the aim to drive consumerism in order to repair economic damage around the time of the great depression. This is an item that for decades was deliberately built by numerous manufacturers to burn out after minimal use, despite the technology being available to make them last a lifetime and to make them more energy-efficient. The lightbulb is a clear example of where technological advancement was deliberately blocked for decades at the expense of the consumer and the environment. The practice became possible in the early 20th century with mass production techniques. There was no necessity to build things as strong and fine as they once were because countless duplicates could now easily be produced. With the exponentially expanding population, demand was increasing out of control, and one could argue in manufacturers' defence that they had no choice. This is why antiques from the times of pre-industry are such valuable and sort after items, but the thousand pound/dollar smartphone becomes worthless in less than a decade; because there are millions more replaced items just like it very slowly decaying in landfills.

Governing society as a whole

When making a move towards forming a world government, the paths of dystopia and utopia become indistinguishable to the naked eye, making the risk of unwittingly accepting totalitarianism greater than ever. Because of this associated risk, the traditional government structure is not suitable for merging into a world government. I hesitate to even call the collaboration of global politics a 'world government' as this conjures up an absolutist dictatorship. I think the term 'international committee' is better suited to what I have in mind. To avoid corruption of individuals leading the entire species to dystopia, the things we need to target are corruption, bribery and self-serving committee members. Please try to remain open-minded as we review global politics and hopefully find some solutions. If we are going to safely and successfully implement many of the financial benefits described above, it is going to require a reform of government structure to make it possible.

It was the French socialist philosopher, and political theorist, Henri de Saint-Simon, (1760-1825), who suggested in his writings that a new world order would be a requirement if we are to stand any chance of attaining a utopian future. Saint-Simon pointed out that the structure of society with a royal family and noble families holding incredible wealth and power as the heads of state was an outdated part of historical social development, that had managed to cling on much longer than it should have done, enabled by a combination of tyranny, and misplaced patriotism from acquiescing subjects. Since Saint-Simon's time, there has been a decline in royal families as primary leaders in society, and an increase in democratically led nations.

The term 'new world order', or as it is sometimes written 'NWO', (once used just to refer to any historical periods of dramatic political change), has been hi-jacked by conspiracy theorists and consequently has a significant associated paranoia, which means any kind of radical social progress suggested is now added to the growing list of things allegedly planned under an apparent malevolent NWO agenda. The list includes things like a cashless society, ID quantum tattoos, facial recognition, state income, removal of private property, removal of family unit, global dictatorship, world army, etc.These are all things that can have good or bad outcomes, depending on the delivery. It is not the technology, science or idea that is good or evil, it is the persons implementing an idea. The binary world view is an oversimplification. In between good and evil there is an infinite spectrum of complexity in every idea.

Let us take a moment to reflect philosophically and remind ourselves that change is inevitable, whereas, change for the better is entirely within our control, and with the economic course correction of capital incentivised socialism, and limits imposed on the power shares created by wealth, the chance of anything suggested being part of a planned benevolent NWO guided by a hidden plutocratic secret society, or cabal, is greatly diminished. The fact is, if a plutocratic cabal is planning an NWO for malevolent purposes, the only way to stop the NWO happening in a dictatorial manner, detrimental to society for the majority, is to redistribute wealth and power urgently. With the masses sharing redistributed financial and political power equally, the perception of the NWO suddenly changes from evil to benign. Merely progress which is positive and beneficial to the masses. An entire book could be filled debating what form an NWO could take, but the only significance for me right now is to show we should not fear change, only ensure we do what we can to make sure change is for the better. By fearing technological, economic and social advances will bring about malevolence, we actually allow the evil to exploit this fearful rejection, and materialise where it otherwise could not.

The way in which the world is governed evolves constantly, and with the formation of hyper states such as the European Union and the United States of America, which operate democratically, we are trending towards a globalised government. This evolution of politics is not something to fear; it is just the natural political evolution of an ever more connected society as technology advances and transport links improve. However, it is important we exercise caution. Royal families, who ruled openly in Saint-Simon's time, formally the richest people in society, wielding absolute power, have been replaced not just by politicians, but by ordinary people of humble origin who have become obscenely wealthy, and therefore politically influential, in a relatively short space of time. As already discussed, plutocratic oligarchies are able to rule over the vast majority of the global population by controlling the economy to the point of monopolisation, should they wish. This is not a conspiracy theory; it is just an economic fact that anyone would be naïve to deny.

Oligarchies can rule openly like kings and queens, or they can rule discreetly under the guise of democracy. The latter being preferable to an oligarchy. Although we have democracy now in the majority of the world, we have to be careful it is not hi-jacked by a hidden plutocratic oligarchy who are serving their own interests, above those of humanity as a whole, with misguided and twisted political views.

In the 21st century, some countries, such as the United Kingdom, still have a royal family. However, the UK also has a democratic government, which is voted into power via the majority during elections. The government of the UK works as a kind of middle man between the royalty and the citizens. It is a hybrid leadership with a prime minister and their members of parliament, not dissimilar from the barons and lords of the feudal system.

Unfortunately, it is very difficult to please everyone and even in democratic governments, the absolutism of the vote, between political parties who market themselves to extreme ends of society, means there are always going to be a good percentage of citizens who feel they are not being represented or benefited. This creates resentment and animosity as a fierce political divide opens up between voting citizens. This is where democracy fails. In today's politics in the UK, for instance, there is a choice from a handful of candidates who can realistically be put forward to represent the majority in the Houses of Parliament, but for a choice of prime minister it normally comes down to only two. Labour Party or Conservative Party. With US presidents it is similarly binary, simplified into extremes, with Democrats or Republicans. When it comes to referendums, they are nearly always black and white too. It is either one or the other, yes or no. There is no compromise, no intermediate, no suggestions, no mitigation and little or no debate involving the general public. Politics is oversimplified to extreme left or extreme right because it is an attention grabbing and vote winning tactic to represent an extreme opinion. It divides opinion, with a clean-cut and the outcome is rarely positive, with most voters lacking the wisdom and unity to demand a compromise. Any political parties who do try and fill the gap in the market for a happy medium, often are met with a lack of enthusiasm, distrust or frustration at their apparent 'on the fence' position in debates when failing to commit to picking a side.

Whilst we have significant political divide, we can never reach H-utopia, as, by definition, H-utopia is a place where all of humanity's interests are served. Not half, not most, but all.

Is it realistic to make everyone feel represented? I believe it is if we are willing to work hard for it, and we all have a duty to try. Let us take a look at some alternative government structures to see if we can draw wisdom that can help us achieve this dream of political unity.

Noocracy - "aristocracy of the wise" was Plato's dream of a society governed by wise philosopher-kings who had undergone years of philosophical training and testing to help them to become worthy to infallibly lead a species to greatness. With all the best intentions for the good of humanity, theoretically, there would be no requirement for society dividing votes. However, you do not have to be one of Plato's trained philosopher-kings to be wise enough to see the idea is unrealistic, idealist and dangerously prone to producing communist dictator style leaders. Who chooses these philosopher-kings, who is to stop them serving their own self-interests, and once they are in power, what if they won't surrender it? If the public has to choose which amongst potential candidates are wise enough or have the most integrity, then this is just like what we already have, except we are voting in dictators rather than democratic leaders. Plato's idea had good intentions, but it would never have worked...until now. Thanks to the invention of computers, we now have the technology that would allow this to be implemented in an unbiased way. For instance, if a noocratic committee could be selected via artificial intelligence, based on mandatory testing of the whole population, to determine their levels of empathy, emotional intelligence, philosophical ideals, integrity, etc. Allowing politics to choose people, instead of the other way around is one way to combat political corruption.

Cyberocracy – a cyberocractic government would theoretically operate by extrapolating all information and coming to logical, presumably peaceful, decisions that serve the interests of the vast majority, whilst preserving the wellbeing of the species as a whole. Utilising state of the art technologies to observe and communicate on a global scale, a cyberocractic system would be able to make first-hand factual observations, analyse strengths, weaknesses, opportunities and threats, identifying the root causes of any problems, and offering solutions to fix them. Once artificial intelligence becomes sophisticated enough, human governors would surely be replaced by an all-powerful artificial intelligence. Imagine an AI life form as the head of state for the whole world! This idea of an all-powerful, super-intelligent logical decision-making machine is something taken straight out of science-fiction. My concern is that it would be found on the side of the genre that leans towards disastrous dystopian futures. Suppose the AI gets hacked by a terrorist organisation. Who programs the AI in the first place? What is to stop them inputting their own agendas? In a cyberocracy, facial recognition would replace paper documents, and credits would replace all forms of currency. In this kind of a 'Big Brother' state, it would be very easy to be cut off from society if you did not conform to any rules, no matter how tyrannical they become. It is not that I am advocating technophobic response to AI, but I would prefer to believe in the power of humans for the future of politics. Our goal for H-utopia is to develop into a wise, ethical and hyper-intelligent species. Our goal is not to build a machine to do all the thinking for us and enslave us; a machine that could potentially be a threat to us with emotionless logic. Therefore, AI should never be humanity's ultimate decision-maker in any way.

Technocracy - in a technocratic government, parliamentary, political specialists are not voted in as the primary decision-makers. Instead, the decision-makers are selected based on their expertise, reputation and knowledge in whatever specific field of work is relevant to the decision that needs making for society. This form of government makes a lot of sense as it uses the entire workforce to their strengths and grants the wisest and most knowledgeable of us the power to make informed decisions. It does not necessarily imply eliminating elected political representatives, but their absolute power would be reduced in favour of the collaboration with technical, scientific experts. It is important the 'experts' in their field are part of a committee of many, from a variety of backgrounds, not working alone, to avoid the risk of rash decisions being made on false information. Also, the committee should be constantly refreshed, changing its members, from decision to decision, to aid us in reducing corruption associated with traditional political governments to influence the expert's decisions.

Demarchy - a novel vision of government, in which the state is governed by randomly selected decision-makers who have been selected from a lottery. Although this makes for an interesting scenario to explore in fiction, I do not think it has any serious place in the formation of a stable government in reality. Any delegates selected would likely be overwhelmed by the sudden power, and would only end up being influenced by the strongest characters around, who have *their* own agendas.

Planetary government/world committee - there are three stages to achieve globalisation before a world committee designed to oversee global politics could be introduced: first, cultural globalisation, then economic globalisation, and finally, political globalisation. It is the final political stage that would prove most challenging because there are leaders around the world that would never willingly surrender their supposed ultimate right to rule over their nations. For those who think globalisation will never happen, you only have to look around you, and you will realise society has been tiptoeing towards it for centuries. For as long as humans have had the ability to traverse, and communicate across great distances, we have been trying to centralise power for a more effective rule. Centralisation of power is most evident today with the formation of the European Economic Area, the European Union, and the United States of America. If we continue with the current trend, the logical outcome is a global government. Will it help humanity to achieve security, prosperity and peace on a global scale? Or will it lead humanity straight into a dystopian 'Big Brother' state similar to that in George Orwell's *Nineteen Eighty Four*? How severely a planetary government could be exploited for evil may depend on our acceptance of such an idea. If we form it during a time of peace, there is little chance for exploitation. Whereas, if we are handed it forcibly as a last resort to maintain law and order in a nightmarish future where democracy has failed to deliver solutions during times of warmongering and/or scaremongering, it could be dictatorial and draconian by nature. Let us review the pros and cons of a planetary society.

Free worldwide trade - consumers would be able to purchase goods from anywhere in the world without extra taxes to pay because there would not be individual national laws that could place restrictions on imports and exports.

More cultural interaction and understanding - when people have the ability to communicate with one another freely, and the artificial barriers between us are removed, there will be more cultural interaction which will reduce xenophobic behaviours, improve worldwide cooperation, and remove intolerances. Better interaction means more information, which means better-informed decision making.

Crackdown on tax havens - as I have already suggested, there should be globally agreed tax brackets to prevent businesses from avoiding paying their fair share of tax in the locations they operate from. These should be implemented, globalised government or not. Globalisation would leave no room for the so-called 'tax havens' where company CEOs and directors prosper at the expense of the rest of the population who have filled their pockets for them.

Eliminating economic manipulation and increasing financial stability - some countries manipulate their currencies to benefit their own economy. All it takes is the prime minister or chancellor to make a statement about the nation's currency, and it can alter the exchange rate. With globalisation and a world currency, there would be no opportunity for manipulating currencies for price advantages, which would benefit consumers.

Development of the poorest areas in the world - globalisation will give the developing countries struggling on the verge of industrialisation the investment needed to catch up with the rest of the world. The removal of the individual nation will mean the removal of poverty, as all countries will have access to the same opportunities. Every part of the world's economic success will be a matter of global responsibility and every nation benefits as all are part of one big society.

Fulfilling human potential with cooperation rather than competition - an example is space exploration. Ask anyone from 50 or 60 years ago, around the time of the Apollo missions to the moon, and many of them would have bet good money us mining the moon and having colonies on Mars by the millennium. Although great things have been achieved, (we cannot take that away from the many scientists, engineers, mathematicians and astronauts involved), it is fair to say we have not fulfilled our potential. Suppose we had pooled resources into one global space agency instead of having multiple smaller agencies all trying to do the same thing with limited investment and public support, who knows where we could have been by now. The next step towards deeper space exploration is learning to live in space, and that is what is currently happening on the International Space Station, which is a testament to the great things nations can achieve when they collaborate instead of compete, demonstrated with the coming together of historic space race competitors, the USA and Russia, along with Canada, Japan, Denmark, Belgium, Germany, France, Norway, Spain, Switzerland, Sweden, Italy, The Netherlands, and the United Kingdom.

There are many positives to a global government, but we cannot overlook the risks:

It could mean slowly losing our identity - we talked about more cultural interaction as a positive, but we need to be careful that in a stateless world, we maintain our individuality and cultural identities. Even if we do not identify as the same nationality as our parents or grandparents, we all have genetic heritage and family history that is unique, and differing cultural practises. This is a good thing that we must hold on to. There is evidence that in large combined states where cultures merge, identities can become blurred. The citizens of the USA, for example, have an incredibly diverse heritage; a second or third-generation immigrant could have large percentages of Irish, German, Italian and English in them and could live in the state of California, but would likely just identify as American, rather than calling themselves Irish German American or Italian English American or Californian Italian German.

The formation of a world government could be biased - the officials of the world government would likely be appointed from only the richest nations. When it came to forming the world government, the super powers of the world would get the most say and the smaller, quieter countries could be completely absorbed with no fair representation or influence in the globalisation. This could mean some nations act like dictators whilst other areas are oppressed or exploited.

The disastrous potential of pandemics - diseases that can spread throughout the world cause us great concern from time to time and the implications go far deeper than just loss of life. Even today, with millions of people travelling internationally every year, it only takes a matter of weeks for an epidemic in one country to become a pandemic. In a globalised future, that has even fewer restrictions on travel and trade, the control we currently have over diseases such as Ebola, influenza or other respiratory viruses such as MERS and SARS could be lost. Mandatory temperature scanners at every airport, every school and every office or food-based workplace could be implemented to help combat this. If a fever is recorded, then no travel or school allowed. Of course, many people are carriers, or asymptomatic, so this almost certainly will not be enough. However, if we had a globally shared economy, then this would not put pressure on countries with sick populations to carry on trading during an epidemic. Therefore, travel in and out of any infected country could be strictly banned until the epidemic is contained. Currently, shutting off a country from the rest of the world would destroy its economy and it is not something we can realistically do. However, in a global society, it would be the duty of the rest of the world to support the afflicted area economically. Currently, in our competitive world, countries displaying signs of an outbreak may desperately try to hide the outbreak from the rest of the world for as long as possible, so they can carry on competing and do not fall behind economically. A disastrous tactic that is doomed to backfire. Viruses pose a far greater threat to humanity than just illness alone. Pandemic threats could always be dangled over humanity to instil fear and therefore increase control measures in society. Scare people enough, and they will not just allow authority to remove liberty, they will demand it and comply with it, due to the crippling anxiety and obsession with death that humans have. We briefly discussed earlier on how this weakness in the human psyche can be combatted from childhood to prevent it being exploited in such situations, but nevertheless, it remains a threat for now.

Absolute power corrupts absolutely - dealing with pandemics and maintaining our diversity is something that we could plan for and overcome. The real threat and a major concern would be the consequences of corruption in a global government. The simpler the power hierarchy and the more widespread the area and resources that power controls, the easier it is to become corrupt and get away with it. Even when power is given to the people proportionally, and we have small localised governments and committees forming, we still observe corruption; only it is on a smaller, less damaging scale. If we multiply corruption up to a globalised scale where we just have one government, one person, or one group of people, controlling every aspect of everything that happens on Earth, the chance of our leaders suffering from God complexes becomes greatly heightened. In a global government, the individual has much less say in what happens. The larger the empire, the less effective democracy is. The chances are, a true global government would inadvertently slip into a more dictatorial kind of rule, much like an empire, rather than a democratic system and there would not be much us normal citizens of the Earth would be able to do about it at that point.

Although there would be many benefits to a globalised society, there would also be many drawbacks and pitfalls, which we would need to navigate around carefully, and with total transparency, if globalisation were to be beneficial for all.

One interesting way we could navigate it successfully is by expanding on and combining the ideas of noocracy, demarchy and technocracy in order to select temporary leaders, logically, not randomly, depending on what decisions need making. Expert representatives from each and every country across the world could then collaborate. In a modern, less random take on demarchy, computerised systems could select the most suitable politically minded leaders from the entire human population to have their chance at being part of a global council or international committee to work alongside the selected 'experts' to ensure they don't become dictatorial in manner.

Selecting people whose ideals align best with the ideals of H-utopia will only work if the aptitude, emotional intelligence, mental ability, empathy, psychology, and ethics, of everyone on Earth, is assessed and recorded, (perhaps with a mandatory mental screening that everyone on Earth has to complete at regular intervals upon turning 21 for instance). Politics choosing people, rather than people choosing politics would minimise the risk of corrupt people getting into politics only to serve themselves. Candidates could turn down the duty if selected, but the duty would only ever be temporary.

To negate even more risk of corruption, we can expand further on the idea of ordinary people running the world with '**proportional representation**'. Imagine a worldwide government where everyone on Earth *is* the government. We would no longer require thousands of paid politicians, or binary, extremist candidates to vote for in order to represent a majority, as the majority would represent themselves as the complex individuals they are. There would be far less chance for corruption as everyone in the world, (of a certain age and with the exception of the incarcerated), would have an equal chance to make global decisions. Debates and presentations could all be broadcast globally online, and as long as someone was registered and viewed the entire presentation, they would be eligible to vote on any matters raised via petitions, etc. We would probably find a population far more interested, involved, and most importantly trusting, in politics than we have today. It would be hard work, but if laziness is all that is holding us back, then is this a good enough reason to stick with a flawed system just for its simplicity?

To conclude, I have hypothesised **'capital incentivised socialism'** as our economic system, and for the sake of argument, we could dub my hybrid international governing system **'tech-noo-marchracy', with 'proportional representation'** in place to ensure everyone on Earth can remain masters of their own destiny. With these three rational social, economic and political changes combining together at once, humanity retains control of engineering its own, peaceful and benevolent **new world order** in a globally collaborating society.

Is there another way?

If you are not sold on the idea of an international committee with expert decision-makers and temporary elected leaders based on aptitude tests, combined with proportional representation for everyone on Earth, and limits imposed on capitalism with excess earnings funding solutions for social problems worldwide instead of increasing power share for the minority, then fear not. I am sure the suggestions so far are not the only way, just one path based on logic and good intentions. To see if it is possible to achieve global harmony and maintain H-utopia without globalisation or any radical economic changes, let us have a look at some of the most socially successful countries in the world today.

Fundamentally, the countries leading the way in development all run their societies with this simple philosophy: the nation looks after its citizens and the citizens look after their nation. The following countries are financially successful, educate and treat their citizens exceptionally well, have powerful workforces and generally manage to avoid the conflict that other parts of the world dirty their hands with: Norway, Switzerland, Finland, Denmark, Netherlands, Canada, Australia and New Zealand. These countries are living proof that nations adopting socialist aspects in a capital incentivised environment, investing in welfare and focusing on educating their people, can successfully compete internationally. It is also no coincidence that these top socially successful countries are amongst the least religious in the world, with Norway hosting one of the world's most convinced atheist populations. Norway, Finland and Denmark have some of the best welfare systems in the world and the best education systems in the world, with their ethos being equality.   In Finland, there are no tuition fees, and there are free meals for students. In 2018, research into human development showed that, along with Norway, Estonia, Latvia, and around 20 other countries, Finland had a 100 per cent literate population. The UK did not even have 100 per cent, and the USA only had around 86 per cent literacy. The Scandinavian countries also continue to have the highest standards of living out of any of the European countries.

Interestingly, despite being surrounded by EU countries, Norway is not a member of the European Union, showing that separatism can work for a country and that we do not need a world government to attain something better than we have today if we can all follow their examples. Another interesting example of an independent European state with 100 per cent literate population is Andorra. This is thanks to the Andorran government managing to provide free schooling and dedicating a significant investment in children up to the secondary level of education. It is enlightening that children in Andorra are only legally required to attend school for ten years, between the ages of six and sixteen. Because of this, Andorra came in at a disappointing 35th place on the Human Development Index, (HDI), in 2018. With 100 per cent literacy, the schooling may be shorter than some other countries, although evidently, it is efficient, raising the question of how long do children really need to spend in schools if their schooling is carried out to maximum efficiency?

It is relevant to make clear at this stage that countries such as Norway, Finland and New Zealand have to sustain a population only around 10-15 per cent of that of the UK, France and Germany. So making comparisons is difficult, but there are no doubts these countries are well managed; and in 2018, the Human Development Index, (which takes into account, life expectancy, quality/length of schooling and average income), put Norway at the number 1 spot in the world. The statistics do not lie, and we all need to be following the example of these countries that are leading the way in human development. Others ranked in the top 10 included Hong Kong, Australia, Iceland and Singapore. The common theme that is linking most of these countries is their population does not overwhelm their resources. Australia and Canada are two of the least densely populated countries in the world, so it is no surprise they are socially thriving.

The population of Australia is just over a third of that of the UK's, and in Canada, the population is just over half of the UK's.   Incidentally, the UK came in at 14th place on the HDI in 2018, with average national income being its Achilles heel. The UK was the only country in the top 15 that had an average gross national income of less than 40,000. It is evident that if this was rectified and raised to around 50,000, making it on par with the others, then the UK would make an impressive jump into the top 5. For the size of the country in relation to the population it is trying to sustain, it has done well to reach this far up in the HDI. In fact, in the top 20 countries in 2018, the only countries that had populations to sustain of more than 20 million were: The UK, Australia, Germany, Canada, USA and Japan. Like the UK, Canada also has a free healthcare service and a good life expectancy into the 80s, but the average gross national income lets it down, putting it at 12th position, just above the USA in 13th. Germany came in at an impressive 5th place in the HDI. Considering it had at least 60 million more people to sustain than any of the others in the top 10, one could argue that Germany deserved the top spot as the most socially successful country in the world.

In 2018, New Zealand came in at 16th on the HDI, and had by far the lowest gross national income out of the top 20 countries at only 33,000. However, the welfare system in the country is extensive, offering support for housing, unemployment, healthcare, childcare, and education. So although officially free market, New Zealand, Canada and the UK have adopted many of the characteristics of a socialist country. The only dilemma is, their overwhelmed welfare systems meant the countries were overspending, not achieving equilibrium financially, and therefore not where they deserved to be developmentally.

It is very easy to get lost in a sea of statistics, neatly ordering everything into leaderboards, but we should not regard human development as a competition. Those at the top of the HDI should not become complacent either. Thanks to the unstable socio-economic climate capitalism creates, nations are prone to wild fluctuation during periods of economic turmoil. By the time you are reading this, it is likely the HDI will look very different. What the HDI should do, is highlight for us, the mammoth gulf in quality of life between top and bottom and how wrong this is. It should also be noted that whilst the Scandinavian countries are socially successful and high ranking in the

HDI, they have some of the highest tax rates in Europe. In contrast, Andorra is considered a tax haven, with some of the lowest taxation rates in the world. Although a nation that has no army and only 70 thousand people to support should not need to collect much tax. This may work for Andorra and some other mini-states whose citizens can benefit from low taxation, but if the rest of the world tried to live like this, dividing up into small separatist states, especially with no army to protect them from the neighbouring states who may try to expand their territory, civilisation would be liable to collapse into barbaric tribalism, and we would all be back to square one.

In some progressive African countries, tribalism is the disruptive influence that divides and conquers the people living there, continually destroying the roots of social progression before they have a chance to expand and grow. It urgently needs to be addressed so these countries can take their place in the developed world, but this is easier said than done, and there is no quick fix for this in a world of separatists. Efforts have been largely in vain so far, with tribal identity even intensifying in some nations, because of a defensive xenophobic response to potential cultural loss when outsiders are seen to be interfering. The fear of losing one's culture or country is nothing unique to the African continent, of course. Even in the most socially developed parts world, people are xenophobic, particularly of those from poorer parts of the world who may be seen by the ignorant and insecure as a threat, coming to steal their jobs or to impose religious agendas.

The negative attitude towards immigration is witnessed everywhere, even from countries with socialist philosophies that supposedly want to do their bit to help global society. There is growing perception that a country's domestic problems, such as unemployment, are the fault of immigrants, rather than shortcomings of the individuals, who do not actively make an effort to remain in employment. There is a xenophobic response to immigrants from all around the world, who bring their own cultures with them. Many natives do embrace the free movement of people, or at least tolerate it, but there are a large number who resent it and commit sickening hate crimes, and racist protests, as well as ignorant and pathetic attempts to scare off people of different religions, (who are not even necessarily immigrants), such as putting bacon on the door handles of Mosques which they resent even being built in 'their' Christian country.

Ironically, with its Jewish background, pork is forbidden to be eaten by Christianity also, if practised strictly. However, we do not witness Islamic people leaving packets of pork scratchings on church pews. Truth be told, it is not even about race or religion. It is about nostalgia, traditionalism and fear. Fear of change, fear of the unknown, fear of being attacked, fear that property will fall in value if immigrants move too close. There is a difference between disagreeing ethnicities and warring tribes. Such ignorance stems from a tribal mentality. The perpetrators of hate crime rarely know their victims; they have not bothered taking the time to get to know them, nor do they want to. All they know is the newcomers are slightly different in how they dress, look or talk. To make matters worse, thanks to a predominantly biased media, many people have perhaps drawn misinformed conclusions about the faith of some immigrants being responsible for extremist terrorism or surges in other crime. This leads the xenophobe to the deluded conclusion that everyone affiliated with this faith or ethnicity deserves to be tormented in their personal lives. Those who think it is acceptable to behave like this should realise this is a terrorist act borne out of extremism and absolutism. Far-right political extremism manifesting as hate crime, targeting completely innocent people. Are these extremist acts labelled in the media as Christian or white extremism though? Of course not, because the tribal mindset does not stop with your average caveman. It is deep inset genetically into all of us, and although these xenophobic acts sicken the majority of people, they naturally do not anger people as much as crimes against the native ethnic majority of a country. It is likely that even the most politically left-winged and tolerant individuals have the potential to react or think in this hostile way when they feel that they, or their families, are directly threatened. Beating our xenophobic genes is just harder for some when the environment they grew up in, or currently live in, reinforces or encourages the negative aspects of our nature.

There is a lesson here, and it is to not let our differences divide us, so we cannot be conquered. If we go back in time a hundred years or so, the UK was an almost entirely Christian country, but if we go back in time a bit further, before it was a Christian country, it was occupied by Pagan's who incidentally were killed or converted to Christianity. The reason? It certainly was not individual Christians came over to Britain and committed terrorism. It was the powerful Roman empire wanted it imposed. Growing in popularity at the time, Christianity, a single religion with a single God was seen as the perfect way to unite an empire and achieve military success by the Roman Emperor Constantine. It did not happen overnight; the takeover took hundreds of years. Christianity was a minority religion in the UK right up until Augustine's mission in 597AD when the Catholic Church and King Aethelbert created a strong alliance between Christianity and British royalty. In the decades and centuries that followed, the Christians 'took over' and built all of *'their'* churches, destroying the native Pagan faith almost entirely, even having the cheek to steal their winter festival, celebrating the winter solstice and rebirth of the sun, combining it with the Roman's Saturnalia, morphing it into what we now celebrate as our Christmas Holiday. I do not wish to digress further back to religion which I have already covered in enough detail for the purposes of this essay. The point is, we have to remove this tribal mentality that we all still harbour to some degree, as the only winners in this war are the few that use conflict to gain political advantage at the expense of progression, holding 'culture loss' over us as a threat. They are the ones that will ultimately choose which faith is imposed, if any, and not the innocent believers, who do not have the power to do this. It is the empire leaders who care not for truth, only for power and the most secure and convenient way to achieve it. We would be naïve to think otherwise. The less distinct groups there are in society, the easier it is to keep control over. Localisation and separatism pose a threat to the centralisation of power, which is why even entirely non-religious ethnic majorities have concerns over globalisation. As the power of the central body grows, or if it feels threatened, the inputs of distinct cultural, ethnic or political groups are cut further.

This kind of political coup where the few get in power and then use their power to influence the many by exploiting differences, whilst bringing the majority around to their way of thinking, is not just something from the ancient history books. The Ethiopian government, for example, is dominated by the Tigrayan ethnic minority and has been since the fall of the communism in 1991, (the social structure that had ruled there since 1974). At my time of writing, Tigrayans in Ethiopia account for only around 6 per cent of its 110 million and growing population. Their goal is to retain power, convert the rest of the population of Ethiopia to their way of thinking, eliminating other languages, values, and historic beliefs present in Ethiopia's ethnonational groups. The largest being the Oromo at just over a third, and the Amhara at just over a quarter, who were in power under the Ethiopian monarchy before the communist committee overthrew it in 1974. Many of the 80 plus culturally distinct groups do not even recognise Ethiopia as a legitimate country, preferring themselves to be referred to as separate nations. After gaining independence from their former European colonists, many developing Sub-Saharan African countries have not developed as was expected, (by mimicking political systems of countries in the developed world). Communist dictatorships, secessionist movements and military governments formed instead. As of 2019 out of all of the sub-Saharan states, very few have democratic governments with different political parties that have equal chances of coming to power when voted for.

We can see from the extreme separatist modern-day example of Ethiopia alone, the political confusion and turmoil that can arise from attempting to centralise governments forcefully. People will never all agree with the centralising body's views, especially when religious belief is involved. The human condition is constantly striving for further separatism out of pride, desperately fearful of losing cultural or tribal identities. Even in the UK, despite the name 'United' Kingdom, there have been many proposed autonomous movements throughout its history, (some successful). England, Scotland, Wales, Northern Ireland, Isle of Man, Orkney, Shetland, and contained within these, even smaller breakaways have been proposed by some political groups. These include Na h-Eileanan Siar (Outer Hebrides), Yorkshire, Wessex, Mercia and Cornwall. So you see, even in one of the most developed countries in the world, the people are yearning for localisation, with their own laws, languages and forms of currency. Welsh and Gaelic language is still widely spoken in Wales and Ireland, and Scottish and Northern Irish banknotes can be used in all parts of the UK.

An interesting case of extreme economic localisation is the Bristol Pound, which can be used in both paper and electronic format. Introduced in 2012, and to be spent only in and around the city of Bristol in England. The idea was to take advantage of the multiplier effect in a circular economy, to boost local wealth by keeping money within the city limits. Using a local currency that cannot be spent elsewhere in the country was proposed to help stimulate local business and trading. For example, the owners of shops and market stalls can purchase their goods from other local businesses, which in turn can pay their council tax and business rates with the money. Most notably, the mayor of Bristol took his entire annual salary in Bristol pounds as a testament to the scheme. The participation of shops and businesses in the scheme remains entirely voluntary. There is no obligation to accept the money as it is not classed as legal tender. It is an ambitious project to be admired that has been hailed a success by some studies, but the long-term effects remain to be seen. In the grand scheme of things, it currently does not make much of a dent in the economy, with an estimated 1 million Bristol pounds being spent annually in the city.

To conclude, I believe a unified planetary society will one day become a reality, but not for a long time. It does not appear to be a necessity for a stable economy, and it is still possible to work towards our H-utopian goals without globalising everything. Some decisions definitely need global agreement, and for this, we have international committees. The mentality of our species is not yet mature enough for cooperation on such a grand scale and to attempt a whole planetary society would be running before we learned to walk. Ideas such as The European Union have been undermined by the likes of the 'Brexit' vote to leave the EU, made by the UK in 2016. The historic vote proved that national pride and independence were valued by over half of the population. It will be hard to convince this half that a planetary society could be a good thing, even if done tactfully. It certainly needs to be welcomed at a time of peace and harmony, not forced upon society as a desperate solution to problems that we cannot be bothered to fix the hard way.

Those who oppose unification may be swayed by fears surrounding immigration, not an attitude suited to H-utopia. However, we cannot blame people from already overpopulated countries for having genuine concerns about even more people coming. The solution is to allow the movement of people, but not force the movement of people who only move because they are left with no other option due to domestic problems in their native countries. War, famine, poverty, broken economy need to be resolved if we really want to reduce the movement of people. For this reason, I do believe we should introduce a global currency, to replace all individual currencies. This way, every country's financial success would be a matter of global interest.

Combined with guaranteed income, globally agreed tax brackets, the introduction of the political hybrid system of technoomarchracey, proportional representation, capital incentivised socialism and the single credit account per person, this will significantly reduce the number of people that move from their homes, or commit crimes out of desperation or frustration, seriously reducing the burden and racial tension that immigration can cause in the nation accepting immigrants. Furthermore, these measures will eradicate tax evasion, encourage global trade, stop booms and busts, reduce poverty everywhere, reduce criminal activity and resolve many other complications that are caused when a civilisation splits itself into hundreds of small states that use so many different currencies and types of cash in order to compete with each other rather than cooperate.

Despite fears that such a move towards globalisation could leave us susceptible to suffering draconian measures, due to over-dependency on authority and simplification of society making it easier to control, we should not abandon the idea of a planetary government. I think it is definitely something to work towards as a longer-term goal. Although there is much resistance to the idea, and I appreciate the anxiety people have, it does have benefits worth considering, that go beyond just stabilising an economy. We will consider these benefits in the remainder of the essay.

War and peace

"Never think that war, no matter how necessary, nor how justified, is not a crime."

- Ernest Hemingway 1899-1961.

Hemingway was just 18 years old when he volunteered to be an ambulance driver in WWI. The horrors he encountered during his time in the conflict left him physically and mentally traumatised. He used his literary abilities and wide demographic reach as a novelist to highlight the criminality of war.

...our default reaction is vengeance rather than rationally responding with forgiveness and looking for the solution that results in the least violence. I do not mean let criminals off the hook, but rather to show offending warmongers that attempting to manipulate conflict from political events such as assassinations is not going to work because guess what...we will find the strength to forgive this, and we will not let you use this as an excuse for more violence...

Since the dawn of civilisation, war has cast its evil shadow over humanity. Consequently, no utopia has ever existed in history - certainly not one that historians are aware of. In human societies, governed by coercion, the instinct for warfare has been a driving force for millennia. In the continents of Europe, Asia and Africa, where people bathed in the blood of their enemies, (sometimes literally), societies revelled in glorifying warfare, whilst elevating their greatest soldiers and generals to godlike status.

There is only one exception of a notable civilisation which managed to flourish for hundreds of years, whilst remaining peaceful. Although not entirely free from violence, it is widely accepted that the art of war was not practised by the enigmatic civilisation of the Indus valley, which flourished from about 2600 to 1900 BCE, spanning parts of modern-day Pakistan, Afghanistan and India. Could the ancient and mysterious Indus civilisation have been closer to maintaining a functional utopian society than anyone before or after them?

Their cities showed no obvious fortification. Archaeological digs have turned up no military attire or weaponry associated with them. The Indus civilisation did not avoid war by isolation or poverty either. There is clear evidence of trade exports with the war-hungry Mesopotamian civilisation via the Arabian Sea, so the Indus had a commerce system and would not have been immune to greed and corruption had the leaders allowed it to consume them. There is also archaeological evidence that the Indus were capable engineers and gifted craftsmen. They created beautiful precision-made jewellery and took on ambitious engineering projects to provide plumbing for their largest cities. Town planners were far from primitive and clearly appreciated the importance of having a healthy and hygienic population, fulfilling another criterion for utopia. They had sewage systems, water tanks and even toilets. They even had the foresight to raise buildings and streets above potential flood levels. Although evidently capable architects and builders, they decided against wasting materials on building palaces and temples that could have been envied by both their own citizens and potential usurping invaders. Instead, they opted for the egalitarian approach of modest but perfectly adequate homes for all, regardless of wealth.

The final thing that really distinguishes the Indus as a far wiser people than their contemporaries, (or their successors), is a total absence of slavery in their society. Just about every other civilisation, all the way up to very modern times built itself on the immoral practise of slavery. The Indus did not tolerate slavery. What we see with the Indus was a civilisation relatively free from jealousy and greed, and therefore violence and suffering. They were neither threatened by war nor did they engage in it. Certainly not on a large scale, with weapons only suited to hunting ever discovered at Indus archaeological sites. We can envision their leaders must have been close to embodying Plato's philosopher-kings; a council of Buddhist-like enlightened ones who detested violence and accumulation of wealth by individuals, whilst the majority remained impoverished.

It is known that the Indus way of running a society did not rub off on the rest of the ancient world though, or the rest of history up until now would have been incomparably different. So what went wrong, and why did this potential utopia ultimately fail?

An inherently peaceful people can only survive and progress to a certain point before they start to become a point of envy in a world of people living with contrary values, motivated by greed. No one knows for sure what happened to the Indus, theories include climate change induced flooding which made their cities less viable, but it is equally as likely this under defended people met with a violent fate. The ideology of the Indus was a mindset of the minority for the time, against the selfish nature of human beings, and perhaps the ideology proved threatening for those more powerful who desired war, not peace, as a means of establishing and maintaining their power.

Thirst for conflict

Aggression, greed, destructiveness, cruelty - these enablers of war are all negative characteristics our species evolved over millions of years, as a consequence of our ancestors enduring unforgiving environmental stresses, whilst competing with animals and other humans alike for survival. These selfish traits helped to ensure the genetic survival of those who had them in excess. Our long lost cousins who were placid, overly trusting, selfless and did not display as much aggression would have been out-competed during skirmishes with natural enemies, (including other hominids), often before they had the chance to breed and pass on their more peaceful and meeker genes to the next generation. Aggressive, selfish genes instead were passed on by those who displayed more powerful emotional responses to abnormally high stress levels; the kind that our ancestors would have encountered, escaping becoming a predator's lunch, or fighting for dominance in a mating group.

Aggression is a self-preserving, basic instinct incited by fear. It is by no means our primary instinct though, and as a self-domesticating species, it is up to us to train ourselves to master control over our primal instincts. Unfortunately, engraved deep within the human subconscious is a thirst for conflict that we may never be able to fully quench. The roots of which can be traced to the simple and ancient, reptilian part of the human brain that provokes irrational, murderous and selfish response to threatening situations. To shoot first and ask questions later.

This primal response is merely the *enabler* of war. After all, every other creature on Earth evolved according to survival of the fittest and often most ruthless; yet we do not observe pre-meditated warfare from any other creatures. Animals will defend themselves if attacked in skirmishes, or battle one another for the right to eat or mate of course, but the only exception of unprovoked organised war is observed with some species of ants that attack their own kind to expand one colony's territory. With the exception of these evolutionary freaks, generally, all creatures avoid prolonging conflict at all costs. Ants can be excused for their behaviour for obvious reasons. Human beings cannot be pardoned so easily. We are the only species ever to have existed on Earth that actively seeks to provoke and prolong avoidable conflict, and the only species to commit murder in such an unnecessary and creative fashion. Nature provides the enabler, but the true causes of war are social, economic and political ones that exploit our natural aggression to help accomplish agendas of the political and/or financial beneficiaries of a war.

The ironic thing about the formation of civilisation is, it has allowed us to act more *uncivilised* than any of our ancient reptilian, or mammalian ancestors. For the last millennia or so, thanks to the invention of defensive technology and weaponry, humans have removed the threat of all natural enemies, apart from each other, and sadly this is exactly where we have been exploited into brutally channelling our pathological aggression for the last two thousand years or so, resulting in 100s of millions of avoidable deaths in wars throughout history. The deadliest and bloodiest of which happened in living memory, demonstrating that we are still not as civilised as we may think. Upper estimates for the death toll of World War II, 1939 to 1945, are in the region of 80 million. This includes deaths from famine and disease as a direct consequence of the war. A sizeable chunk of this figure comes from the Nazi's state-sponsored attempt at genocide, known as the Holocaust. Most sources put the number of people who perished in Nazi concentration camps at 6 million, but the actual figure is considered to be much higher, in what was one of the most sickening examples of hatred witnessed in human history.

Nazi ideology did not disappear with their defeat at the end of WWII; remaining even today in the form of Neo-Nazism that still poses a threat to society with far-right political movements sometimes adopting Nazi philosophies into their manifestos. People with far-right political views tend to be absolutists and will derogatively label anyone not in absolute agreement with them, (no matter where they sit on the political spectrum), as 'lefties' or 'commies' out of ignorance, fear, hatred, and an outrage that anyone dares express a contrary opinion to them. The term 'lefty' is now commonly used alongside terms such as 'snowflake' to insult someone because they are perceived to be easily offended by old fashioned views, or because their opinion is not extreme, or because they are promoting tolerance whilst condemning oppression, prejudice and violence, no matter what the subject matter is.

Perceptions of what is right and wrong evolve over time, and it is important that anyone throwing these terms around viciously, first considers that this is exactly the type of insult that would have been directed by slave traders towards the minority of the population, during the time of the slave trade, who had the courage to publicly voice protest against what the slave traders were doing.

Anyone who clings to extreme views should also consider that a society which only moves right or only moves left is doomed to go around in circles like a rowing boat with only one oar. Only by powering *forward,* by applying equal effort in both oars, can we hope to stop circling back to repeat mistakes of the past.

Slavery and Nazism are both examples of just how dangerous extremism and absolutism can be. Both were the result of xenophobia, intolerance, greed and cruelty being allowed to evolve into their very worst forms during the pursuit of wealth and power by those who arrogantly believed they were so much better than the rest of their species.

The Nazi orchestrated Holocaust went much deeper than just racial intolerance; during the four years of the Holocaust between, 1941 and 1945, it was not just the Jewish persecuted. Nazi authorities also targeted other groups because of their perceived 'inferiority', including Gypsies, Polish, Russians, Communists, Socialists, Jehovah's Witnesses, disabled people and homosexuals. But how does a single leader's evil agenda become imposed on an entire nation? A war needs support from the public. Emotions are often played to in the media to provoke responses of sadness, anger, defensiveness, fear and tribal pride.

For generations, people have been programmed by manipulation only to see extremes during times of conflict; to celebrate wars won as glorious affairs whilst demonising perceived enemies. Organised, strategic warfare as we know it today is the result of nationality, and in return, nationality owes its existence to war. Throughout recorded history, since the dawn of civilisation, individuals, nations or governments have gained power through the use of war as a political tool.

One of the earliest documented civilisations in the world,

Mesopotamia, was plagued with conflict. The first war we know of was fought in 2700 BCE between Elam, (situated in modern-day Iran), and Sumer, under the command of King Enembaragesi of Kish. The Sumerians triumphed over the Elamites in battle. Although this was the first *recorded* war, we can be almost certain it was not the first war ever. The archaeologically determined range for the first known battle is between 4000 BCE and 3500 BCE at the ancient city of Hamoukar, which falls in the present-day Jazira region of Syria. The Uruks of southern Mesopotamia travelled north along the Tigris and Euphrates rivers, eventually reaching Hamoukar, which they invaded and absorbed into their empire. Settlements along the Tigris and Euphrates were desirable due to the ease of agriculture at these locations, so it is not surprising they were fought over by competing civilisations attempting to upsurge their resources and expand their empires.

Jericho, named as one of the oldest cities on Earth, was established at least 9000 years ago. The fact that Jericho was a city strongly fortified with walls of three meters thick and four meters high, surrounded by a wide moat, is evidence that suggests defence against warring invaders was an important necessity even at this early point in human civilisation, if you had something worth taking. It seems people have always wanted what is not theirs and have always done unspeakable things to make it theirs.

Historically, the outcome of war is often the unification, sometimes even the formation, of entire nations, and world history would have been very different without this unification in the following examples of successful civilisations that owed their very existence to warfare:

- Early Dynastic Egypt - thought to have risen from war when the unifying Pharaoh Menes, (or Narmer), of the south, supposedly conquered the region of northern Egypt.

- The Zhou Dynasty in China - gained power through battle in 1046 BCE and the conflict was ongoing until eventually resolved when the State of Qin defeated the other contending states in battle, unifying China under the rule of emperor Shi Huangti in 220 BCE.

- Ancient Greece - under the rule of Philip II of Macedon. He united the individual city-states of Greece, becoming the head of state in an enormous empire.

Warring peoples have either been destroyed or, more desirably, unified by conflict throughout history, with opportunist individuals taking the chance to attain or enhance political power by offering order out of the chaos that war causes - a political tactic famous in its Latin form *"ordo ab chao"*. It is a scenario that has been played out again and again. For as long as humans have been able to build walls and fashion crude weapons, opposing factions have settled their disputes on the battlefield in the name of their leaders and for the honour of their tribe or nation. The only thing that has changed over the centuries is the weaponry. The commodities of war constantly become more powerful and sophisticated as the life and death competition incentivises everyone to push the limits of their technological capabilities. Advancements in weaponry and defence for the purpose of war, along with devices of torture were some of the few technologies that were not suppressed between the middle ages and the 18th century. Humans had cannons and makeshift bombs as early as the 13th century. However, the chemistry and physics involved in these devices would not be allowed to re-emerge in human knowledge, to be used for scientific reasoning about the nature of the Universe, until hundreds of years after.

The earliest wars we know of in ancient Mesopotamia were fought by infantry shock troops right up until the introduction of the composite bow from the Hyksos in 1720 BCE. The Hyksos were masters of war, infiltrating Ancient Egypt at around this time. As well as the composite bow with a firing range of 200 meters, they brought with them metallic weapons, chariots and revolutionary strategic planning. This led to advantageous changes in battle formations and the development of military tactics, later utilised by the armies of the Roman and Greek empires, helping them to become two of the most unstoppable superpowers in the ancient world.

So it seems war is the tool that unified the world and formed the political order we have today. War is no doubt an unavoidable and inevitable part of development for any emerging intelligence forming a civilisation in the Universe. We cannot alter this inevitability, or undo the sacrifices of the past, but at some point, an intelligent species should get to a stage where it realises it has outgrown war and I believe we are at that stage now in our development. However, before we can overcome it, we have to fully understand the motives of war and combat the provokers. Without the stresses of war, the need for defence, building cities bigger, fortifications stronger, training armies more powerful and vaster, and creating more advanced technologies, modern-day superstates like the European Union and the United States of America may never have been forced into formation. For as long as we allow it to, war continues to push us further and further into larger hyper states in an attempt to find world peace. Some argue that whilst we are significantly divided, there is too much potential for the exploitation of our tribal mentality by the opportunists in this world, and the wars will likely continue indefinitely.

War, whether conventional or otherwise, is leading humanity to the inevitable outcome of unification that it has been gradually marching towards for millennia; and it should be of no surprise, as the purpose of war was always to grow empires. Whether we trust the idea of a globalised society or not, advocates claim it is the best chance humanity has for world peace and prosperity. However, as we have already discussed, hypocritically attempting to force peace by provoking war comes with severe associated risks.

There are two ways globalisation could happen: we could accept it willingly as a good thing, and all work together to let it happen out of good will. Or we could be forced into it as a last resort to stop us killing each other, (even though it is our governments and the treaties they sign that take us into wars, not the strong will of the average individual).

Globalisation out of desperation will only give those in charge of the globalised hyper state an excuse to remove freedoms from society, in order to "control violence, keep us safe, and prevent the return of those damn wars from our traumatic history". A consequence of a sudden forced unification could result in a totalitarian empire, rather than a harmonised planetary society. The less extreme compromise that would be preferable to total globalisation, is just creating a global currency, without having to form a global government. The idea of war between nations that share the same economy is ludicrous, as there would be no profits for the winning side because they would suffer the effects of a shifting economic climate equally. The financial success of every nation would be a matter of global interest in a world that shares the same currency. In theory, globalising currency, but nothing else, could be the most efficient way to put an end to wars without risking totalitarianism. This has been suggested by humanitarians for a long time, but alas, those profiting most from chaos and financial complexity/obscurity are the ones who have the power to stall such peaceful decisions.

What power do we really have as individuals to prevent war, when the enablers of war are in our very genes, and the provokers of war are often the most powerful people in society? What we can do is prevent the enablers being exploited anymore by collectively exercising our human rationale and questioning the motives of warmongering leaders, demanding they are subjected to scrutiny.

WWI is the best example in recent history of how one person and one bad decision can destroy an entire world when our default reaction is vengeance rather than rationally responding with forgiveness and looking for the solution that results in the least violence. I do not mean let criminal acts go unpunished, but rather to show offending warmongers that attempting to manipulate conflict from political events such as assassinations is not going to work because guess what...we will find the strength to forgive this, and we will not let you use this as an excuse for more violence. It takes a wiser and stronger leader to show your nation to be the bigger people and respond peacefully in this way, rather than react with blind rage because of damaged pride or fear.

Spiralling political tension can be wound so tight that a single death at the wrong time and place can result in a spark that ignites a worldwide conflict. The decision of 18 year old Bosnian Serb nationalist Gavrilo Princip to assassinate Archduke Franz Ferdinand of Austria, and his wife Sophie, during an official visit to the Bosnian capital of Sarajevo in July 1914, did not have to mean millions more would die. But this is what happened because the single spark was all that was needed as an excuse to set off a rapid chain of events after Austria-Hungary, desiring vengeance, immediately blamed the Serbian government for the attack. Rationally speaking, one frustrated teenager's actions should not have been powerful enough to start a world war that killed millions. It was though because the rational desire to resolve peacefully and avoid more death was not there from those with over-inflated egos, or from those in power who stood to gain politically and financially from a world war. If it had not happened in this way, then no doubt something else would have triggered it sooner or later. One could argue that a world war was inevitable after the industrial revolution presented humanity with the capability to mass-produce the commodities of war.

Over 65 million men volunteered or were conscripted to fight in armies during WWI, and millions of civilians also contributed by working the industrial and agricultural vacancies left behind by the enlisted. Victory was absolutely dependent on patriotism and public support for vengeance. This was achieved by grouping together and demonising the character of entire diverse nations with stereotyping propaganda, to make slaughtering them easier to stomach. Another cowardly military tactic used by both sides was to try and make nations surrender by diminishing morale with attacks on defenceless civilians. Made possible by propaganda that demonises entire populations and races of people, this rarely spoken about tactic demonstrates no nation is glorious in war. People will do what they must to survive. As the saying goes: *"all is fair in love and war."*

Public perception and the glorification of war

In our informed modern world, war today would just not be possible without public support. Long gone are the days where the monarch would say the word and the able-bodied men of the land would follow on horseback blindly to their glorious deaths for king and country. The best way to get the backing of the general public nowadays is by drawing out and exploiting xenophobia with the clever use of propaganda.

By definition, propaganda is biased information used to influence its audience towards supporting the desired agenda of the user. Propaganda advertising in the media will pick and choose which facts to show to the public, sometimes embellishing or stretching the truth, taking things out of context to deliberately provoke an emotional reaction, rather than a rational response. In a wise population thoroughly educated in real history, cultural interaction, philosophy, sociology and theology, this sneaky, manipulative tactic could never again be used as a tool to divide humanity. But during the times of WWI and WWII, when education was far from a priority, and cultural interaction was minimal, the masses were kept ignorant of world affairs, except what they were allowed to know. With the level of cultural interaction and worldwide communication nowadays, propaganda is not as blatant as it once was, but make no mistake, it is still used extensively and effectively nonetheless, exploiting the admirable human traits of loyalty, nationalism and patriotism.

Many people who have a strong sense of patriotic nationalism may never have met 99 per cent of their fellow countrymen, may never have visited 99 per cent of their nation, may have no political understanding or knowledge of their nation's history or any idea of their leader's true motives, but the xenophobic response to an unfamiliar threat genetically hardwired into all humans, coupled with the manipulative use of language in propaganda campaigns, is strong enough to provoke sudden rage, and it is heavily played on to justify prolonged involvement in conflict; it can make a normally peaceful person want to violently protect what they proudly call *their* home and *their* people, against a demonised enemy.

Although there is evidence for the use of propaganda, in a primitive form, dating back at least 1500 years, propaganda is generally thought of as a more recent phenomenon, that only became effective with the emergence of literate and politically active societies that are kept informed by a mass media. The rulers over these more sophisticated and politically involved societies realised there was a vital requirement for public support in favour of their policies, in order for an agenda to be successful. Heads of state have always been managed by their subjects and not the other way around, but by the 19th century, the general population was getting wiser, and starting to realise this, making them more difficult to manipulate into doing the bidding of the people in power. The masses now needed a bit more convincing that it was in their personal interest, before following the leader to their demise, or at least turning a blind eye to suffering that their leader may have been inflicting on people in other parts of the world.

One of the earliest notable examples of media exaggerating the truth as a tool to gain political support from the masses was during the Indian Rebellion of 1857, where Indian Sepoys rebelled against the authority of the British EIC, (East India Company), who were occupying India at the time. Accusations of the Indian rebels raping English girls as young as ten years old were greatly exaggerated by the British newspapers, in order to provoke an outraged emotional reaction from the public in Britain, who demanded their military delivered justice. This kind of reaction helped to justify continued British presence in the Indian subcontinent. The propaganda did its job, quelling escalating murmurs of public disapproval about Britain's actions. It did eventually come to light that some of the accounts were fabricated, playing on common stereotypes at the time that the natives were savages who needed to be 'civilised' by the British and saved from themselves. Nevertheless, the propaganda had already done its job, proving to be hugely effective, and would be used again on a larger scale, by both sides during WWI and WWII.

In 1914, at the outbreak of WWI, thanks to the use of film as a new media, a greatly widened audience could be reached by the propaganda campaigns. Governments on both sides of the conflict successfully persuaded their populations, with the use of war glorifying, absolutist propaganda campaigns that exploited national patriotism, to volunteer willingly for a fight against the evil enemy, who had been relentlessly demonised in national media. In the UK those who did not volunteer for the army, pacifists whose conscience would not allow them to kill, or those who saw through the exaggerations in the media and objected on moral grounds, were hated worse than the enemy and shunned in society. In Nazi Germany, in WWII, those who refused to fight on moral grounds were treated even worse, with some being arrested and executed.

The media was the reason wars became worldwide affairs in the 20th century. Without propaganda in mainstream media, and the broadcast of speeches by Winston Churchill and Adolf Hitler, WWII probably would never have happened. The German Nazi Party would likely never have risen to power in the years leading up to WWII, and even if they did, it would not have been possible for the Nazi party to justify their evil policies to their public, many of whom would naturally have had even worse memories of WWI than the winning side did. But this was a new generation; the children of WWI survivors were now being sent to their deaths.

The atrocities committed during WWII are an extreme example of how one individual's insane agenda can be pushed onto an entire nation of millions, when the persuasion is strong enough, the propaganda is cunning enough, and the people feel they have no choice. It is no coincidence that there were no wars that involved the whole world's involvement before the 20th century, when the inventions arrived that allowed worldwide media broadcasts to be received by the masses. Even if people were illiterate, they could listen to the radio, look at inspirationally designed posters, or watch films.

The crucial role of the media in justifying war does not end when the war does. The winning side naturally tends to glorify and celebrate any war, no matter how bloody, as a great and historic achievement, ensuring to teach about it in schools for generations. It is important children be taught about wars, but this should be seized as a perfect opportunity to impartially debate human actions in philosophical study. To make sure the mistakes of the past never reoccur, rather than just re-spawning ancient propaganda to instil blind patriotism in new generations, by painting a deliberately blinkered view of historical events. It is vital to understand the motivation of the individual and to empathise with oppressed or brainwashed 'enemies' who were often forced to keep fighting for an evil leader because if they tried to do the right thing then they would be killed or they knew their families would have been killed, or at least socially exiled. During WWI, both sides executed their own soldiers for desertion. They had to have a zero-tolerance approach, or everyone would have refused to keep fighting and submitting the madness of their authority.

If in the place of a soldier in the trenches in WWI, I wonder how many people could honestly say they would stand up and stop fighting, knowing they would be executed and that the fighting would carry on anyway. To refuse to fight took a much greater and different kind of courage, and it was witnessed with the WWI Christmas Truce in 1914. An extraordinary event that embodied the true feelings of the individual soldiers on both sides of the conflict. It has become one of the most famous events of WWI, or of any war for that matter. Late on Christmas Eve in 1914, men of the British Expeditionary Force heard German troops in the trenches opposite them singing carols and saw they had decorated along their trenches with lanterns and fir trees. During the evening, messages were called out between the trenches, and on Christmas day, British and German soldiers alike emerged from their trenches to meet peacefully in No Man's Land as equal human beings, not enemies. They exchanged gifts, shook hands, took photographs and some even played games of football. They also buried their dead comrades and repaired trenches and dugouts. It could have been a triumphant turning point in human history, but alas, the truce did not spread. Elsewhere the fighting continued on Christmas Day, and the truce came to an end the following day as officers re-focused their troops, worried that such an event would undermine fighting spirit, which of course it would have. Even after this, there were smaller, less famous truces that occurred in isolated areas, but the military leaders on both sides desperately tried to prevent any truces of this magnitude ever happening again. Some British soldiers would later face punishment for their part in the Christmas truce as an example had to be made out of peace brokers.

As individuals, we generally do not glorify war. This is especially true of the front-line soldiers that have witnessed wars first-hand. But as a society, certainly, in the wealthiest nations that have the most powerful militaries, participation in war is viewed as a glorious thing to be proud of. This view is reinforced not just in documentary journalism, but in fictional media also. For as long as Hollywood has been making movies, there have been movies about war. War films are timelessly popular and could be considered as the ultimate propaganda. For a film to be successful and turn a profit for its makers, it has to be about a popular subject and has to have a good storyline. Even for a pacifist, it is easy to get caught up in the action of violent films, overlooking that the compelling storyline with a happy ending is rarely realistic. Even so-called true stories, or films based on real events, do not accurately portray real life, do not demonstrate the true lasting traumas of war accurately, and are generally biased to one side's point of view, simplifying the fictional world into absolutes, (just as many people find comfort doing in real life). We are told which side are the 'goodies' and which are the 'baddies'. The goodies are magnanimous, honourable, skilled and brave, displaying no fatal flaws, whilst the baddies are portrayed as ruthless, cowardly, backstabbing and seriously flawed. Simplifying our world view like this makes it a lot easier on the brain to cope with, and fun-filled fast-paced action evokes interest and admiration in a powerfully irresistible way.

Who would want to go and watch a film that would make them physically sick or leave them traumatised questioning their world view? Spending two hours immersed in a concentration camp or watching gruesome realistic images where thousands of children get blown apart by explosives would only appeal to an insane minority I would imagine. We enjoy action films; but a heroic and fun action, following the story of the infallible good guys as they save their comrades from peril and deliver an overdue comeuppance to the stereotyped, caricatured 'baddies' who had it coming. The typical war film scenario usually follows a small, charismatic and flawlessly trained team of soldiers who single-handedly take down an impossibly colossal enemy, and ultimately save the world from oppression. It fills us with an overwhelming sense of patriotism when the credits roll and we are left feeling proud and great about something that in reality would be total unethical carnage and absolutely nothing like what we watched. The same can also be applied to role=playing war-themed video games.

Of course, we cannot ignore the fact that it is not just trained volunteers who are killed and injured in wars. Many innocent civilians and children are caught up in conflicts, getting attacked, tortured and killed. As a society that still practices warfare, we have learned to live with the questionable things, that even the 'good guys' do to win a war, justifying to ourselves that any 'collateral damage' caused is for the greater good, and the end justifies the means.

The reality we do not see

The victims of war are not just the civilians and soldiers killed or physically injured. Post Traumatic Stress Disorder, (PTSD), is a psychological response that can affect those who lived through the life-threatening traumas, experiencing them first-hand. PTSD does not discriminate, it can affect anyone, and although thought of as a modern phenomenon, it has affected humans throughout history. As sentient beings who are very overly aware of our own mortality and who form strong emotional bonds with friends, we are extremely vulnerable to the disorder.

Before being properly diagnosed in modern times, the condition has gone by many names over the centuries, such as 'shell shock' or 'combat fatigue', but it was not until after the Vietnam war that the potential for the stress condition to develop into long-term Post Traumatic Stress Disorder was taken more seriously. If left undiagnosed and untreated, in some instances, the afflicted person can suffer for the rest of their lives, rendering them unable to function properly in society again, with the nightmarish memories materialising over and over as intrusive thoughts, accompanied with sensory re-enactments of the traumatic event(s), making it difficult to focus on day to day life. These recurring thoughts are not normal memories, they are known as 'flashbacks' and although psychological, can cause symptomatic physical responses, such as cold sweats, irritability, increased heart rate, insomnia, muscle tension and can even provoke over the top violent or selfish behaviour in situations that do not appear to warrant such a reaction from the perspective of someone who does not have PTSD.

Sadly, many people suffering from the condition do not seek out the professional psychiatric help they need or are not taken seriously when they do, with some becoming hooked on prescription drugs and others self-medicating with mind-numbing illicit substances as a coping mechanism, developing drug or alcohol dependency. These symptom blockers only worsen the root causes of the disorder, isolating the sufferer further from society, by making it difficult to form or maintain lasting relationships or contribute in a place of work. Sufferers can be obsessive, compulsive, and aggressive in an attempt to control potential threats, no matter how big or small. Anger, incited by fear will often be the 'go-to' response to a new or difficult situation, and they can appear to have reduced empathy and become disconnected from friends and family who feel constantly pushed away or unloved.

With millions of people estimated to be suffering from PTSD and with the symptoms psychologically or emotionally damaging for people around the sufferer, whether they be colleagues, friends or family members, it is like a contagious negativity that ripples through society. In severe cases that do not get better on their own, the root causes need to be addressed. Reasons the PTSD fails to alleviate can include confusion about what happened, why it was allowed to happen, not being able to process what was witnessed, or oversimplifying the world into extreme good and extreme evil, thus removing all the grey areas of mitigation. A sufferer may even have personal feelings of guilt or responsibility for what they did or what they could not do. Cognitive restructuring therapy sessions can help to overcome the emotions of fear and guilt by challenging the authenticity of the remembered events, identifying the triggers for flashbacks, working out the relevancy of them, then painting a more realistic picture of events and culpability of the individual, thus removing feelings of responsibility for events they could not possibly be held responsible for.

Thankfully, a majority of people do not experience war first-hand, but this makes it all too easy to underestimate how traumatising war really is. Our opinions of war are formed by the media, and most of us only see the bits we are *allowed* to see; the more patriotic heroic elements that give us national unity and inspire us to join together to confront who we are told is our mutual enemy. The average citizen would not be motivated to fight for the real political reasons, that are mainly for the financial benefit of faceless conglomerates and world leaders. So the mainstream media companies, (who by the way, are often owned or at least influenced by the beneficiaries of conflict), embellish the truth. If we think our way of life is threatened, or our friends and family are in mortal danger, it provokes an emotional, personable response. So, it is really not war itself that is glorified; it is the emotional response of people that take part because they are willing to endanger or sacrifice themselves for the safety and security of their loved ones and strangers alike. War and the ones who incite it may be a disgrace, but the people who volunteer to sacrifice their lives for the rest of society are certainly anything but that.

There is a further phycological explanation for why people may be so willing to participate in war. Most people will be born, live and die without contributing anything particularly memorable or special to society. Not everyone can cure diseases or walk on the moon. We humans are complex animals, and we search for something more than merely existing, to make us content. We crave meaning and a purpose, so people search for a chance to serve society and for some, this purpose may be sacrificing themselves for others to fulfil a sense of duty.

Because war is something that has become an accepted part of society through manipulative political and psychological conditioning over millennia, to un-condition ourselves is something that will take time and unprecedented global cooperation. Despite all the conditioning, humans are by no means a lost cause. In modern warfare of the 20th century, apart from the Christmas Truce in WWI that I already mentioned, there are many great examples of moral sanity. Instances where infantry have reported never firing a shot, or deliberately delivering non-lethal shots during close quarters combat. Nowadays much of the killing is carried out from long distance; airstrikes/bombings, where those delivering the lethal blows, never meet their victims. Homicide on a mass scale from a distance is apparently easier to stomach than one personable kill. Although peace is desired by many and it is theoretically possible to end wars, sadly the strong moral compass of individual infantryman is not going to be enough, and to make a difficult challenge harder, there are many who do not aspire for world peace and will go to great lengths to prevent it.

Of course, those who desire war more than any, are those who benefit the most from it. Those whose livelihood is manufacturing the commodities of war, profiting from both sides, as they unscrupulously sell to the highest bidders. With many governments spending more on military than on social development and education combined, it is one of the most lucrative businesses on Earth. Many arms merchants maintain that their industry is justified because it is essential for international relations, self-defence, and a successful global economy. But this is just self-justifying nonsense. Demonising one client so that sales can be increased to another, whilst prolonging avoidable conflict, is not forming good international relations. The following are codes of conduct that arms dealers should adhere to:

- Not selling arms to non-democratic countries.

- Not selling arms to regimes that will use the weapons to commit crimes against human rights.

- Not selling arms in places where conflicts may be fuelled and exacerbated. Escalating civil wars in developing countries will only further delay social development and increase poverty there.

Unfortunately, the weapon industry is one of the most corrupt in the world and does not attract the most ethical of people who happily abide by these codes of conduct out of high moral standards alone. The arms dealers of the world continue to sell to human rights abusers and developing countries, despite joint efforts made by Amnesty International, the International Action Network on Small Arms, and Oxfam since the 1990s with the 'Control Arms Campaign'.   The solid wall of defence we come up against when combatting war and the vendors of war goes back to the flaws of a greedy capitalist society without limits on an individual's power share, and an economic structure that allows for financial obscurity and anonymity. A lack of financial transparency from the dealers, (many of whom are just middlemen with laptops), allows them to dodge tax by banking in multiple accounts offshore in tax havens. The USA is the biggest offender for bypassing the codes of conduct, criticised along with France, the UK, Israel, Switzerland, and Germany for selling weapons, either to known violators of human rights, or to developing countries that have weaker arms export controls, meaning the weapons will most likely be used to escalate domestic conflicts in those countries. Arms dealing is as bad as drug dealing for the negative ripple effects it has on global social development. The main difference being, drug dealing has been made illegal for its detrimental effects on humanity and society.

National militaries are a proud, controlled, disciplined part of society that keep millions of people employed in legitimate work around the world. They are officially there for 'defence' and keeping the peace, not to start conflict, but of course, this purpose can be twisted, and over the decades as each country expands their own military, the others race to keep up, feeling threatened, and it is a vicious circle. As I already wrote about earlier on, this is how a handful of countries have ended up with enough nuclear weapons to blow up the Earth many times over. I argued at the start of my study on war and peace that I believe we have reached a point now where our human civilisation is mature enough to realise it has outgrown war. But how do we go about ending it? Of course, every military around the world aren't going to just surrender their immense arsenals, link arms and break out in harmonious singing. But, what we can work on is triggering a 'reverse arms race', starting with the most devastating weapons.

Nuclear disarmament and world peace

If our aim is to reduce weapon production, with a goal of one day being able to stop it altogether, we should start with the biggest and most devastating.

Nuclear disarmament is the act of reducing and ultimately eliminating nuclear weapons worldwide. There have been many groups formed over the years including Greenpeace, Global Zero, the International Physicians for the Prevention of Nuclear War, the International Campaign to Abolish Nuclear Weapons (ICAN), and the Nuclear Age Peace Foundation, all of whom continue to campaign towards abolishing nuclear weapons.

The arguments for and against nuclear weapons, ultimately, are simple: those in favour of nuclear disarmament argue the probability of an apocalyptic war occurring, intentionally or by accident, is too high for them to be possessed by anyone and they are too immoral to be used in warfare on any level. Those against nuclear disarmament say that it would undermine the deterrence that nuclear weapons have provided - basically implying that the threat alone has helped to maintain relative peace since they were used for the first time on a military target, during WWII. If it were true that we had been living in peace since the end of WWII, then maybe more people would be inclined to agree with this ridiculous notion. In reality, there have been hundreds of conflicts, skirmishes and full-blown wars, some of which are ongoing, involving hundreds of nations from around the world.

On August 6, 1945, the 'Little Boy' nuclear device was detonated, by the United States Air Force, over the Japanese city of Hiroshima, destroying nearly 50,000 buildings. Some were tactical targets like the headquarters of the 2nd General Army and Fifth Division, but most were civilian. 70,000 - 80,000 people were killed outright, including innocent men, women and children. Three days later the second device, 'Fat Man', was detonated over Nagasaki, destroying over half of the city and killing another 35,000 - 40,000 people outright. Combined with the Soviet invasion of Manchuria, this led to Japan surrendering. The nuclear threat alone from the US was a major contributor to the end of WWII less than one month later. For fear of future retaliation from Japan, the US occupiers imposed a pacifist constitution on Japan after the war. To this day, after witnessing the destruction first-hand, Japan has never possessed nuclear weapons.

In the decades following the war, the rest of the countries in the world, that were economically capable of keeping up in an arms race, grew their nuclear weapon stockpiles in an attempt to possess the most bombs, or devices with the most powerful megatonnage, in an effort to become the world's most feared military superpower.

The shocking effects that the weapons had on Nagasaki and Hiroshima should have shown the world that these weapons had no place in a civilised society, but sadly they had the opposite effect. Less than a year after using them on an enemy, the US military was ready to test more nuclear weapons, in Operation Crossroads. The test was to see the effect of nuclear weapons on naval ships. The scientists who worked on the Manhattan Project, and helped to develop the bombs used in WWII, protested against further use of the bombs, arguing it was unnecessary, not to mention damaging to the environment, causing the vicinity they were detonated in to become radioactive. The tests went ahead anyway. This would not have been so bad, except the parts of the pacific ocean where they conducted these tests were inhabited by native islanders! The US military at least had the decency to evict and re-locate them first, (all be it to smaller less habitable islands).

The testing continued without much public knowledge until 1954 when a hydrogen bomb test in the Pacific resulted in the crew of a Japanese fishing boat becoming contaminated, developing radiation sickness. One of the fishermen died in Japan months later from the effects of the radiation. Finally, the world awoke to the unstable power, and the immorality, of these weapons. Realising humanity was being led down an avenue of doom; the anti-nuclear weapon movements began forming around the world. The problem was it was too late. By this point, the cold war was in full force. The world was gripped in geopolitical tension that manifested in absolutist terms as East versus West. The Soviet Union versus the USA and its allies in Western Europe.

The cold war lasted from the late 1940s up until communism fell in Eastern Europe in 1991 and the Soviet Union collapsed. During this time, the USA and the USSR had continued to flex their nuclear muscles, with the USA testing over 1000 nuclear devices and the USSR over 700. Other countries allied to either the USA or the USSR were conducting their own tests as well over this time, but they pale in comparison. For example, the UK officially conducted only 88 nuclear tests and have not done any since 1991. China conducted around 47 tests and none since 1996. As of writing, Pakistan, India and North Korea have set off less than 20 devices between the 3 of them and none of them anywhere near as powerful as the tests done by the US or USSR. The largest Hydrogen bomb tested by North Korea is 100 kilotons. In comparison, the USA's largest was 15 Megatons, and the USSR detonated a 50 Megaton monster, Tsar Bomba, in 1961! North Korea, since 2006, has been hypocritically demonised in Western media for its supposed nuclear threat. The reason being, North Korea were still actively testing well into the 21st century, whereas the rest of the nuclear-armed countries have not tested since the 1990s. I am not defending the actions of any countries testing nuclear bombs, even 'little' ones. To possess any of these abominable weapons is a national disgrace, but it does put things in perspective when we realise the firepower that some nations have compared with others.

North Korea, along with Pakistan and India are the only three countries yet to sign the Comprehensive Nuclear-Test-Ban Treaty (CTBT). Getting these last three to sign and join the rest of the world would be the next step towards total disarmament. However, we would still be a long way off the goal. The politics at play are complex, and even if all countries signed the treaty agreeing not to test the weapons, that does not mean they would not use them if provoked. So, sadly the current disarmament stalemates will likely persist unless there is a positive precedent-setting change in global politics. Even if the planet was technically at peace, with officially no wars going on anywhere, whilst we hold nuclear threats over each other, the peace would only be out of fear, and therefore not real or sustainable.

World War III

After the horrors humanity faced during the first two world wars, there has always been a fear that history will repeat itself, and global conflict will break out again. The world has never been entirely conflict free, and there is always the threat that localised conflicts can escalate into a global one. If tensions are high enough, one wrong word spoken can start a chain of events that change the course of history. The Cold War, the war on terror in the Middle East following the 9/11 attacks in the USA, tensions between military superpowers such as the USA and China. Obvious examples that spring to mind when predicting how WWIII could have started. But consider for a moment that the kind of conflict we recognise as warfare from WWI and WWII with guns, bullets and patriotic volunteers rushing to enlist becomes a thing of the past. This does not mean we would be safe, though. The wars of the future could be fought in a less violent way, but no less devastating to humanity. Biological warfare disastrous to organic life, technological warfare targeting anything electronic, satellite controlled, or computerised, and psychological warfare, the most effective and devious type of war to destroy the morale of an enemy and this can be applied in all types of war by controlling that most valuable commodity – information and data.

It is not always obvious that you are being targeted as an enemy, or being conditioned as an unwitting ally for that matter, during psychological warfare. It has been hypothesised that WWIII may even be fought covertly with psychology alone, without a single shot fired from a conventional weapon. Although less devastating to life initially, a world war fought with psychology would ultimately prove just as socially destructive and traumatic, if not more so, than previous world wars combined.

Psychological warfare is the tactical use of propaganda, threats, or other techniques that affect the enemies psyche, during wars or even geopolitical turbulence. The aim is to mislead, bring down morale, intimidate, or influence the thinking or behaviour of the target.

Psychological warfare tactics use fear as a weapon of choice to break down the psychological well-being of an opponent. The tactics used during a psychological war include:

- Spreading of misinformation and deception.
- Guilt tripping/ emotional blackmail.
- Attempting to humiliate, or socially isolate people.
- Spouting of impressive-sounding empty rhetoric.
- Presentation of false sincerity.
- Relentless fear-mongering.
- Creating deliberate political doom/racial divides.
- Intentionally committing logical fallacy. Contradicting all rationale and reason.
- Activation of 'The Lucifer Effect'. Dehumanisation and removal of individuality.

The following are all ways to spread uncertainty, fear, and terror in a psychological attack on an enemy:

News Outlets - the news is a large information source that all can tap into. The news has the ability to spread whichever information it chooses about whomever it chooses. By infiltrating a news source, an enemy population could be exposed to volatile information, misinformation, or repetition of morale damaging information. If it is repeated enough over and over again, even outrageous untruths will be accepted as genuine by the majority of a target audience. There will be a minority of people, that are naturally suspicious and sceptical by nature, who question all information given, but so long as they remain in the minority, and the 'official' version of events is stuck to and repeated enough in media, these sceptics will be treated as paranoid social pariahs and will not be successful in countering the influence of the mass media.

Threats – these can be threats of violence, threats to job security, money, food supply, or restrictions of freedom. These can be made to instil so much fear in people that a primal survival response is triggered and most will comply to secure their own survival. The threats could be bluffs or with intention; either way threatening people, exacerbating anxieties and fears that are already present in the human psyche can further psychologically damage the recipients over time, putting them in a state of terror, rendering them vulnerable to their enemy's control.

Objects - using objects such as t-shirts, posters, hats, badges, etc. Objects can become radicalised, idolised or latched onto as symbols religious or political symbols. Particularly objects such as badges and uniforms can be used as tools to de-humanise people as individuals and make them all appear the same. Anyone who is then seen to be standing out as different can be targeted as an enemy of the uniformed.

False flag - a false flag is when a group releases false information or carries out a faked incident or attack to frighten people or provoke an emotional response from the general public. The blame for the incident or attack is put on a targeted group or organisation to shift public opinion in support of an agenda that may otherwise be rejected.

The most effective weapons to arm ourselves with during a psychological war are critical rationale, calm logic, freedom of speech, forgiveness, courage and empathetic kindness to others. With this defence, provokers of a psychological war are doomed to lose, and casualties will remain minimal. With psychological warfare tactics disarmed, all other types of warfare are less likely to escalate, and WWIII will, (hopefully), never come to pass.

Is world peace achievable?

A world without nuclear weapons would be a great stride in the direction of world peace. It is possible and desired by most of us, and although it is not something we have been given a chance to vote on democratically as individual citizens of the world, the United Nations launched a historic international treaty banning nuclear weapons, in 2017, where 122/124 countries voted in favour of the total ban. This revolutionary treaty plans to make it illegal under international law to develop, test, manufacture, buy, sell, use, or even threaten to use nuclear weapons. Remember it is only a hand full of countries which posses these weapons. The UK, USA, Russia, France, China, India, Pakistan, Israel, and North Korea. The agreed disarmament is blocked by these nine countries ultimately. Obviously, not every country in the world was part of this vote, and unfortunately, these nine were not. Amongst the countries who voted in favour of the treaty were South Africa and Kazakhstan, both of which formerly possessed nuclear weapons and had admirably surrendered them voluntarily, proving to world it is a possibility to take this brave step into a better future.

The less strict 1996 Comprehensive Nuclear-Test-Ban Treaty (CTBT) is the treaty banning all nuclear test detonations. Unlike the 2017 treaty, this is not a total ban of developing and trading nuclear arsenal, just a ban on setting them off to test. This treaty was negotiated at the Conference on Disarmament in Geneva in September 1996, and most countries around the world have now fully agreed to abide by this treaty, including some of those in possession of the weapons, France, the UK, and Russia included. In the world today there are 44 designated nuclear-capable states, and as of writing this, eight of those states have not ratified the treaty: China, Egypt, Iran, Israel and the United States have signed, but not ratified. India, North Korea and Pakistan have not even signed it, and all three have tested the weapons since the 1996 treaty came into place.

Although great progress has been made with these treaties, and there is overwhelming support from humanitarian activists, (and the general public globally), the nine nations that still possess these weapons have no agreed plan for disarmament.

So, how do we help these nine countries get the ball rolling on total disarmament? One part of society that is holding back support, not just for nuclear disarmament, but for weapon disarmament in general, is the business community. This again comes back to the problems of a capitalist society without limits. War is good from the perspective of the various research facilities and manufacturers that provide us with the commodities of war. Their very livelihood's are dependent on continuing conflict. It is scary to think they would regard approaching world peace as a dark cloud looming over them. With any other business, when trade is dwindling, the business owner would desperately try to drum up some trade by any means they can. It is naïve to think well-established warmongers would not go to the same efforts to stay in business.

Public awareness about the horrors of nuclear weapons is not the issue. Everyone knows how immoral and devastating these weapons are and how horrific the aftereffects of radiation are. What needs more exposure is the companies that are putting financial self-interest above the good of humanity. That being said, H-utopia is for everyone, even the out of work weapon manufacturers. Therefore, we need conversion plans for weapons facilities, to convert them for peaceful uses, so they can continue generating revenue for their investors. This will help to sway the opinion of those who work and invest in weapon facilities. Instead of seeing disarmament as a threat to their communities and livelihoods, they may then appreciate it as an opportunity to go down in history as having done something truly great for humanity, but without having to totally sacrifice their personal wealth doing so.

I am sure disarmament will happen, but we need to come at it from all angles and ensure everyone is represented, *especially* those who stand to lose out most from it. We need entire nations in agreement, pushing relentlessly for disarmament, and the disarmament groups who have been working tirelessly for years also have to up their game and accept responsibility for publicly addressing the fundamental obstacles raised that stand in the way of disarmament:

- Nuclear weapons act as a deterrent to war and help to maintain order.

- Maintaining disarmament is unenforceable, as some countries will secretly develop the weapons again with a plan to dominate the rest of the world.

- Disarmament is dangerous and undermines nuclear alliances.

- It is impossible to rid the world entirely of nuclear weapons because certain countries will never willingly comply.

- Disarmament would only lead to an expensive increase in conventional arms instead, and pave the way for more conventional warfare, potentially leading us back into WWI type warfare.

These may sound logical and convincing arguments for keeping nuclear weapons, but each and every one of these put forward as reasons against disarmament can be strongly contested with counter-arguments. They are not contested publicly enough though, instead being accepted by society as issues so difficult that they cannot realistically be overcome, so we have to make the best of it, get on with our lives and hope someone does not do or say something that results in us all getting obliterated. This unbelievable laziness in the face of annihilation boggles the mind.

Human initiative is more than capable of overcoming all of the above reasons and any other arguments that are put forward in favour of keeping nuclear weapons. For instance, all of the reasons above would become null and void just by introducing a global currency and changing our socio-economic systems from the extreme capitalist or extreme communist dictatorial ends of the socio-economic spectrum that we currently choose between as if they are the only options. We know extremism rarely benefits society and I have already suggested a globally financially unified society; socialist at the core, but with a limited capital incentive available to everyone in electronic format.

With a globalised economy/currency, public companies would not be interested in profiting from weapons for the purposes of war because the economy of the world would be shared and so any nation producing weapons to start a war with would quite literally be shooting themselves in the foot! As for preventing private companies from filling the gap in the market, perhaps making it illegal to profit from weapons is an option to explore, so they are only ever produced in quantities sufficient for civil defence by public companies, not for full-scale wars, and private manufacturers by law would have to forfeit all net profits after paying their employees. This would help to start the ball rolling on the 'reverse arms race' already suggested.

Without making radical changes to the socio-economic structure of the world, disarmament could still happen. France and the UK closed their nuclear test sites and have both stopped producing fissile material for weapons. These steps at least show the willingness to work towards disarmament but progress painstakingly slow, and it cannot be just one or two countries cooperating. All those who still possess the weapons need to formulate and agree on unanimous actions. A disarmament agreement that is irreversible and universally legally binding will do far more than any other single initiative to help us reach H-utopia. The only guarantee against these weapons being used is the total elimination of them and I for one would rather take my chances in a world where no single head of state can dangle that much instant destruction over the heads of millions of innocent people.

As for preventing conventional warfare from breaking out as much as possible during the reverse arms race, the targets are national prejudice and the sources of shameful propaganda campaigns. These provide psychological enablers for the soldier whilst justifying continued conflict by exacerbating hatred and division amongst civilians. By recognising and remembering that irrational xenophobia can taint nationalism, and we are all equal around the world, we will be less receptive to manipulation from propaganda campaigns. A nation, after all is just an enigma; there is no black and white definition. A nation is not a race of people, a religion practised, a language spoken, a single area of land or sea occupied; for many nations have a great multitude of variety contained within them. A nation, in fact, only becomes defined during wartime. It is certainly not political or social unanimity either that defines a nation. There are many conflicts where nations have fought amongst themselves in civil wars, often due to political disagreement. One singular thing nations do tend to fall back on is an independent economy/currency. As already suggested, if the entire world had a single shared economy with a single and simplified currency, there would be limited or no financial benefit for any partakers in any kind of war. The only wars that could arise would be civil political ones, and equally economically destructive for both sides of any conflict, therefore would be avoided at all costs and short-lived if they did occur. I cannot claim the result would be world peace *per se*, but if we want to rid the world of war completely, this could be as close as humanity will ever realistically be able to get.

I will now move on to explore what actions we can take to reduce violence, hate crime, and other illegal activity, without resorting to desperate measures of extreme authoritarian control.

Crime and punishment

"When a man is denied the right to live the life he believes in, he has no choice but to become an outlaw."

- Nelson Mandela 1918-2013.

...journalists have a greater responsibility than people may realise; to refrain from publishing anything that may incite panic or that lacks integrity. To underestimate this responsibility by publishing biased news stories, smear campaigns, gossip, false news, even misleading articles that manipulate people with twisted words and sensationalist headlines, is nothing less than a crime against humanity...

There are many theories on what makes a criminal. Some theories are based on experiences of hatred, jealousy, xenophobia, frustration, desperation or a poor upbringing deprived of love. Other scientific based theories suggest genetics play a dominant part, and people are born with psychological traits that produce a criminal mindset no matter what environment they are raised in. Generally, it is accepted that the reasons for exerting criminal behaviours are a combination of complex neurological issues, and survival instincts manifesting in a society humans were not evolved for, rather than one specific trait or motive. To find some answers, we can analyse what chemistry is going on in the brain of a habitual criminal.

In terms of violent crime, testosterone, the hormone linked to levels of aggression, is certainly a suspect, and serotonin, a neurotransmitter that affects mood is another. The raw potential is provided by nature, but on the nurture side, we also have some suspicious suspects. Research has suggested poor levels of nutrition in infancy are directly linked to higher levels of aggression in a person when they are an adult. Child poverty, in general is a significant concern because a child's development during this crucial infancy stage lays the foundation for the rest of their life. As I have stressed right from the beginning of this essay, humans denied lower biological needs, such as food, shelter and love are not going to fully appreciate the importance of higher human needs, such as knowledge, respect, expression and social progress. Therefore, it is of the utmost importance that children must be given the best possible start in life.

Forgive the old cliché, but children are the future, and what chance does the future have to reach H-utopia, if the children we are raising now are not being raised to be the best human beings they can be? It cannot be overstated enough how important it is that children are raised with a strong moral compass, combined with the encouragement and love they need to motivate them into chasing higher biological needs, rather than just surviving using their primal instincts. As I stated right at the beginning of this essay, what is the point in trying to create the 'perfect' person if they are destined to be immersed in an environment/society that we have not managed to get anywhere near perfect?

When the very most basic needs of a human are not being satisfied, and our very lives are threatened, nature will overpower nurturing, and negative behaviours will prevail as instinctive survival responses. The most primitive and deep subconscious phycology at work in the human brain does not tolerate altruism like our more advanced primate areas. This older and more sinister, mostly subliminal, part of the human brain serves only itself, and it can be expressed thus: *"If others have to die or suffer so that I can survive, and prosper, then that's fine because I must survive by securing excess for myself at all costs"*. In times of severe emotional stress, this built-in survival mechanism can manifest itself in extremely unpleasant ways, including murder and vigilante witch hunts. The fear of death and of the unknown is a strong motivator for many to act immorally and commit heinous crime or hate against others if they perceive doing so will in any way aid their own selfish chances of survival. This is a strength that has allowed our species to survive up until this point as animals. However, it is a hindrance that has prevented us from advancing further socially as humans. We cannot deny our nature, but we can raise our children to respond rationally to emotional stress rather than react to it by allowing fear to take control.

Income and social status of a family should not determine the levels of integrity with which a child is raised. There is no reason the parents from families of differing social status cannot raise their children with the same ideas of right and wrong. However, there currently is a difference. On average, children raised in families with greater material goods enjoy more secure living conditions, more stability in family life, greater access to a range of educational opportunities and are statistically less likely to be involved in criminal activity. Whereas children from low-income families or living in low-income neighbourhoods, statistically have poorer health outcomes, are more likely to be involved in criminal activity in adulthood and tend to have fewer legitimate chances in life. It is all too easy for a child to become swept up in a life of crime when they are surrounded by it growing up, normalising the criminal behaviour during a time in their life when they are learning how to behave and react to situations by observing the people around them. Allowing children to grow up thinking criminal behaviour is normal is a crime in itself; causing children self-conflict and unacceptable amounts of stress as they learn from others that what their parents are doing is illegal and immoral. Serial offenders of any crime who are supposed to be responsible role models for children should perhaps be subject to harsher sentencing, as psychological child abuse should be added to the list of charges.

Continuing our investigation into criminal mindsets, the anatomy of the brain could be an accomplice to hormones. The part of the brain associated with emotions is called the Amygdala. Physical damage to this part of the brain is believed to be a cause of criminal behaviour, possibly because the afflicted person would have a reduced fear response, and therefore the fear of repercussions for their actions would not deter them from indulging in their criminal activity. Also, their sensitivity to the feeling of guilt would be reduced. If a person really wants something, such as money, a better lifestyle, a new car, an exotic holiday, or even a person, in the case of kidnappers and sexual predators, but they do not have the aptitude to attain their desires virtuously, then this causes dissatisfaction and resentment against the people who have what they want. They will have little or no remorse about getting these things through unscrupulous means; stealing, drug dealing, blackmailing, even murdering and kidnapping. So, what can we do about crime? More arrests, more prisons and putting more people in prison for petty crimes? I do not think this is the answer.

Crime prevention failure

Over 11 million people are held in penal institutions globally according to the World Prison Population List (WPPL), researched by Roy Walmsley and published in November 2018 by the Institute for Criminal Policy Research (ICPR), at Birkbeck, University of London. That is roughly the same amount of people in prison as the population of Finland and Norway combined! Not to mention the rest that have served their time and recently been released back into the general population, or those who are still to be sentenced and due to serve for their crimes. I am sure we can make an improvement on this figure or at least stop it rising, by combatting crime from the roots.

In theory, it is quite possible to drastically cut this number with relatively simple measures. One thing we need is a reformation of how prisons operate. Some may argue that prison is clearly not enough of a deterrent as criminal activity is rife. In some country's prisons, life has been deemed too comfortable for prisoners, with some convicts actually claiming to prefer life in prison, even re-offending just to get put back in there to have an easier life. This completely undermines the justice system and makes a mockery of it, but sadly it is true. On the outside, ex-convicts have to support themselves again in a society that will always exercise prejudgement over them. In prison they have provided for them: television, games consoles, gyms, food, drink, education, bed and board, visits from partners and some even get supervised trips out of the prison/day release from time to time. Make no mistake; everything is not provided for free, with the prisoners just lounging around all day. The prisoners do have to work in prison, contributing to the day to day running of the facility, and in return, all of the above mentioned comforts are provided. But this is not really punishment though because it is just like the rest of us. We all have to work to earn money to secure these things and to survive. However, in prison, the societal structure is more like egalitarian communism, there is no accumulation of wealth, and no matter who they were on the outside, the inmates are equal inside the prison walls as far as the authority is concerned.

The limits of freedom are obviously significantly reduced compared to people living on the outside of course, but arguably the main deterring aspect of prison is the shared company; often violent or unpleasant people all congregated in one place, forced to live in close quarters with one another for years at a time can mean non-violent criminals must adapt their personalities, becoming aggressive to fit in. This is a failure of what prisons are meant to do though, which is rehabilitate criminals so they are able to function in society again after release. But in order to survive prison, the prisoners often have to become overly aggressive. Consequently, after completing their sentences, many people leave prison more psychologically disturbed, hardened or traumatised than they were before they went in. Someone can go into prison as a one time offender who would never have broken the law again if given a second chance and leave after serving their time, having developed into a habitual, hardened criminal because of the people they were exposed to during their sentence. What good does that do for society? Yes, there needs to be justice for wrongdoers, but not at the expense of society. Where possible the justice should be delivered outside of prisons. This will anger people who desire to see all wrongdoers locked away, but the long-term adverse effects on society that come from locking up non-violent criminals are not worth the satisfaction of seeing people behind bars.

For some countries, simply imprisoning criminals for life is not enough. Parts of Africa, Asia and North America still retain the death penalty for consideration in criminal trials, (although it is usually reserved only for the most heinous crimes). The majority of nations have completely abolished the death penalty though, opting instead to imprison people, even if it has to be for the remainder of their lives. Despite the wasted contribution to mankind and the incarceration being financially burdensome, it is the humane and right thing to do. It was possibly Mahatma Gandhi who said *"An eye for an eye leaves the whole world blind."* Regardless of who said it, they were right and wise to caution the dangers of bloodthirsty retribution against those who have done wrong. Remember, a thirst for vengeance is the trait that provoked World War I.

Our ancestors were far less tolerant towards criminality than we are today. The 'eye for an eye' punishment was practised quite literally in medieval Europe and the suffering reached a sickening level, with torture and execution so brutal that one can only imagine the degree of psychopathy at play in the minds of those imposing it. Certainly, it had to be as bad, or worse, than that going on in the minds of the most violent criminals at the time. The harsh punishments were not even reserved for just violent crimes. People would often face gruesome death or lifetime imprisonment in hideous, filthy conditions for non-violent crimes, such as stealing food to feed their starving families, or criticising authority.

Even this kind of extreme intolerance to lawbreakers did not work as a deterrent though, as the desperate will do what they must to survive, and the psychopaths will kill when provoked to, without thinking of the consequences during that moment of weakness. It is a simple philosophy; we should exercise forgiveness but not to the extent of forgetfulness. There has to be a consequence for committing a crime, of course. However, an eye for an eye, or tit for tat, only prolongs and reciprocates the suffering, passing on the negativity, engulfing the lives of more people as it spreads and grows. It is far more preferable to find a non-violent solution, exercising mercy and forgiveness, as this is the only thing that will truly extinguish the violence from the base and avoid it spreading in society.

As early as the Victorian era in Great Britain, it was becoming obvious that capital punishment did not have any place in the kind of future the Victorians were trying to build towards. Although the Victorians firmly believed in punishing criminals, the punishments moved away from executions, with fewer hangings. Instead, criminals were deported to the British penal colonies overseas. The Victorians also began looking at rehabilitation programs and considering how prisoners could still contribute to society. Investment in prisons meant a convict could be released a better person rather than a broken person whose only choice was to re-offend. Prisons were never designed to be nice places to live but the new prison buildings of the 19th century had to meet certain, minimum, requirements following new legislation, including gender and age separation, and the facilities had to be kept in a clean, well-maintained condition. Prisons often contained a chapel and had a chaplain to give moral guidance as part of the rehabilitation. Sometimes the prisons even included areas to exercise. Prior to this, prisoners were left to fester. With the new rules, it ensured that prisoners were made to wash regularly and wore a uniform to help keep them clean and prevent the spread of disease and parasites. They were fed a basic diet, and were even educated. People who went into prison illiterate were taught to read and write in order to help them contribute in better ways if released.

Nowadays, there is a growing feeling that prisons in many countries have become overly comfortable, with too many amenities available that some of us on the outside world cannot even afford regularly, such as the use of fully equipped gyms, medical care, food for every meal and heating whenever it is cold. To an extent, I agree with this notion, but the fact some people cannot afford these basics on the outside of prison is not the fault of prisoners, but rather a separate government failure that I have already acknowledged. Furthermore, considering that even when prisons were just a cold, dark stone dungeon with a bucket for a toilet, where the prisoners would be left to rot, it did not stop criminal behaviour. No matter what the condition of the prison, the desperate or socially damaged will always do what they must to survive or satisfy their needs.

The main deterrent techniques for reducing criminal behaviour needs to target the roots with violence reduction and rehabilitation schemes for current prisoners. Couple this with socialist efforts to make sure struggling parents are supported with troubled children, recognising the early warning signs of criminality and pre-emptively treating them by helping those who are desperate to get what they need through legitimate channels and by peacefully programming people from birth, (through education and philosophical training), with the *desire* to do the right thing even in the face of adversity.

Without doing this, we are always going to be leaving it to chance that badly raised, poorly educated people will do the right thing simply out of fear of what could happen if they do the wrong thing and get caught, which we know from experience does not work effectively. We need to prevent as many criminal mindsets from forming in the first place, rather than accepting the inevitability of it all and punishing criminals that society allowed to materialise and commit their crimes because of system failures. It is too late when the damage is already done, and the suffering has been caused. It gives us pleasure to see guilty people receive justice or 'karma', but it should give us greater pleasure to see a bad person transformed into good and to stop the crimes being committed in the first place as our civilisation advances socially, recognising risks and negating them successfully. This should be our focus area when it comes to crime and punishment, not thinking of how we can make long-term prisoners' lives more miserable and pointless than they already are.

Non-violent, first-time offenders, will not benefit from prison. If anything, it is likely to turn them into re-offending, harder criminals. Therefore, I believe there is only a requirement for people to be in prison who are dangerous to others, have caused suffering to others intentionally/through severe negligence of their own, or those who do not respond to rehabilitation, continuing to re-offend.

As an alternative to prison, non-violent offenders could be sent to correctional therapy centres, where they would be assessed psychologically, have their motivations fully understood, be made to confront their wrongdoings and to work on legitimate life plans for correcting their course in the future. If deemed safe and genuinely remorseful, they could be released back into society to complete their 'sentence', which could be contributing on humanitarian projects whilst being 'electronic tag' monitored for a fixed length of time to deter partaking in further crime. The months or years that their location has to be monitored would be part of their sentence, and if this sentence is completed satisfactorily, without incident, then there would be no prison for that offender.

Some criminals are so dangerous that they *have* to be locked away for the safety of the general public. If violent criminals are released from prisons, they could be monitored for the rest of their lives to minimise the risk they pose to the general public. Permanent tagging, or microchipping, could be an alternative to prison for repeat offenders of non-violent crimes too. With this type of punishment, there is a significantly reduced burden on the taxpayer compared with incarceration for longer periods of time.

For extremely violent criminals, such as terrorists and murderers, many may remain inclined to advocate the death penalty that some countries around the world still use, so as to further reduce the population in prisons and increase public safety. However effective the death penalty is at reducing prison populations, this practice has no place in our H-utopian future, or even in our current world. We cannot kill defenceless incarcerated people, no matter how evil, without absorbing the evil ourselves, creating a bloodthirsty, uncivilised society akin to the pitchfork-wielding simpletons of the middle ages. This is not to mention the tragic instances where wrongly convicted people have been sentenced to death, only for new evidence to come to light and clear them of the crime when it was too late.

Continuing with my anti-extremist philosophy, the death penalty is out of the question. The solution will not come from the death of evil, as it is doomed to re-spawn no matter how many times it is killed. The focus should be on preventing evil materialising in the first place. It has been estimated at least 3 per cent of the population are born with strong psychopathic tendencies, but they will be far less likely to become psychopaths if the environment they grow up in is nurturing and positive. With the correct education, parenting, therapy and chances in life, even the natural born psychopath is likely to be benign and go onto to be successful in their lives, never to harm anyone. So why do we think it is beyond our capabilities to prevent petty criminals from manifesting in society? If we get the basics right by looking after our citizens financially, educating them properly, and recognising criminal tendencies in children from a young age, then crime will be far less of an issue in the future than it is today.

Safest country in the world

Not convinced that taking the softer approach towards criminals will work? Do not take my word for it. We can look to Finland which has been ranked as the safest country in the world, because of extraordinarily low crime rates, and crucially, a respectful and trusting relationship between police/authority and the general public. At a time when rising crime rates around the world are putting pressure on governments to push for harsher prison conditions and longer sentences, Finland has saved millions in taxpayer money, prevented human suffering and advanced socially by doing the exact opposite. Prison is seen as an absolute last resort in Finland. Even when it is used, sentences are shorter than most countries, outside relationships are allowed, the inmates have frequent visitation rights and time outside of prison. In some facilities, prisoners can work or study at any education level, with hired specialists coming into classrooms and teaching convicted murderers and drug dealers, (in unguarded rooms), vocational skills, such as cutting and styling hair. Regardless of their crime, prisoners are treated like individuals and actual human beings. They are treated with dignity, allowed to wear civilian clothes, and are given the chance of getting to know facility staff on a level that traditional prisons discourage. This trust that comes from familiarity is how they are able to have murderers attending educational classes without armed guards present. Trust and respect work both ways, and no matter what our opinions are on how fair or 'just' this is, we cannot argue with the success of Finland's justice system at work. The fact is, with the exception of the most heinous, remorseless, dangerous minority, most criminals will be released sooner or later, and they need to be reformed and prepared to re-enter society. Otherwise, any money and time put into their incarceration is wasteful and inefficient.

The fact Finland can have one of the softest approaches to criminals in the world, yet have the lowest crime rate, again shows that prisons first and foremost were never a deterrent for crime, but rather a convenience for locking away misfits that society is too lazy to rehabilitate; opting to hide them from society, brushing them under the carpet. When someone who knows they have done wrong, and feels they do not deserve help or trust, is given it, they will receive it as the greatest gift possible.

It gives many people great pleasure to see prisoners suffering, (the worse, the better), and those calling for prison reform, better conditions, rehabilitation schemes, and lighter sentences, are branded 'lefty' liberals and hated worse than the criminals. However, what Finland and many other countries who have taken this softer approach realised a long time ago, is it does not matter how miserable you make prisoners, it will never prevent or undo their crime. Only fulfilling the duty of care for all of our citizens will truly remove the criminal mindset. Remember, prisons are there for people who have already committed their crimes. To prevent the crimes occurring in the first place is the goal, and to prevent criminals from re-offending. Many low to medium-security prisons built in Finland since the reform, several decades ago, do not fit the stereotypical prison image. They have no guardhouses, no sniper towers, no barbed wire fences, etc. They have escape prevention and detection, but they are not placed in clear view. Buried wires in the perimeter that detect motion and trigger alarms are the preferred option to avoid undermining trust. To even refer to these facilities as prisons, is wrong. They are open institutions, where inmates are allowed to work and travel in the community, so long as they return when required to. Finland's justice system is only free to operate in this way because they have reduced prison populations to an absolute minimum and manageable amount by the nation's leaders committing to fulfilling their duty of care to their citizens, educating them properly and drilling in the philosophy of mutual respect and trust.

In contrast, most countries are overwhelmed by their prisoners and cannot afford to rehabilitate them effectively, because merely housing and feeding them is exhaustive. Finland's 'open institutions' are a way even violent criminals coming to the end of long sentences can prepare to re-enter society slowly, instead of just being dumped back onto the streets after decades away from society. To help with the transition back into normal life, and to reduce that chance of re-offending to a minimum, prisoners first have the chance to transfer from their high-security prisons to finish their sentences in these far more lenient 'halfway houses'.

Even after release, ex-prisoners are still given lots of attention with extensive use of parole. Ex-convicts are supervised whilst they re-establish themselves in legitimate society and are given support to find work and homes. The ex-convicts learn they are going to be responsible for providing their own living again, but with the authorities supporting in directing them onto a legitimate path from here on out, rather than just leaving it to chance whether they sink or swim.

A final testament to Finland's justice system: whereas many countries suffer from constant prison riots and insane violence, putting prison staff at risk, in Finland's prisons violence is extremely rare. This is again because of the ethos of mutual respect and trust between authority and inmates, but also because prisoners are given regular direct contact with family, friends, and as many law-abiding people on the outside as possible. There is even the option of home leave for those who pose no physical threat to return to their families and neighbourhoods for a few days a year. This may sound crazy and irresponsible, but it is considered by the authorities as crucial, to avoid dehumanisation of the prisoners and loss of basic social skills, whilst offering incentive to reform.

Eradicating crime - is it a possibility, and what would it mean?

So, to achieve our goal of preventing crime before it is allowed to happen, just how strict do we need to be with immoral behaviour? Is it realistic or even desirable, for that matter, to eradicate 100 per cent of crime? What would living in a world with no crime of any kind actually be like?

I have made clear that any kind of extremism will only lead to dystopia, and this is what we risk trying to achieve unrealistic goals by force or taking draconian short cuts that restrict the liberty of the general population as an easy way to stop crime quickly. Short of dystopian fantasies such as mind control, or the extreme and undesirable measure of microchipping all humans at birth, there is nothing physical available that will help to see a complete end to all crime.

Say there was a way to physically stop all crime with some as yet undiscovered technology or genetic modification that renders human beings incapable of wrongdoing. What would complete eradication of crime mean, with no room for exceptions or mitigation? A world where humans cannot possess a certain herb or plant that is deemed illegal by an authority, or have an abortion, or display affection in public, or exercise a right to protest peacefully, or go outside during an authority imposed curfew. A world where one cannot even criticise authority without fear of persecution for the crime of treason, terrorism or disturbing the peace. Depending on the circumstances, committing such a 'crime' as free speech could even leave people victim to verbal or physical abuse from other oppressed people who do not know or do not care they are oppressed, because they are suffering from Stockholm Syndrome due to the nature of overly controlling authorities that can use fear to relentlessly torment and reassure a general public during periods of fluctuating chaos and order, danger and safety, panic and calm, hardship and comfort.

We can begin to imagine how an attempt at complete eradication of 'crime' can lead to the worst kind of injustice and corruption imaginable, as crime is just a point of view. In the present day, each society has their own definition of what constitutes criminal activity. Most would agree on murder, rape and stealing of course, but what about consuming alcohol in Dubai, publicly displaying affection in Saudi Arabia or publicly practising any religion other than Islam there? Certain circumstances can also change whether something is a crime or not. For example, someone driving an emergency vehicle may break the speed limit without suffering a penalty. A police officer can commit murder if he or she decides such force is needed to overcome a criminal threat. Even a homeowner can commit murder in self-defence if someone has illegally broken into their home.

The definition of crime has also changed with time. There are outdated crimes such as prohibition, adultery and homosexuality, as well as the emergence of entirely new categories of crime, including cyber-crime and credit card fraud. Consider also, in the not too distant past, that slavery was legal all over the world! The definition of crime will continue to evolve and who knows what will be considered illegal in the future that is acceptable now and what is illegal now but will be acceptable in the future.

It is apparent that complete and absolute crime prevention is not possible or desirable in our H-utopian future, as it would require an 'Orwellian' style, mind-probing dictatorship to enforce. As we have discovered, there are, however, steps we can take to drastically reduce crime to a minimal level whilst retaining our whimsical human flaws at the same time.

Most criminal activity imaginable can be traced back to these root causes: desperation, fear, frustration, abusive parenting, or just plain bad parenting. If you want to kill a weed, you must pull it from the root. The same is true of criminal behaviour. It nearly always begins in early childhood, and if not nipped in the bud, it will grow out of control. Behind the mortal exterior of a habitual criminal, is usually a heart deprived of love. When human beings are raised in an environment lacking love, (and a respectful role model as a moral compass), they will start feeding on anger, hatred, envy and other negative emotions. This manipulates their behaviour, making them unrighteous, dishonourable and selfish. These are the ingredients for creating an evil, bitter personality, and being fed these ingredients leads to casual routine criminality, aggression and a lack of empathy for any victims, as a lifetime of abuse leaves the afflicted individuals becoming desensitised to the suffering of others. It is alarming to think that all is needed to create a petty criminal out of a child is:

1) Absence of good role models - *"My parents steal stuff all the time. They say it's easier than working and it's okay if you don't get caught"*.
2) Motivation - *"I need stuff I don't have because other people have it and I should be happy too"*.
3) Target - For instance, trying on a pair of trainers in a high street store and walking out wearing them.

This kind of situation is just a minor example of what growing up in an immoral environment costs society. An environment where a child may learn that stealing is a normal and easy way to get what they want fast.

Even people who may appear not to fit the stereotypical image of a criminal, fooling society with their well put together facade, can engage in regular immoral/illegal activity. For example, purchasing stolen goods, knowing they are stolen, and selling them for a profit, or even having the cheek to return the goods to a store for a refund or exchange. Or, people who lie or exaggerate the truth on insurance claims for compensation; this is called insurance fraud and is no petty crime. Nonetheless, people who appear otherwise legitimate can easily succumb to these kinds of crime. Why? Because they are easy to get away with, not personable, (they cannot see their victims), and the temptation to make a quick buck can be too much in a society that is every man for himself. These kinds of petty criminals may believe they are not harming anyone, but their crimes are far from victimless. The victims are every human being on Earth. Petty theft from a multi-billionaire company or exaggerating an incident or accident to claim some additional compensation may seem like they have no effect on society, but one has to consider that the money has to be recovered from somewhere. Most companies have insurance they claim on in such circumstances. They pay into premiums and the insurance companies, pre-empting that this kind of activity goes on in society, raise their premiums to account for it. High street stores and supermarkets raise the price of their goods too, to account for stealing that. As crime goes up, insurance premiums go up, and the cost of goods go up, to account for any thefts. So ultimately, everyone pays back what they have taken in the end. If these kinds of crimes did not happen, life would be a lot cheaper for everyone.

Hate Crime

Who is responsible for hateful attacks on others? If we are honest, it is probably every single one of us at some point in our lives. Whether it was joining in with bullying in the school playground or cyberbullying online, taunting celebrities, or anyone for that matter, on social media sites such as Instagram and Twitter for how they look or what they have said, making idle threats over trivial matters, sabotaging businesses or service givers by writing overly critical reviews out of spite or as a form of subtle blackmail to receive compensation, creating discord either online in forums or in real life to incite conflict, discriminating against someone's sexual preference, political views or religious beliefs, either to their face or behind their back. An extremist may decide to take this hatred even further, seeking to cause physical harm to people out of this animalistic response to what is ultimately fear, ignorance and perhaps frustration. Because hate crime comes in so many forms, it is the easiest to commit and probably the most commonly committed crime. This means it is also the hardest to police. In mild forms, we can police it ourselves with behavioural correction and education. In its most severe forms of terrorism, assassinations and pre-meditated murder, it warrants the harshest punishments the authorities allow to protect the general public.

It is not just individuals who commit hate crimes. Entire organisations do it in plain sight on a national scale, with political parties being some of the worst offenders. Successful politicians are often wealthy and therefore, influential. Some may even have connections in mainstream media organisations, turning once reputable newspapers and broadcasters into unwitting hate criminals as they are relentlessly exploited to commit slander, by running smear campaigns that take facts out of context or may just entirely fabricate stories for convenience. It is a tactic that has been used since democracy first formed - find a molehill of dirt on your opponent, turn it into a mountain and then crush them with it. This example is set by the people who are meant to be in charge of improving our society. When the rule-makers become law-breakers, what chance have the rest of us got following this example of squabbling hatred as it spreads down into society and we begin to fight amongst ourselves over which candidate is the least dishonest and deserving of our vote?

The problem with hate crime is, by the time a serial hater has already committed their first spree, it is difficult to change their perception on life and get across to them the importance of rational debate and tolerance. We have to combat this quarrelsome mindset from the bottom up, starting with young children in school. As already suggested we need to be establishing children to deal with conflicting viewpoints in a positive and rational manner, so they are able to accept varying opinions as a positive thing for society, rather than reacting with emotional fear responses which are often primal and aggressive by nature. We can hope to make progress with this by opening up philosophical debate in the classroom wherever possible and by being more stringent when it comes to correcting violent tendencies or hateful outbursts in young children.

Making excuses for children and not correcting hatred and ignorance early on is one of the biggest failures in society. All crime begins with hate and fear, so we must target these emotional responses as much as possible by training our children to accept others as equals. We live in a society of extremists because of acute hate and fear, but if we can train ourselves from youth to live more rationally, always incentivised to find common ground and compromise, rather than allowing exploitation of extremist hatred, then maybe we will stop spiralling helplessly towards dystopia, regain control, and begin accelerating up towards H-utopia.

Crimes against humanity – the worst offender

Here we have another category of crime that can range from petty all the way up to terrorism. Sometimes the perpetrators may not even realise they are committing a crime against humanity and none are more guilty of this crime than media outlets.

Media can sway the opinions of entire generations, inciting hysteria, manipulating political outcomes, socially traumatising children, provoking wars, and causing avoidable deaths, including suicides. With the rise of smartphones and WIFI in the 2010s, most people now have easy 24-hour access to the internet in the palms of their hands, wherever they may be. This is seen as a great technological achievement and certainly a life-changing convenience. However, we should exercise caution.

Never has it been easier to manipulate an entire population via the media. We already touched on how the media can inflict Stockholm Syndrome on an entire population, and we reviewed how propaganda was used during World War II to impose one individual's evil agenda on an entire nation, and this was even before media was easily accessed by everyone at any time of day. 24-hour access to media is a very new phenomenon, and we are yet to realise its full potential, good or bad. Even a decade ago, in 2010, it was not the case one could easily get onto the internet from any location. But nowadays we are absolutely bombarded 24/7 with updates from news outlets, social media, forums, YouTube, advertisements, etc. Many of us even have apps or alerts on our phones to inform us of an update. Social media, in particular, is full of speculative journalism as people obsessed with 'shares' and 'likes' create deliberate controversy with sensationalism and 'clickbait'. Debate is healthy, but on social media and forums, partly thanks to anonymity, it is rarely rational debate, usually descending into chaotic hate speech, inciting violence. Unless someone makes a real conscious effort to do so, it is unavoidable to be influenced by all of this media output.

The scary thing about media companies is, how they operate

can be likened to arms dealers: they profit most during times of frenzy, crisis and misery. Doom and scaremongering sells more papers and achieves more 'clicks' or 'shares' than any 'good news' story. The media thrives on suffering, hysteria, sensationalism and frenzied chaos. They are often biased and extremely manipulative in the way they write, simplifying a situation to deliberately divide opinion into binary extremes. In the interest of protecting their reputation, a media outlet may 'test the waters' for the majority opinion on a subject matter, then demonise the minority in their writing, instead of debating both points of view impartially . This is particularly true of mainstream media outlets. The dividing of society is exacerbated further by online algorithms picking and choosing what they think we want to see on social media, based on our internet searches. This then ends up creating an overly simplistic, extremist view of society by limiting what news people are exposed to, (unless the target audience makes a conscious effort to research the 'other side' of the story, then they will never be exposed to it, and it will hold no influence over them. Then, when someone from the contrary extreme opinion brings it up, it challenges their world view, at which point medieval-style mob mentality rears its ugly head.

Unscrupulous journalism thrives on all of the hate and division that we should be desperately trying to avoid on our way to H-utopia. Media is important to keep us informed. However, it should be regulated far better, not by authority, as this will undermine freedom of speech, but by ourselves with our own integrity and rationale, and we should practice researching all sides of a story, not just what the algorithm on our device tells us is our most likely opinion.

Particularly since the invention of social media, YouTube, and similar platforms, everyone is a journalist and everyone can have their say, but journalists have a greater responsibility than people may realise; to refrain from publishing anything that may incite panic or that lacks integrity. To underestimate this responsibility by publishing biased news stories, smear campaigns, gossip, false news, even misleading articles that manipulate people with twisted words and sensationalist headlines, is nothing less than a crime against humanity. A crime, they will likely never be held to account for by any authority, but that we as the audience can police, by not receiving and accepting it as we are expected to.

Generally, people have a high degree of trust in mainstream

media as it acts as a liaison for updates from authority, and can come across very official. But the same 'official' media also crops out the bits that do not suit a story, embellishes and deliberately misleads to attract more attention for something that may otherwise not have been as interesting or shocking to hear about. Media companies can even take it one step further and deliberately influence world events by pushing the right buttons and prodding in the right places to achieve a desired outcome. The pen is mightier than the sword, and it is a dangerous weapon, drenched in the blood of millions.

Alternative media outlets, generally online only, have a far lower demographic than mainstream, and therefore anything they publish that is contrary to what mainstream has already informed us, is automatically branded as 'fake news', and will have to fight tooth and nail to be proven true. The problem is there is so much 'fake news' and a lot of it really is fake, but say, for instance, 20 per cent of the news branded as fake really is true, then it is worth sifting through the misinformation to find the truth. Freedom of speech must be retained at all costs, and any attempts to undermine individual journalists striving to deliver truth is another crime against humanity. Sadly, many lone journalists undermine themselves by falling for sensationalism or conspiracy to get noticed. It is like the boy that cried wolf: when an independent journalist does stumble across a vital truth, no one will believe it because of how many times they have fooled people in the past.

To reiterate, whenever we post a video on the internet or share something on social media, we are all dabbling in journalism, and it is absolutely vital we dabble with integrity to avoid freedom of speech becoming tarnished by ignorance. Equally, the rest of us, as the target audience, have a duty to question everything, exercise rational debate and strive to get all sides to every story by corroborating any information fed to us, with our own independent research before reacting. Doing anything less would be foolish and naïve. It is up to all of us not to let media outlets get away with fracturing society, using fear as a weapon of hatred. Malcom X said it best:

"If you're not careful, the newspapers will have you hating the people who are being oppressed, and loving the people who are doing the oppressing."

The effects of recreational drugs on society

If you are an adult who has never tried recreational drugs, you are in the minority. Most adults have tried at least one kind of mind-altering substance at some point in their life. It has become accepted as normal, and if someone is discovered to be in the minority that does not drink alcohol for example, or has never tried smoking marijuana, they may receive a funny look as if *they* have the problem.

Marijuana has become almost as mainstream as alcohol consumption, and the trend is on the up. Some may use the drug as a quick and easy way to relieve tension or anxiety caused by an ever more overwhelming day to day life. However, this drug has a rebound effect that will make the anxiety more intense after it wears off. This can lead to dependency, which then begins to interfere with everyday life; and prolonged drug use because of dependency can trigger deeper psychological problems. Many people will identify as 'social smokers' or 'social drinkers', meaning they only take the drug in the company of friends, to reduce inhibition, making it easier to fit in and mix well with others, not necessarily because they enjoy the drug and cannot live without it. However, this also demonstrates a mental weakness and sadly many long-term addicts will begin with this casual self-justification.

So, even a drug as commonplace and apparently harmless as marijuana can systematically compromise an individual's motivation, corrupt their morals and cripple their potential. Many people do not realise they have a problem, and unfortunately, there is a stigma around mental health, especially self-inflicted mental health problems caused by excessive drug use. We can combat this stigma with better education on the subject and talking more about it, as already suggested earlier on in the essay. If the approach to parenting and schooling that I have already laid out is followed, then people are going to be far less likely to succumb to drug addictions in the first place.

Long-term drug addicts left to spiral out of control often get into financial difficulties and can end up homeless, fully dependent on government support. This is a literal personification of social failure as further judgement is cast on these people making their situations even more helpless. It is a common myth that an addict has to hit 'rock bottom' before they have a realisation, get help and can begin the road to recovery. Because of this myth, sometimes friends and family members will allow the addict to carry on making their mistakes without intervening. A personality that craves excess or something outside of the norm does not have to be unhealthy. Doctors are there to help addicts as much as any physically sick person, but sadly, many addicts leave it until it is too late. Unable to cooperate with treatment plans, they consequently relapse.

The impact of drugs on society is worse when we look at the bigger picture. We can all have good intentions to build towards something greater, but as I have already stated, the personal desires of the individual, even in the knowledge they are damaging the future for their children, are nearly always prioritised above social progress. Even with the strongest minded and most ethical individuals, this is often the case, so what hope have the helplessly addicted got? This is why it is vital steps are taken to drastically reduce drug, (and alcohol), abuse as these are root causes of many problems that will misdirect the human race on its road to H-utopia. These include: child neglect and/or child abuse, poverty, homelessness or poor quality of life, increased violent crime, mental health problems, spiralling anxiety, paranoia, increased burden on the health and social care industry and an increased burden on taxpayers to pay for incarcerated individuals convicted of drug-related crimes. Perhaps the most tragic, which covers all of the above, is not fulfilling individual human potential, because the brain cannot help but prioritise where its 'fix' is coming from above all else.

Another pressing issue is damage to the economy, where parts of it are lost to drug money that is not taxed, and in extreme cases is hoarded by multi-billionaires such as notorious Colombian drug overlord, Pablo Escobar who was worth an estimated 30 billion US dollars at the time of his death, and Mexican, Amado Carrillo Fuentes, who was worth an estimated 25 billion dollars at the time of his death. Although the chosen lifestyle of these two extreme cases resulted in their untimely demises, some billionaire drug overlords are still alive today and profiting off of human suffering, whilst listed as fugitives. They remain free because of the influence their extreme wealth gives them, and by being careful not to directly incriminate themselves, getting others to perform the 'dirty work'. When they are eventually brought to justice, the authorities will seize their assets and money. Just like industrial-scale war, or human illness, the sale of narcotics is a massive business. But what is the cost to humanity?

Drug abuse and alcohol abuse correlates directly with increased violent crime and theft. Even if you do not personally know someone who is abusing drugs, everyone is impacted by drugs at least indirectly. Whether it is through our taxes going towards medical care for drug-related illness, covering the cost of incarceration for drug-related convicts, or paying higher insurance premiums. Financially, the estimates for how much drug and alcohol abuse costs society are between 500 billion and 1 trillion US dollars a year, which means even seizing a fortune the size of Escobar's would not make much of a dent in compensating the expense. We are talking about something more important than money here, though. We are talking about our sanity, our humanity, the safety and wellbeing of our children and the long-term effects on the future of our species. The mental and physical side effects that come from dealing with drug and alcohol-related abuse, either directly, or indirectly in the case of abused or neglected children, requires tireless support and endless resources from the health and social care industries. The more selfish individuals there are who abuse drugs, the more we pay for it as a society. It drains the health care industry, which is responsible for rehabilitation programs, taking resources away from saving the lives of those who have not caused their own illnesses.

Furthermore, drug abuse tears social development apart from the inside by destroying families which in turn has a negative impact on the rest of society. A parent abusing drugs leads to their children receiving poorer care and higher amounts of emotional neglect, resulting in a reduced performance at school and causing lasting psychological knock-on effects that may make it hard for them to function in society properly as adults - in some cases, even adopting the addicted lifestyle themselves as a coping mechanism. If a mother is the drug user and used the drug whilst pregnant, her child is even more likely to become addicted to that drug. Children living with parents who are drug addicts or alcoholics often try to take on the responsibility of the parental role. The unfair burden put on these neglected children is an unacceptable disgrace on the part of the parents who allow their children to go without basic necessities, including adequate nutrition, hygiene, health care and education. Research suggests 80 per cent of all child abuse and neglect cases are strongly related to drug or alcohol abuse, and it is the number one reason for children being removed from a family and put into foster care.

It is not just parents taking drugs themselves that causes neglect, and passes on a drug dependency; a child or young adult from a family of otherwise non-drug users can get into drug-related activity from an external source, and this one family member's problem can then cause stress and anxiety amongst all the other family members. Parenting efforts and financial resources tend to go toward helping the child with the problem, inadvertently neglecting other children in the family. The 'stable' children are denied their fair share of attention, fail to be pushed to fulfil their potential and may even turn to drugs themselves as a way of getting attention or coping with neglect and trauma growing up in households with high levels of criticism, drama, misdirected anger and negativity. The messy end result is a generation of socially inept young adults, suffering from anxiety issues and complexes that could hinder the rest of their lives. The issues roll into adulthood and into the workplace where the effects of drugs continue to negatively affect the economy through reduced productivity. Some estimates of lost revenue, directly related to decreased productivity from drug users, runs into 100s of billions a year!

It is almost like the negativity is contagious. Drug abusers in the workplace will begin bringing down the productivity and morale of the rest of the workforce too. Drugs are not always the obvious reason for an employee's underperformance, and it can take time for an employer to manage the problem, balancing efficiency with compassion. In the meantime, the drug user affects the business with poor timekeeping and regular absences. They will appear to have reduced capability and be less responsive to training, leaving other employees to pick up the slack for their drug-abusing colleague's lack of productivity. This causes tension and irritation in the workplace which has a knock-on effect that can cause the rest of the workforce to develop personal issues that they then take home with them to their families, and ultimately this will reduce their performance too in school and in other work. So, having drug users around you, even if you do not know they are drug users, can take its toll, and the negativity spreads like a disease throughout society. The whole world is affected by this ripple effect, but what can we do about it?

The pandemic of drug abuse has become this widespread thanks to a capitalist world without limits, failed economic systems and unscrupulous, selfish, opportunist mindsets, from individuals who have exploited human weaknesses for their own personal gain, with complete disregard to the next generation, or social development. In 1920, American president Herbert Hoover delivered what he called "a great social and economic experiment", known as prohibition. This was a ban preventing alcohol from being made, transported or sold in the USA. Astonishingly it remained in force for 13 years. However, banning substances entirely clearly does not stop their distribution; most recreational drugs are illegal in most countries, and yet the pandemic remains. Prohibiting things from sale just leaves the doorway open for underhanded Machiavellians to waltz through and profit off the desperately dependent, and it is nearly impossible to police possession of drugs for personal use. Because of underground activity during prohibition, the USA actually saw an increased crime rate! So is the answer to make all drugs legal, taxing and regulating them? No, I do not think this is the answer either. This would be an extreme and unnecessarily risky approach.

Our best chance has already been suggested earlier on in the essay. We can change our socio-economic system to a capital incentivised socialism with a limit to how much money individuals can accumulate and stockpile. We could also swap all national currencies for 'Earth Credits', and remove cash, as we know it, to stop counterfeiting and deter criminal transactions in general. These actions could be combined with agreed global tax brackets to stop tax evasion and money laundering. I am not claiming this alone will remove the drug problem entirely. There is still the opportunity to barter for drugs, and there is the 'dark web' or 'deep web' where, amongst other nasties, untraceable drug deals can be carried out electronically and posted in vacuum-sealed parcels to avoid detection at sorting offices. For this reason, some have claimed that a society without cash would only make a drug dealer's life easier. But this is wrongly assuming several things:

1) That law enforcement does not use the dark web and is incapable of policing/baiting it.
2) That everything else with our economic system would stay the same in a future without large amounts of paper cash, and shady electronic transactions would be allowed to continue.
3) That the evolution of technology available for investigatory bureaus to police this kind of cyber-crime has reached its peak

and will somehow now fall behind the criminal's technology.

4) That postal/courier service changes could not be implemented, such as compulsory sender ID checks and sender contact details when posting parcels, combined with random illegal activity detection checks at sorting offices, leaving any senders and recipients at risk of being caught with every transaction.

With the removal of cash, the clarity of all credit transactions would have to be improved upon also. As already suggested, everyone could be assigned a single credit account at birth, and these accounts would obviously be monitored for suspicious amounts of activity as normal bank accounts are anyway. Like any part of human society, there is an underground or 'seedy' side and the internet is no different of course. However, despite what Hollywood or media hype may have us believe, there is no conspiracy with the dark web. It is just another part of the internet, and the formation of it was an inevitable stage in the evolution of crime. The anonymous nature of the internet, in general, makes it ideal for criminal activity, but obviously, no intelligent criminal is going to advertise on social media or search engines on the clear web. So, the dark web was created, obscured from view in normal internet searches through the use of encryption, and to access it requires the use of purpose-built routers.

In our H-utopian future, we can hope to severely reduce the amount of crime by taking the steps already laid out in this essay anyway. It is likely in the distant future that technology will become available to remove unwanted addictive or psychopathic tendencies all together from the human genome. However, the goal is to attain H-utopia the ethical, long way around. It would be wise to steer clear of eugenics as history has taught us this can severely backfire in the wrong hands. There should be no requirement for it anyway if we get everything else right. H-utopia is not about surrendering free will or eradicating traits *some* opinions deem undesirable. This makes us human and to forcibly try to change our nature and control humanity by physically altering genes is a recipe for a totalitarian dystopia.

Creatures of great responsibility

"We are made wise not by the recollection of our past, but by the responsibility for our future"

- George Bernard Shaw, 1856 – 1950.

...People of great responsibility are not let off lightly when they do not live up to the potential imagined, and the immortal memory of them can become tarnished, no matter how good their intentions were...

It is apparent that the failures start from the moment we are born, and they continue throughout childhood into our adolescence, spreading like a disease into every corner of society as we become adults who are significantly flawed or traumatised. Inadequate education, failed parenting, religious dogma, political scaremongering, economic burden, ease of access to narcotics, restricted access to basic needs and ineffective justice systems are just some of the problems we have reviewed that are responsible for the traumas. As children grow up, they learn their ethics and how to behave from the people around them, and many of the remedies discussed come back to looking after the children of society better than we currently do, and pushing education to its maximum potential. Based on what is possible, public education is currently only delivering a fraction of what it could and should.

To stand a chance of reaching H-utopia, (or any future better than we have today for that matter), it is up to all of us, as role models for the next generation, to set a respectable precedent. The many actions that have been discussed during this essay need to come together simultaneously and unanimously for H-utopia to realistically succeed. The planning has to begin with our newborn children, and the examples we set as they grow and develop in a man-made world, contrary in many ways to what nature evolved them for. New humans are born as a blank canvas, and it is up to us whether we paint a nightmare or a dream. We all have a responsibility to nurturing future generations in how to cope with this world we created for them - no one is exempt from that responsibility. Remember, no one ever asks to be born. For this reason, those of us already here and creating small self-aware replicas of ourselves have an obligation to constantly strive to improve ourselves and the world around us in any way we can.

Combining the steps to H-utopia

The following is a simplified summary of some actions discussed throughout this essay. Actions, in no particular order, that, if combined and followed, will allow our children to not only reach the golden age of H-utopia but sustain it indefinitely.

[If the reader has skipped ahead for a spoiler, I urge you to fully read to this point before reading through the steps below, as without the due deserved context and explanation that is rationalised throughout, each of these bold sounding ideas will appear utterly quixotic and perhaps even detrimental to society.]

Simultaneous global disarmament of nuclear weapons between the remaining countries that possess them. These cowardly weapons are the mark of a socially immature civilisation, and we will never reach H-utopia until this evil, threatening hold we have over each other has been removed. The noble and historic act of unanimous nuclear disarmament will be an opportunity to spark the beginning of a reverse arms race, that will see the gradual reduction in all weapon production around the world. It may take decades, but that is fine. Sources of antagonising propaganda will need targeting with better regulation during this delicate time to avoid conventional warfare from breaking out.

Morphing society into one where enhancing mental ability and mental health, with an aim to fulfil individual human potential, is treasured above all else. The introduction of in-depth philosophical study, phycology and sociology as a part of the mainstream curriculum in every country from a young age, to aid children in coping with matters of both life and death. We also should invest in a complete reformation of the school system, to align it better with human nature, and to bridge the gap between the quality of schooling given to different socio-economic groups of the world. The vision statement is simple: create a better society through better education by making the basic education standard high globally. High standard of education allows for a well-balanced, well-adjusted, and well-informed people to function and be happy in society, and in their interpersonal relationships. A more focused, consistent education system is less likely to fail when it comes to discovering and nurturing geniuses, so they are able to contribute their full potential to society.

We must come to terms with our own mortality to form a better relationship with death. Whether it is faith in a Shaman, or an obligation to monarchy, offering up loyalty and/or freedoms in return for protection and survival is a deal our ancestors have always made, and we continue to make without even realising it. Freedom of thought, critical thinking, equality and liberty must be retained and prioritised at all costs. As upsetting as death may be, as long as there is new life, it will never be the end. The importance of having a healthy relationship with death must not be underestimated if we wish to reach H-utopia. Unless we work on our anxiety surrounding the unknown, we will always be too easy to manipulate by opportunists offering comfort at a cost, and there will always be a demonised enemy for us to attack in order to save ourselves, (witch hunts). Whilst we are so preoccupied with death, many of the positive social changes such as guaranteed incomes and the removal of cash are too risky because, with this innate human fear, there is too much chance for the exploitation of people. If we train our children now, with the opportunity we never had, to embrace life's natural cycle rather than fear it, then it will protect them against future malevolent powers that may otherwise exploit human obsession around mortality.

Menial jobs to be phased out of the human workplace. These should not be removed suddenly, just not preserved unnaturally. Machines and androids are being developed wherever possible. We cannot allow technophobia or nostalgia to stand in the way of progress. With increased technological advancement and a reformed education system, new and challenging work opportunities will replace outdated manual jobs. I suspect that there were objectors, on superstitious grounds, at the first use of the wheel. A scary new invention at the time no doubt, as it proved far more efficient than human feet for transportation. Progress is inevitable, and I am sure none of us would wish to go back to a time of no wheels or vehicles, to bring employment to the thousands of people that would be needed to drag giant stone blocks up and down the motorways, instead of just having a single HGV driver do the same job.

Aim for quality, not quantity with our children. For a fixed time, a maximum of one child per person, (two per couple), should be introduced as an international guideline for the sake of humanity. This should not be required to be imposed in a dictatorial manner, as we are all anxious about the looming issues of overpopulation. Despite the urgency of this matter, we must retain free will to avoid dystopia, so it is important the two-child guideline is implemented with benefits for following it, rather than punishments for breaking it. For example, the first two children could receive free education to a tertiary level as a kind of 'scholarship for humanity', funding for childcare, and free health care. For subsequent children, parents would only receive partial benefits or be subject to population tax, dependent on household income. We also need to work on removing stigma around abortion, via education and perhaps by lowering the legal limit for the procedure slightly. A further measure is to offer financial incentives for people who are already parents, to have vasectomies or tubal ligation to prevent further unwanted pregnancies. The cost of these sterilisation procedures are several thousand, but even with this cost absorbed by the taxpayer, plus the incentives paid to the patients, society would profit massively in the long term from this initiative if it were successful at reducing the rate at which the population is growing to a more sustainable level. If we do not take the initiative to limit human reproduction ourselves, then this will be done for us, either by nature or an authority that will at some point have to grow a backbone on this. The population of the world currently increases by about 200,000 every single day. It does not take a mathematician to work out that this is not sustainable. Not stopping at two children because we are too ignorant or selfish will mean all of the children we are having will suffer a horrific future of draconian measures to control the population. In the developing world, political and social support is needed as a matter of international emergency. High infant mortality is not an acceptable form of population control, and this needs to be addressed urgently, with medical intervention, education and development schemes, and it needs international cooperation from governments around the world. This responsibility should not fall to charity and philanthropy to handle alone.

Reformation of capitalism which could be labelled 'capital incentivised socialism', drawing the best aspects and wisdom from all ways of running a society, with a limit imposed on how much money an individual can control. This will have to be enforced with strict regulation, forcing the surplus money back into a centralised trust-fund for humanity, with re-investment schemes and projects for the good of the species as a whole. There should be limits imposed on organisations too, (including religious ones, who currently benefit from tax exemption, which will have to re-addressed). For this change to be achievable, paper cash would need to be abolished, to be replaced with a global credit as sole currency. The abolition of cash and different competing currencies would be most beneficial if it were to be combined with the introduction of a single credit account that is assigned at birth to every person, instead of people opting for private banking in multiple accounts. The removal of paper cash should *significantly* reduce illegal activity, that has serious negative ripple effects on society, such as illegal drug dealing, counterfeiting, and tax evasion. Drugs are the root cause for much of the world's evil and child abuse, which has dire knock-on effects that echo throughout society. The removal of cash and enhancing financial clarity with only one credit account per person is a way to significantly reduce this evil. Removal of cash and switching to 'credits' will also help with global cooperation and will put a stop to the anti-social, non-contributory way of life that some underhanded people, unfortunately, adopt as their philosophy. It will also put an end to poverty in developing nations, and minimise international wars, by making building economic security in every country a matter of global interest and financially beneficial to every other country on Earth because the wealth is pooled and shared globally. Where you are born and how rich or poor the country is, must not determine if you get to have access to human rights and whether you have the chance to fulfil your personal potential.

Reduction of the inefficient practise of farming animals for their meat, with the goal to eventually stop completely in the future as alternatives are perfected, and consumer preferences change. We should be investing fully in alternatives, including lab-produced meat, that will contain all of the goodness and none of the bad bits of the real thing, will last longer without spoiling or harbouring harmful bacteria and viruses that can result in pandemics. On top of all this, it will have the added bonus of being environmentally friendly, animal-friendly and solving world hunger. The idea is already being explored by some philanthropic individuals and great scientists, but this is a matter of global interest and needs more government collaboration with private companies to be successful.

We need to be allowed to end our own lives free of charge through the practice of euthanasia when we are suffering from incurable illnesses or facing imminent death. There is a stigma around suicide, maybe because we arrogantly consider ourselves too important or maybe we think only God has the power to end human life. It is already legal in some forward-thinking countries, but the procedure often comes with a hefty price tag. The rest of the world needs to follow their example, but with the aim to make it a free service one day.

Forming an agnostic society where we either embrace atheism or can embrace tolerance of all peaceful, spiritual beliefs. A sudden abandonment of religion to form a secular society is not beneficial. On the contrary, out of historical respect alone, it is important theology be taught even more thoroughly than it is now, (although, in an unbiased way). It is important children are raised tolerant of all beliefs without being pressured to follow one in particular. Instead, children need to be allowed to study all aspects of religion and science from a young age, enabling them to make informed decisions on their own as to what they believe. Children should always be taught to respect their elders, but should never to be afraid to challenge them in rational debate. This theoretically should be one of the easiest changes on our list, but I think it will prove to be the hardest, perhaps taking several generations to fully cleanse spirituality of dogma and intolerance.

Attempt a clean and determined break away from fossil fuels, with a heavy investment into renewable, cheap energy sources that can realistically fulfil large portions of the demand, such as tidal energy and fusion energy. Such technologies are not beyond our capabilities and can produce all of our global power needs efficiently, cleanly and inexpensively, (after the initial investment). Currently, they are just not being invested in enough due to the amount of money that fossil fuels are still making for energy conglomerates.

Provide every adult on Earth with their basic human rights free of charge as an 'H-utopian Global Allowance'. This is the most vital action, and the investment in humanity is guaranteed to pay off in the future if it is orchestrated correctly. It could work like so: every human being is assigned one, (and only one), credit account at birth that they can use to start saving into from birth, much like everyone is issued a national insurance/social security number that stays with them for life. Upon turning 18 years old, an individual is assigned a *second* credit account - this one, governmental. The minimum credits required to pay for minimum food, water and shelter to give a basic quality of life can be paid into every adult's 'government credit account' at regular intervals. The credits in this second account would have to be distinguishable from regular credits that circulate in primary accounts, to ensure the money is not misspent by those who are helplessly addicted to luxury items. These credits would have to be restricted to food items, prescription medicines, utilities, mortgage repayments to certified lenders, etc. These government credits could be available to withdraw in limited amounts of paper cash format, to satisfy anxiety surrounding cards being declined in a cashless society, but the paper cash would have to be limited, date restricted, or person-specific to avoid counterfeiting and criminal activity re-emerging. Additional credits can be earned by working, and these would be paid into an individual's primary credit account to be spent wherever desired. Of course, additional benefits would still have to be paid to those who are genuinely unable to contribute in any way due to severe health problems. For anyone who thinks this is financially impossible, remember, 'credits' are just electronic figures. In an economic system where no physical gold or silver needs to exist, the 'H-utopian Global Allowance' could, in theory, be produced from thin air and as a rule, be exempt from any economic strife that the rest of the economy would be subject to. In other words, there would always be credits available for every adult on Earth to get their most basic needs. In theory, this would actually prevent severe economic strife from escalating because everyone would always have credits to keep topping up the economy with and to keep themselves from becoming a burden to society. This is a vital last step that will take us into H-utopia, as we can never expect humans to be concerned with higher societal needs, such as knowledge, expression, and world peace if their own lower primal needs are not even secured.

For those who may be questioning the steps so far, wary of the human race accepting such a dependency on authority, you need not worry. Remember in the list above we have ensured two very crucial changes in society that will make it impossible to allow a few to rule over the many. The first is to reduce fear, especially of death and the unknown, and therefore reduce the effectiveness of exploitation of our species.

Another crucial step is to redistribute wealth more fairly so it would no longer be possible to have 1 per cent owning more than the rest of the 99 per cent put together, as we currently do. This is not just about equality; it is about preventing the formation of dangerous plutocratic oligarchies. If this does not offer enough reassurance, then to put your mind at rest, even more, there is a final exciting and important step that can ensure liberty is retained in H-utopia: to fashion a new way of running the world with proportional representation on global decision making. Imagine a worldwide government where everyone on Earth *is* the government. We would no longer require paid politicians or candidates to vote for in order to represent a majority, as the majority would represent themselves as individuals. There would be far less chance for corruption as everyone in the world, (of a certain age and with the exception of the incarcerated), would have an equal chance to make global decisions. Debates and presentations could all be broadcast globally online, and as long as someone was registered and viewed the entire presentation, they would be eligible to vote on any matters raised via petitions, etc. Running the world like this, we would find a population far more interested, involved, and most importantly, trusting, in politics than we have today. Furthermore, with proportional representation, war would be a thing that remained firmly in the history books, as the masses grouped proportionally would never choose to go to war against one another.

We would still need someone in charge though, right? To lead the debates, review laws, regulate, and make the final decisions official. Well, here we evoke the blossoming symbiotic relationship of mankind and machine. Utilising specialists at the top of their fields for finalising the detail on decisions relevant to their industry, expanding on the ideas of noocracy, demarchy and technocracy in order to select *temporary* subject experts and politically minded leaders, logically, not randomly, depending on what decisions needed making. The vital part is that they are strictly temporary, to avoid one person ever wielding too much power.

Computerised systems could even select the most suitable leaders from the entire human population to have their chance at being part of a global council or international committee to further reduce the risk of any elected specialists from becoming dictatorial. To be able to select people whose ideals align best with the ideals of H-utopia would only work if the aptitude, emotional intelligence, mental ability, empathy, psychology, and integrity of everyone on Earth is assessed and recorded, (perhaps with a mandatory mental screening that everyone on Earth has to complete at regular intervals upon turning 21 for instance). Politics choosing people, rather than people choosing politics would minimise the risk of corrupt people getting into positions of political power only to serve themselves. Candidates could turn down the duty if selected, but the duty would only ever be temporary.

The above is way more complicated than any political system we have today, but it is the only way to achieve democracy in the truest sense of the word. Without taking bold steps to defeat political obscurity, there will only ever be corrupt dictatorships masquerading as democracy. To think otherwise is to kid ourselves.

So, to conclude, we have '**capital incentivised socialism**' as our economic system, and for the sake of argument, we could call the combined governing system a '**tech-noo-marchracy**', which would operate as a global council, and we have '**proportional representation**' in place to ensure everyone on Earth can remain masters of their own destiny.

I strongly believe that with the above actions, we will be able to complete our journey to a sustainable H-utopia. Some of the suggestions may sound controversial or impossible from our blinkered point of view today, but actually none of the above is beyond possibility or unrealistic even to achieve within *my* own lifetime. There is nothing extreme or out of the question here, only rational choices that will be for the greater good of humanity in the grand scheme of things.

It would be stubborn, selfish and downright lazy of us not to attempt to make the future better for our children and grandchildren just because it is inconvenient for us now, or different from the comfort of familiarity. Our own short existence may be smoother and quieter if we accept the way things are, live selfishly, choosing to bury our heads in the sand. To carry on going about our daily lives ignoring how wrong many aspects of reality are because we think there is nothing we can do about it, or because actually, we like living as we currently do, and do not desire change. But what is the point in living our lives excessively now, if our children are going to suffer in the future because of us? Most people casually say, they would do anything for their children, but if we delve into that statement and begin to test the authenticity of it, we discover it is not true, and the limit of what we will do is set surprisingly low. Many people resent even slightly inconveniencing themselves for their children. We do not live in a static society, but we stubbornly resist change as if we do. At the very least, we allow those in the social hierarchy above us average folk to resist change whilst they are benefitting at the expense of the many below them in the hierarchy.

The future belongs to societies that dare to challenge the status quo and invest in political and social upheaval, whilst taking steps to safeguard it from corruption. It may be difficult at first for some of us, but it will pay off in the long-term for the entire species. The time has come, (it is overdue in fact), to make the so-called 'difficult decisions'. Some of which may inconvenience us or upset those of us who are set in our ways and fear change. The decisions will not kill us or physically hurt us, though, and they will secure a more certain and stable future for our children.

The infamous tale of Emperor Nero playing his lyre and singing whilst Rome was burning is appropriate here. The story is most likely fabricated, nevertheless, this is arguably the historical act Nero is most famous for, whether he really did it or not, demonstrating he was not a greatly admired leader of monumental social progress. If he was a truly great man, it would have made it impossible for this kind of slander to resonate alongside his name throughout history.

People of great responsibility are not let off lightly when they do not live up to the potential imagined, and the immortal memory of them can become tarnished, no matter how good their intentions were. Allowing society to crumble around us is not something I want to resonate alongside our generation's name throughout the rest of time, and I am sure I am not alone in that desire. One day, every human being alive at the time of my writing this will be dead and gone, and how will we be remembered in history?

Like Emperor Nero - a generation that had its back turned whilst the world burned?

Or

Like Marcus Aurelius - the generation that awoke to clear cognizance of the world, and saved it?

Human potential in H-utopia

"Invention is the most important product of man's creative brain. The ultimate purpose is the complete mastery of mind over the material world, the harnessing of human nature to human needs."

-Nikola Tesla, My Inventions, 1919.

...We are playing a universal game of hide and seek with aliens whose chance of existence may be 1 in 500 billion. Needle in a haystack does not even begin to cover it. Perhaps we should stop looking helplessly out into our apparently, mostly empty Universe and focus our attention inward, to a place where truly enlightened life is more likely to exist in abundance...

I am now going to speculate what the human race could achieve in both the short-term and long-term future if we are successful on our journey to H-utopia. With the problems in society raised during this essay fully resolved and overcome, we could finally start to channel our combined human effort into what really matters and undertake truly great ventures.

Nanorobotics and eradicating disease

In H-utopia, where we have successfully controlled our population growth, and our society focuses on reproducing an ethical and well-rounded replacement generation, rather than breeding like animals, inevitably producing a high percentage of neglected, morally flawed, socially doomed people, we will be able to extend human life even further than we do today, without the repercussions of severe overpopulation and social burdening. In our current society, where there are no limits to how many offspring one person can produce, we are causing ourselves an ethical dilemma: our medical scientists cannot be allowed to freely discover how to save everyone who is dying a potentially preventable death because the implications of doing so would be disastrous. It stands to reason, we cannot have life without death, and we cannot have death without life. The two balance each other, and if we do not maintain equilibrium, population growth becomes exponential. If we are able to responsibly control our breeding in a more disciplined way than we currently do, as a species gifted with future planning should be able to, then we can become masters over death, (or at least over disease), with a chance to live longer, healthier lives.

There have been many revolutionary treatments emerge over the last few decades that have not been given enough positive attention and investment. Stem cell therapy, for example, has been deemed risky and controversial, even though it has been shown as effective in treating some serious illnesses. A stem cell is an undifferentiated cell, capable of becoming another specific kind of cell. Stem cell therapy is the use of these cells to treat or prevent diseases and illness. This is usually done by a bone marrow transplant from a compatible living donor, or the stem cells are sourced from umbilical cord blood. Diabetes, heart disease, leukaemia and stroke are some of the common illnesses/causes of death, that stem cell therapy can potentially treat. Furthermore, when we are talking about extending human life, stem cell treatment also has the potential to reduce the symptoms of degenerative illnesses associated with old age, such as Alzheimer's disease and Parkinson's disease.

Stem cell therapy can also help with healing injured joints and muscles by replacing damaged neurons. Scientists have even begun working on bioengineering the entire human gastrointestinal system in a lab, growing the intestines, stomach, and liver from scratch, and even using pluripotent stem cells to grow the complex oesophageal parts. This groundbreaking research could one day lead to regenerative cures for all kinds of birth defects, cancers and diseases of the organs that are currently inoperable or terminal.

The end of diseases such as cancer, heart disease, stroke, diabetes and other illnesses, triggered by a combination of genetics and lifestyle, may not come from cure, but from prevention. There are already tests available to anticipate an individual's likelihood of developing certain illnesses and armed with this knowledge the person can make lifestyle alterations accordingly and attend regular check-ups to specifically monitor for specific illnesses. These tests will only become more thorough and accurate as time goes on, and we now find ourselves heading back down the path of eugenics. If we can accurately predict illness via genetic testing, at this point would we be able to resist taking it one step further and removing chance from the equation by selecting embryos that do not have the gene for certain cancers, or multiple sclerosis, or Alzheimer's disease for example?

Before we get carried away with trying to cure and prevent everything, we need to stop and consider first, should we? Imagine a world with no disease whatsoever. Where cancer, heart disease, HIV, malaria, pneumonia, even the common cold, are all a thing of the past. This is exactly the future many medical scientists are desperately aiming for, with some even attempting to develop a universal flu vaccine for the ever-evolving virus that causes various types of influenza. Although it would be good to have a cure for leukaemia, that robs children of their chance at life, and a cure for dementia that robs the otherwise healthy elderly of their minds, would total eradication of every disease and illness, even the common cold, actually be a good thing for humanity?

I believe we have the ability to cure all disease, given the investment and chance to, and one day this opportunity will come, but when it does, we need to tread carefully. Apart from the obvious implications regarding population growth if people are not dying anymore, there is another argument against ridding the world of all disease and illness. It may be a bad thing for the continued evolution of our species. At least whilst we still have 100 per cent organic bodies anyway.

For millions of years, survival of the fittest drove natural selection positively; responsible for evolving us into the strong and capable beings we are today. If we mess around with the relationship between germs and all other living creatures, then it becomes survival of everyone, fit or unfit. Total immunity to all germs, could mean our species begins evolving negatively. A similar argument has been put forward against having too much medical intervention during childbirth. Our species could slowly move beyond a point of no return, where we can no longer reproduce and survive entirely naturally with our own reproductive and immune systems, becoming overly reliant on scientific, medical intervention. If this intervention was suddenly removed from us, due to a global natural disaster, resulting in a loss of knowledge and/or a long-term loss of power, it could result in the premature end of our species. We are already coming up against challenges caused by previous medical breakthroughs, such as the arms race now going on between bacterial illness and antibiotics. Bacteria are getting stronger all of the time due to overuse of antibiotic medication, which in retaliation to the super-resistant bacteria, has to be made stronger or taken in greater doses to work effectively.

Before we worry about finding cures for every disease, we need to be thinking about making sure the cures and treatments we already have are available to the whole world, so we can create a healthy, energetic and contributing global population. Socio-economic problems in the poorest parts of the world, such as lack of education, out of control reproduction, followed by starvation of children, would be a lot easier to remedy if treatable disease was eradicated there first. For example, malaria in some African countries is so common that the people there are reinfected over and over, meaning they are less able to contribute to society productively.

The most developed parts of the world are decades ahead of these disease and poverty-ridden countries. Millions of people alive today are alive thanks to artificial means. Pacemakers, organ transplants/implants, blood transfusions, medications, vaccinations, caesareans in childbirth, resuscitation and the list goes on. There is only so far we can prolong life in our current stage of evolution. Those who make it into old age, thanks to constant monitoring, medication and treatments, only get to 85-90 years old before their bodies and/or minds start to rapidly deteriorate so much that they cannot support themselves anymore. This places an enormous burden on society. Often when people reach their 80s, and even more so by their 90's, they will have to move into communal homes during their final years, dependent on around the clock care. After only eight or nine decades of life has passed, we become shells of our former selves, ceasing to live, merely existing. Often at this stage, not only do we lose our minds but also our hard-earned homes and savings of a lifetime, to assist in paying for this constant care.

So, what is the answer? One of the most promising ways it may be possible to eradicate disease and prolong life, without the consequences of living to an unnatural old age that we currently experience, is with the medical use of nanobots - robots built on a microscopic scale and programmed to perform a specific function. In this case, repairing and maintaining the human body. The potential for the use of nanobots in human beings is game-changing:

Disease treatment and immune system enhancement - the reason the elderly get so sick and die from illnesses as common as rhinovirus, coronaviruses, influenza and other respiratory infections that the young tend to recover from without treatment, is because as we age, our immune systems deteriorate. Robots the size of blood cells could be programmed to operate like white blood cells, able to support the body's natural immune system as it weakens. Nanobots would compensate for the natural deterioration, tirelessly 'patrolling' the body for viruses, bacteria, blockages forming in arteries/veins, cancerous cells, any pathogens, in fact, eliminating them at the earliest stages before they have a chance to take hold. Even tumours could be cured by nanobots by cutting off blood supply just to the tumour. People would not even have a chance to realise they were getting sick before being cured.

Body repair and rapid healing - even death from massive physical trauma such as knife wounds could be prevented with the use of nanobots. In the event a laceration occurs, the nanobots immediately set to work repairing the damage, creating a clot to stop the person from bleeding to death, closing the wound much faster than the body's normal healing process, and at the same time, destroying any foreign bacteria that may have entered the body via the wound.

Super-humans - nanobots could even remove some of our physical limitations by enhancing the natural bodily processes. By supplying oxygen to the muscles and brain more efficiently than our red blood cells could ever do alone, we would be able to run faster, and for longer distances, hold our breath for longer, it would ease the burden on our organs and reduce the risk of heart disease, stroke, brain aneurisms and even migraines. The nanobots could make other bodily functions more efficient too, such as metabolism/vitamin absorption, so our bodies could run on a lower supply of fuel, (food and water), and this would be a truly magnificent advancement, massively reducing the environmental impact our species causes with food production.

So, with such incredible potential for nanobot application, just in the human body alone, why are we not already making it our number one priority and devoting all the time and funding required to make it a reality?

Well, to an extent we are; tests have already been done in mice, but developing and releasing a finished nanorobotic product suitable for human use is not an easy task to accomplish. The science is still relatively new, and we are quite a way off even prototypes being used for simple one-off tasks such as delivering medication efficiently to a desired part of the body, (thus reducing the dosage of medication required). Even once nanobot treatment is created, it could take years to get from this stage to the point where it has been tested enough and approved by the relevant government agencies, such as the Medicines and Healthcare Products Regulatory Agency in the UK or the Food and Drug Administration in the USA. It also comes down to our willingness to face into the practicability issue we discussed already. Our current society is not focusing its efforts on physically and psychologically preparing for the practical application of this kind of technology. We are preoccupied with war, greed and rising crime rates, neglecting the parts of society that need help to access basic needs. We first need to prove we are mature enough as a species to handle this kind of power. The ultimate goal of nanobots in humans would be the creation of a kind of human robotic hybrid species - a cyborg, capable of super-human activity, that never gets sick, heals quickly, is hyper-intelligent and lives an incredibly long life, whilst retaining mental and physical ability well into old age.

This is not science-fiction but an actual real possibility in the not too distant future. However, if we want our children and grandchildren to be allowed access to this godlike technology and for it to be used successfully to improve and prolong human life, we need to follow the steps to H-utopia first, which include, each and every one of us taking personal responsibility to control our population growth, eradicating war, reducing crime to a minimum, forming a 'technoomarchratic' governing structure, (a combination of technocracy, noocracy, and demarchy), with expert decision-makers and international committees of politicians chosen via humanitarian compatibility testing. We also need to morph pure capitalism into capital incentivised socialism, so our globally cooperative society shares an economy, and therefore benefits from combining all resources.

Doing all of this will not only help to make the technology possible but also will reduce the risk of the technology being manipulated for evil. Imagine the things a malevolent power could do with programmable robots that are inside every human being! Even if it existed right now, we simply could not be allowed access to this technology whilst our world is at war, whilst 1 per cent of individuals control 99 per cent of the world's economy or whilst we are too ignorant or selfish to understand the implications of our overbreeding.

Clean, renewable and unlimited free energy

Earlier we touched on the idea of the 'Dyson Swarm'. A futuristic renewable energy source and one ingenious way a civilisation can get all of its power needs. In the future, it may be a possibility to build structures around our sun that can absorb all of the energy that is otherwise lost to the vacuum of space. It is logical that we should look to the biggest power output in the solar system as a solution to our power needs. But what if we did not need to go to the sun, what if we could create our own mini suns right here on Earth, that could power the world by fusion energy? Fusion reactors would be like mini stars, generating enough ultra-efficient, clean and renewable power for everyone on Earth.

A fusion reaction is when at least two nuclei combine, for example, in the hydrogen atom, deuterium and tritium isotopes fusing together. This is easier said than done, because they are both positively charged, and two positives repel one another in a normal environment. The only way to get them to fuse is to force them together by exerting extreme heat and speed. The sun is hot enough for the fusion to occur naturally, but here on Earth, it is not so easy. We would need to use powerful magnetics to contain plasma in a stable state. Plasma is the fourth state of matter after heating solid into liquid into gas. If we then continue heating gas, it eventually becomes plasma. Plasma is so hot that atoms are split up into electrons and ions, which can move independently from one another. We are talking about heat many times hotter than you would find in the centre of the sun. The plasma would have to be heated to over 100 million degrees Celsius to get the deuterium and tritium nuclei to move fast enough to overcome the repulsion and fuse to generate the energetic particles. Heating the plasma to such a high temperature would take a massive amount of energy in the first place to be fed into a reactor before fusion could even begin. But once it gets going, the fusion process could potentially maintain itself for a long time, allowing us to harness excess heat, turning it into usable electricity from that initial investment.

This is not sci-fi beyond the realms of possibility by any means. We have already started to develop techniques to heat and maintain the temperature of plasma, and ways to construct chambers that can withstand the extreme heat. For example, using liquid metal as the material surrounding the plasma is one possible solution proposed. Or to use powerful magnetic fields to hold the heated plasma in place, surrounded by a soup of subatomic particles, so it does not directly contact the chamber it is housed in. In 2018, scientists in China succeeded in heating plasma to the 100 million degrees required and maintained it for a short time, so we are well on the way to making this a reality. This is a clear testament as to what we can achieve in a society that celebrates new discoveries, rather than suppresses them.

Remember earlier, we discussed the ludicrous time frame involved in the development of an invention as simple as the spectacles. Because of the threats new technology posed to religious orders, who relied on the preservation of social status quo for their power, thousands of years elapsed between first understanding the principles of optics to actually using them for a practical application. Fusion energy, as a principle, was discovered in living memory for some humans alive at the time of me writing this and already we are building working fusion reactors. We can now go from theory to application of something infinitely more complicated than eyeglasses in less than one lifetime. This is one of the most exciting and promising realisations for me during my study of human progress.

Currently, the most comparable form of energy production we have to fusion is fission (nuclear power). As we know all too well, fission can result in an unstoppable chain reaction that can be potentially environmentally disastrous. In a fusion reactor, however, there would be no chance of a meltdown. The worst that would happen if a fusion reactor malfunctioned would be the plasma cools, and the fusion stops. Another benefit fusion has over fission is the fuel for fusion power is much more abundant in nature than Uranium. Deuterium is found in water, and the reactor would actually produce the tritium by neutron activation from Lithium-6. Such a power source would not be reliant on mining and would not benefit only those whose territories happen to be sitting on top of vast deposits, such as those who have taken control of fossil fuels. It would be equally available across the world, and as it is a renewable, clean, and almost limitless supply of energy, the power generated could theoretically eventually be made available free, for a limited residential use at least, as a basic human right.

Before we can turn this too good to be true energy source of the future into a reality, we need to work towards solving scientific problems and overcoming engineering hurdles. Heating the plasma to the required temperature and then maintaining that temperature and the fusion reaction over long periods of time are still problems yet to be fully overcome. Undertaking these kinds of projects are the great ventures I have referred to, that we would be more likely to succeed in sooner with global cooperation and pooled resources.

For as long as our species is around, energy production will never cease to be a concern for us. There is no shortage of scientists and engineers trying to come up with ideas to power the planet indefinitely. In the future, we may have an energy source that has not even been theorised yet. Apart from the ones already discussed, there are some other 'out there' ideas floating around that are worth looking at briefly.

Cold fusion, which is the process I have just described but without the incredible heat requirement. It is just an idea and may even be impossible; estimates suggest we are still decades away from figuring out how to perfect normal fusion reactors, let alone the science behind cold fusion. Nevertheless, there is a chance it might be possible one day.

Another idea that sounds like it is straight out of science-fiction is zero-point energy, also known as ground state energy. The potential of ground state energy was realised as a by-product of quantum physics, based on the idea that on the subatomic level, particles do not behave like single particles, but like waves constantly fluctuating, with virtual particles occupying what looks like the empty vacuum of space. There is disagreement amongst physicists over whether the fluctuations contain the energy claimed and if it would even be possible to tap into that energy. For argument's sake, let us say it is real, that it is a possibility, then given enough time, one-day humans *will* figure it out, and when we do, it could be the equivalent of harnessing the power of multiple stars, giving us so much free energy in abundance that charging for it would be ludicrous. It may be one way we could practically manage interstellar or inter-dimensional travel. However, we do not know how much energy is actually contained in the vacuum. Albert Einstein's theory of general relativity suggests zero-point radiation would spread out throughout the Universe and be reduced to a weak power. Some physicists contradict this, claiming the opposite; that a concentrated amount of zero-point energy the size of a tennis ball would produce enough power to boil all of the water on Earth.

NASA is taking the idea of harnessing zero-point energy seriously and even claim to have successfully tested a 'Quantum Vacuum Plasma Thruster' that utilises the 'Casimir effect' to create propulsion. The Casimir effect is an attractive force that acts between two conducting plates/mirrors on a quantum level in the electromagnetic field. If the mirrors are placed facing each other, then some of the waves will reflect back and forth between them. As the mirrors attract, the longer waves will no longer fit, and the total amount of energy in the vacuum between the plates will be less than the vacuum outside of the mirrors. The idea is if the mirrors move fast enough, then some of the 'virtual' waves in the vacuum can become real waves with real energy, and quantum theory suggests the energy could be infinite! If this could be harnessed, we could theoretically produce spacecraft that take advantage of zero-point energy for propulsion in space and this form of travel would be a solution to the fuel problem that is keeping the door closed on interstellar travel. This kind of energy could realistically open the door to deep space exploration and human colonisation missions to other worlds.

With our energy problems solved, we can turn our attention to powering technologies that are theoretically possible such as teleportation and quantum supercomputers. We reviewed quantum particle entanglement earlier on in *products of time*. It is the theory that Einstein did not want to contemplate, famously calling it "spooky action at a distance". He did not want to believe that the Universe would behave in this way, on a fundamental level, because it did not fit neatly with the unified theory of everything he was pursuing his whole life. Quantum entanglement is a bizarre but very real phenomenon where pairs of particles are generated and interact in ways in which the state of each particle is determined by the other, regardless of proximity to one another. So even if two quantum entangled particles were at opposite ends of the Universe, they would still be affected by one another. The theory has been proven by multiple experiments that lifted the curtain on the magician that is quantum mechanics. The results of the experiments do appear to tell us that the Universe does not exist in a single state until it is observed. Fundamental particles do not exist in a stable form until they are observed and thus are outside of the normal laws of physics. The long-accepted cosmic law that nothing can travel faster than the speed of light does not even apply outside of the normal Universe.

So what would be the most revolutionary practical applications of quantum physics as our knowledge and engineering capabilities improve? Quantum computers are one exciting possibility. A quantum computer is a device that computes and performs operations using quantum-mechanical phenomena, such as superposition and entanglement. Whereas a conventional computer stores information as bits, a quantum computer stores information as 'qubits'. A qubit can represent a 0 and a 1 at the same time. Occupying different parts of space at the same time is the quantum phenomenon, superposition. The consequential application of this is that qubits can conduct an immense amount of calculations simultaneously, therefore increasing efficiency and computing capacity. The principle of quantum computation is that the quantum properties can be used both to represent and to structure data. If it is possible for large-scale quantum computers to be built in the future, they will be ultra-efficient and able to solve problems faster than any of our current computers, because they would be able to trial all possible outcomes simultaneously to find the solution to a problem. Much like particles on a quantum level can appear to be occupying different points in space at the same time.

But what would be the practical applications? The race is already well underway between IBM, Microsoft, Google, Intel and others who all want to build the world's first quantum super-computer that can be practically applied to: encrypt data with unbreakable security, accurately predict weather patterns/climate change and maybe even be able to predict the future or create simulation universes.

I suspect quantum computers will eventually make conventional computing obsolete. The ability to sample a large number of possible combinations is exponential in comparison to conventional computers. To understand how quantum computers are in a different league to conventional computers let me use the commonly referred to analogy of a spinning coin. In a conventional computer processor, a transistor is either up or down, heads or tails, on or off, 1 or 0. However, in a quantum computer, it is the spinning coin that is the power behind it. Whilst the coin is still spinning, there is no heads or tails, only possibility. One might put it another way and say it is both heads *and* tails. If the coin is kept spinning indefinitely and we never get a definite black or white answer then for all intents and purposes the answer is always heads and always tails. So rather than a conventional bit that is either 0 or 1, we have a qubit, that is simultaneously representing 0 and 1 for as long as the qubit keeps 'spinning'; and we can have many hundreds of coins spinning simultaneously to increase the computing power further, potentially creating more possibilities than there are atoms in the Universe! However, there are many hurdles to overcome to make these machines a reality. The main problem is stability; keeping the qubits from collapsing into a fixed state. Much as a coin inevitably will stop spinning and land on either heads or tails, eventually, a qubit would eventually have to make the decision to become either a 1 or a 0. The goal with quantum computing is to keep them from being affected by external stimuli, such as fluctuating temperatures, that can stop them spinning or operating. One possible way is to keep them very cold. By very cold, I mean as close to 'absolute zero' as possible. Absolute zero being -273.15 degrees Celsius, the theoretical temperature that would be impossible to go beyond, because it is the temperature atoms stop moving, allowing only quantum movement to occur.

With quantum computers, human teleportation may become a reality also. Again, this might sound like something out of science-fiction, but it is theoretically possible, using the science behind quantum entanglement to send atoms faster than the speed of light from one point in space to another, and as we are made of atoms it is theoretically possible humans could be teleported in the same way. There is a moral dilemma to consider with teleportation, though. The original item or person is effectively destroyed, or killed when travelling via teleportation. After stepping into an information scanner, and having your pure quantum information downloaded into a quantum mainframe, your body and mind could be sent to the destination where an output device would be used to rebuild you, identical in every way, but you would no longer be the same person that you were born, just a copy. Furthermore, the original 'you' at the starting point would have to be destroyed at the same time the new 'you' appears at the destination to avoid a duplicate of yourself coming into existence every time you travelled via teleportation. On top of the moral dilemma and lack of quantum computers, another problem blocking this invention is the insane amount of energy the teleportation process would require. We need to perfect an unlimited energy source and develop quantum computers to an advanced level first. Teleporting humans is a science that is definitely possible, but I suspect this invention is centuries away from becoming a reality. The moral dilemma alone may prevent us ever pursuing transporting people in this way, but the potential for transporting goods via teleportation is even greater as it would most certainly solve a whole world of environmental issues that come with long journeys by air, sea and road. Currently, it can take weeks, and several methods of polluting transport, just to get a cheap piece of costume jewellery sent all the way from the other side of the world, and conveniently delivered to our home.

Alien contact and colonisation of other worlds

There is an ongoing debate over whether it is wise to be announcing ourselves to the Universe, for fear of who may be listening. Personally, I think we should be able to make contact on our own terms, rather than allow ourselves to be surprised by an alien civilisation that may or may not be hostile. Some scientists claim that any species capable of interstellar travel would long have outgrown xenophobic reaction to other lifeforms and would logically be peaceful. But we cannot be so sure that our logic applies universally. Broadcasting ourselves to the rest of the cosmos, on the assumption that human logic counts for anything in other parts of the galaxy, is not particularly wise. One only has to observe what humans do to other life on Earth that is deemed to be disposable or less worthy than human life.

Judging aliens by our standards, I dread to think how humans would be treated by a species that is a billion years more developed than our own if they needed to exploit our planet's materials or harvest our sun for energy. A civilisation that has left its home planet and is now entirely space-faring would not pass up an opportunity to utilise the resources of a planet like the Earth if they came across it. Humans have disgracefully exploited each other in the past out of ignorance and lust for power. For example, how the Europeans robbed the Native Americans of their homeland, then later, how the American Europeans exported people as slaves from African countries, right up until the 1800s. This is how we treated our own species who lived in slightly less developed parts of the world. When our more technologically advanced ancestors came into contact with slightly less developed peoples around the world, instead of respecting the differing ways of life attempting to learn from them, they just decided, as the slightly more technologically advanced, that they had the right to overpower and dominate the others, forcing their values and beliefs onto them whilst robbing them of their land and resources. So what is to say that aliens a billion years more advanced than us would feel an ounce of conscience exterminating us all like insects if they could benefit from it.

Even if all space-faring aliens are peaceful, we should never meet them for the biological reasons alone. Look how vulnerable we are to diseases that are born of other animals on Earth. An example is HIV, originally found in monkeys as the virus SIV. It was most likely transmitted to humans who were butchering and consuming the meat of infected monkeys in the early 20th century. Imagine how devastating diseases that developed in entirely different parts of the galaxy could be for life on Earth and vice versa, how Earth's pathogens could affect extra-terrestrials. Although one would presume a species that has mastered interstellar travel would be nanobot filled cyborgs as a minimum, maybe even entirely synthetic or electronic and therefore likely to be invulnerable to illness and disease. Perhaps susceptible to computer viruses though!

Once we put our petty differences aside on Earth and stop wasting time and resources on domestic conflicts, we can turn our attention to protecting our entire species and our planet from potential outer space threats, whether that is cloaking ourselves from genocidal aliens, or building defence systems, such as gravity tractors to save us from large asteroid impacts.

Scientists have been suggesting for years the idea of a cloaking device for our planet to make us effectively invisible to potential onlookers. There are several ways it would be possible to mask our presence in the Universe. One way suggested to conceal the Earth is with lasers to compensate for the dip in light from the sun as the Earth passes around it. Checking for dips in light in other stars is the way we are currently searching for exoplanets. If aliens are using the same method, we could fool them into thinking there were no planets in the habitable zone near our sun, by replacing the light lost when the Earth orbits the sun. Another option is to cloak the signatures of life itself rather than the planet, so any alien race observing our vicinity for planets with chemical life signs would be fooled into thinking the planets in our solar system never gave birth to life and were inhospitable.

Honestly, I do not think we have too much cause to worry about this for now, as the broadcasted messages we have sent out into the Universe to potential alien neighbours go back less than a century, and the Milky Way galaxy is so vast, that the first radio waves will only have reached 0.001 per cent of it in that time. With that percentage of coverage, combined with estimates of how many intelligent civilisations there could be in the Milky Way, it makes the odds that one of humanity's signals will be picked up by living aliens, literally astronomical. But why is it so unlikely? If there are billions of stars in the Milky Way and billions of other galaxies in the Universe, where is everyone and why have we not even encountered signal evidence of extra-terrestrial life?

Enrico Fermi, 1901 - 1954 was an Italian physicist who worked on building the world's first nuclear reactor and creating the plutonium that was used in the atomic bombs deployed by the American military in WWII. The insatiable curiosity of this genius led him to address the paradoxical nature of the Universe with his 'Fermi paradox' - with the unfathomable size of the Universe and with numerous planets, even in our own Milky Way galaxy, why is there no evidence for intelligent life besides our own? In an attempt to provide mathematical clarity to the 'Fermi Paradox', astronomer Frank Drake created a mathematical model, the 'Drake Equation', in the early 1960s. His equation was originally as follows:

$$N=(R^*)(fP)(ne)(fL)(fi)(fc)(L)$$

N - The number of contactable civilisations.

R* - The rate at which stars are formed in the Milky Way.

FP - The fraction of stars that have planets orbiting them.

Ne - The fraction of planets that are in the habitable zone for life.

Fl - The fraction of those habitable planets where life actually appears.

Fi - The fraction of planets that are potentially suitable for intelligent life like ours to develop.

Fc - The fraction of civilisations that go on to build detectable technology.

L - The length of time that a civilisation would spend transmitting detectable signals.

When this original formula was worked out, it gave a pretty vague answer of between 53 per cent to a 99.6 per cent chance that ours is the only intelligent civilisation in the galaxy and a 39 to 85 per cent chance that we are the only intelligent life in the whole Universe.

So at first glance, this equation appears to answer the question of why we have not encountered a hint of other intelligent life: because it is potentially so incredibly rare. However, the equation is far from infallible, assuming a lot of things, and is almost certainly not accurate. Drake's equation has been updated and modernised since the 1960s, with the discovery of so many exoplanets in recent years and a change in our understanding of what 'habitable zone' means. It could be that the Universe is teeming with life, and some of it has evolved to intelligence levels equal to or greater than our own. But as I have said above, technologically capable lifeforms would not allow themselves to be observed or contactable for long and would likely begin masking their presence as soon as their technology allowed them to do so.

The following is evidence that life is way more common than Drake's equation would have us believe: it has been discovered that Europa and Ganymede, the large moons of Jupiter, as well as Saturn's Enceladus, may have vast subterranean oceans containing more water than the Earth; and they could potentially host an array of microbial lifeforms. The immense gravitational forces Jupiter and Saturn exert upon their satellites means they are constantly flexing, causing friction to heat them from within, keeping the oceans in a liquid state. Ganymede is the biggest moon in our solar system and actually larger than the planet Mercury. If not caught in orbit around Jupiter it would be a planet in its own right.

There is also evidence that Mars, in its very distant past, was once Earth-like and may have had liquid water flowing on the surface for millions of years. Fossilised ancient riverbeds, estimated to have had water flowing in them 3.7 billion years ago, are still visible on the planet surface. Earth is now confirmed to have had life in its seas over 4.2 billion years ago. So perhaps genesis may have had enough time to occur in the water on Mars too, entirely separately from Earth. It is even possible that life on early Earth came *from* Mars, transported via panspermia.

Genesis was pushed back millions of years earlier than previously thought possible, with the discovery in 2018 of new fossils in Canada showing there were lifeforms already thriving on Earth at least 4.2 billion years ago, living in the 60 degree Celsius oceans; organisms similar to iron-oxidising bacteria found near hydrothermal vents today. It was once thought that life on Earth could never have survived before 3.9 billion years ago because, before this, the planet was undergoing intense meteorite impacts known as the 'Late Heavy Bombardment'. If life is not so fragile after all and was able to evolve and survive not long after the Earth itself had formed and cooled enough for liquid water to collect in deep enough quantity, and if other seemingly inhospitable worlds in our own solar system show significant potential for life, then maybe life is way more common than we ever thought. Further probes to Mars, and to Jupiter's moons, in the future will confirm this in my lifetime, I am sure. Perhaps so long as there is sustainable liquid water, life is sure to find a way given a chance. On the worlds with less extreme conditions, beings like ourselves evolving is the easy bit. As we have seen, once genesis occurs, with the right conditions, enough time and relative stability, life runs away with itself.

On the other hand, consider for a moment that we may be the only *intelligent* life to have evolved in the galaxy. Maybe it really is so rare that life, not only evolves to a sentient level, but then survives long enough to produce technology. The ongoing search for exoplanets has proven there are plenty of Earth-like planets in other parts of the galaxy that are candidates for life, but this still does not make them suitable for intelligent life that can produce technology as sophisticated as we do. It may be that intelligent life not only needs a suitable planet, orbiting around a certain type of star, in a stable solar system, in a quiet part of the galaxy, but also the home planet of any intelligent beings may require a minimum of two large Jupiter and Saturn sized neighbours to stabilise each other's orbits whilst acting as the vacuum cleaners of a solar system, attracting life-ending asteroids away from habitable planets with their immense gravity. Habitable planets may also require a large moon orbiting them to stabilise the climate enough to give intelligence the chance to evolve and build a successful civilisation. The moon that orbits Earth is unusually large in comparison to its host and only exists because a Mars-sized planet was thought to have collided with the early Earth, breaking off to eventually form the moon. Without the moon, Earth's climate today would not be as stable as it is. The planet would be plagued with extreme and relentless climate change, such as regular ice ages every few millennia, striking in different parts of the Earth each time, making it very challenging to sustain a successful civilisation anywhere on the planet. Even if a large moon and large planetary neighbours, like Jupiter and Saturn, are required for an Earth-like planet to evolve intelligent life, with all the hundreds of billions of planets in the galaxy, there almost certainly *will* be other Earth-like planets with Earth-like moons and Jupiter-like neighbours somewhere in the vastness of space.

There are even known to be a number of 'interstellar' planets that are not part of a solar system. Massive Jupiter sized rogue planets that drift freely through space, perhaps failed stars, that have captured planetoids orbiting closely around them. The unimaginable extreme conditions on these truly alien worlds may be perfect laboratories for genesis to occur in liquid on their surfaces. Despite having no star as an external heat source, it is possible these planets have dense, hydrogen-rich atmospheres that insulate them with trapped greenhouse gasses to a point where they are warm enough to have liquids flowing on the surface. Clearly, the hellish dark environments will not be candidates for intelligent life, but these shadowy rogue planets could be spawning life in its simplest form and carrying it through the galaxy. Because these drifting planets are not held captive in solar systems, they will not be destroyed by a host star when it dies, engulfing its own planets. In theory, a free planet like this could drift around for eternity, 'sneezing' microbial life like a disease in all directions on meteorites, some of which could contain extremophiles capable of surviving the vacuum of space long enough to reach worlds suitable to sustain and further evolve the extremophile lifeforms contained within.

Panspermia is one of the few theorised galactic phenomena that actually improves the odds that intelligent life has evolved more than once, as it reduces the number of times life had to spontaneously appear from non-living raw materials. Something that may be impossibly rare - scientists are yet to be able to forcefully create life from scratch in a laboratory, despite mimicking the predicted conditions of early Earth. Their failure may be because the conditions on early Earth were never suitable for genesis to occur, but they *were* suitable for life to evolve that arrived on Earth from somewhere else in the solar system or the galaxy. In which case the aliens are already here and have been all along. Or it may just be that the scientists have not been trying for long enough. Perhaps it takes 100s of millions of years of trying with the same chemicals and environment before genesis occurs by a one in a hundred million chance.

Despite the best efforts of the organisation SETI, (search for extra-terrestrial intelligence), there has never been a substantiated signal detected that proves intelligent life has broadcasted radio signals elsewhere in the galaxy. The reason for the lack of success may simply be that they have not had enough time. We should be wise enough to know we cannot take absence of evidence as evidence of absence. Furthermore, it is arrogant to assume we would even be capable of detecting evidence of aliens. It is the same small-mindedness that allows some of us to believe we have seen evidence of aliens visiting Earth via metallic flying saucers or other forms of aircraft that we recognise as reminiscent of terrestrial engineering. Science writer, Arthur C. Clarke said it better than anyone: "*sufficiently advanced technology is indistinguishable from magic*". How can we be so arrogant as to think intelligent aliens who are millions, or even billions, of years older than our species, would be the slightest bit interested in visiting Earth, flying around it in tin cans with blinking lights, or broadcasting in a primitive way that we could understand and interpret.

I have no doubt that one day we will find irrefutable evidence of alien life, as for intelligent life, I am less optimistic. I am sure it exists elsewhere, but I doubt truly intelligent life wants to be found. To be able to produce detectable signals, an alien race would have to be equal to or more advanced than we are. We are playing a universal game of hide and seek with aliens whose chance of existence may be 1 in 500 billion. Needle in a haystack does not even begin to cover it. Perhaps we should stop looking helplessly out into our apparently, mostly empty Universe and focus our attention inward, to a place where truly enlightened life is more likely to exist in abundance.

Surviving the trial of the Universe

"All this long human story, most passionate and tragic in the living, was but an unimportant, a seemingly barren and negligible effort, lasting only for a few moments in the life of the galaxy. When it was over, the host of the planetary systems still lived on, with here and there a casualty, and here and there among the stars a new planetary birth, and here and there a fresh disaster."

- Olaf Stapledon, Star Maker, 1937.

Thank you, the reader, for taking the time to read my study of human potential. I want to leave you with a final sobering thought of the seemingly impossible places righteous paths can lead us.

The humble ending

Approximately 5 billion years from now, the sun will end its life. Everything that has ever lived, every material possession ever made or owned, every ancient monument ever constructed, and every piece of priceless art ever created will become worthless, ceasing to exist. Every event that has ever occurred on our planet or in our solar system will no longer matter. What is more, no one will even know the Earth existed. For all intents and purposes, everything may as well never have existed in the first place.

The sun ending its life and consuming our planet in the process may sound like a pretty definitive end for us, but what if there was a way around it? A way we could have already secured our survival long before the death of the sun. I do not mean becoming space-faring, colonising other worlds. Even if we had successfully done that, and some humans, (or rather the descendants of humans), were living on and telling the tale of humanity in other parts of the galaxy, they would still be faced with the end of every other solar system they reached. We cannot run forever; even if we abandoned the dangerous idea of relying on vulnerable planet dwelling and became capable of creating planetoid sized vessels that contain within them replicas of Earth's eco-system, in order to sustain entire populations indefinitely in an artificial environment, they would still ultimately face the end of the Universe. Most scientists agree that our Universe is not eternal and will one day either contract back to a singularity, destroying everything and starting from scratch, or that it will dissipate into nothingness, void of life, elements and energy. New stars will stop being born, and expansion will have taken everything so far apart that any creatures still alive in the elderly Universe, standing on their planets, looking up at a clear night sky would see total darkness. They would be isolated from the rest of the Universe and would have no way of knowing anything exists beyond their own star system. Hypothetically speaking, it is likely at this point, any intelligent creatures left alive would have long reverted back to superstitious belief and religious preservation as their primary focus.

The only way we could theoretically beat our fate and cheat death is via extra-dimensional exploration - to 'transcend' into another reality. Something that actually may be a lot less effort than interstellar travel and an entirely more logical outcome for any intelligent civilisation in the Universe who are wise enough to overcome petty differences on their own planet, threats from outer space, maintain their society through a utopian age of engineering and invention, in order to give them the power and knowledge to **survive the trial of the Universe.**

One fascinating theory, known as 'transcension hypothesis', is credited to the futurist, John Smart. Smart proposes that the logical ultimate end game for any advanced civilisation, should they survive long enough, is to 'transcend' into 'inner space'. The concept is, that given the natural course of fairly predictable developmental processes, combined with evolution and enough time, many intelligent beings would eventually surpass even the stage of exploring outer space. The civilisation, realising the Universe would eventually reach old age and effectively die, would stop looking out for salvation and start looking inwards, at the increasingly dense, miniaturised scales of space, time, energy, and matter, ultimately leaving this dimension entirely, via a black hole-like portal or universe replicator, continuing to go on existing in a different plane of reality.

Our descendants may long since have had to of abandoned their organic bodies for this to be a possibility, perhaps even becoming pure consciousness on what we can only imagine to be an impossibly complex and godlike level. These godlike beings may even master the ability to create their own universes and be able to watch them play out as our own did. Although technically an artificial reality, these new universes would feel as real as this one. The combined consciousness of the creators may even be able to interact with the new universe it creates, downloading itself back into multiple 'mortal' forms in order to experience the infinite variety of surviving a universe once again.

As 'out there' as this theory may sound, we cannot rule out the idea that this will be perfectly possible, and may already have actually happened at least once somewhere deep in the past. Nothing observed in the universe so far can totally disprove that we are living in just such an artificial reality right now. A reality forged by a previous intelligence that learned the ability of creation, evolving to this higher level of existence an immeasurably long time ago and has even divided its consciousness into numerous mortal forms to exist physically again as it once did.

In the transcension hypothesis, simpler civilisations that resist transcension by staying in their birth dimension until their demise would be considered developmental failures. Logically speaking, everything wants to survive; the very Universe itself is one big reproduction cycle. On the largest scale, down to the smallest scale, everything is reproducing, and it is survival of the fittest, the cleverest, the luckiest and the wisest. Everything reproduces to keep life going. So it stands to reason that even the Universe must reproduce, for one day it will reach old age, becoming sterile and void. If nothing ever stood a chance of surviving beyond a certain point to carry on the legacy of this Universe, then there would be no point to anything ever.

If transcension is a real developmental process, it could mean we may never encounter a truly wise and enlightened alien civilisation in this Universe, as the ones left behind would be the genocidal, parasitic cyborgs that are desperately trying to prolong their existence in space by any means necessary, their integrity and empathy long since compromised by the knowledge of their impending doom. It is possible, and what is more, it is logical that intelligence eventually evolves into one of two things:

1) Physical lifeforms that are 99-100 per cent robotic, living extraordinarily long lives but ultimately mortal and trapped in one universe, perishing along with it at the end of time.

2) Pure 'electronic' consciousness that can move between dimensions and exist for eternity.

The latter, being the more desirable outcome for our species clearly. All of this is just a theory of course and may never come to pass or even have the chance to be proved possible, but if it *is* possible, much like having access to all of the godlike technology and science discussed, it will only be in a future that has passed through an enlightened era of cooperation and unity akin to the H-utopia I have described.

Transcension into pure consciousness and immortality may sound like an impossible fantasy, but something similar is already being worked on. Not immortality per se, but something that may be achieved in my lifetime, has been dubbed Whole Brain Emulation (WBE), or to put it literally, mind upload.

Transhumanists are pursuing a way to upload their personalities and memories into a computer, to preserve their 'souls' on Earth for eternity. To achieve such a thing, would mean families would never truly lose loved ones to death, as they could always enter the 'matrix' to continue interacting with the consciousness of anyone lost after their mortal forms had failed them, so long as they took the time to upload their minds to a mainframe containing a virtual reality. In this artificial 'afterlife' humanity could discover limitless virtual experiences and achieve immortality. If nothing else, this comfort could significantly reduce the fear of death and loss. A fear that is currently exploited for evil purposes. For many futurists, this form of mental immortality is more practical than trying to preserve mortal physical forms, to keep consciousness trapped in the third dimension, via artificially grown replacement organs, and anti-ageing therapies. The question of whether these avatars of our former selves would actually be considered living or 'real' could be one that will keep philosophers of the future entertained. However, with the methods currently proposed, this matrix of the dead would be more like a complex memorial of a person's consciousness rather than evolving consciousness itself. But who knows what the future will bring. Perhaps any stored consciousness will one day be able to be downloaded back into mortal form to begin experiencing reality again, accumulating further knowledge.

I fear now, after reaching the end of the Universe and the transcension of humankind, I have digressed far enough and shall hastily return back to present-day Earth in order to conclude with the point I have been making throughout. This whole study on human potential, and building a prosperous, sustainable future for all of humanity, has just been a single idea out of infinite variables and possibilities available to us. It is merely a point of view, stemming from the consciousness of one sentient individual out of literally billions that have existed just on this planet alone, demonstrating the mindset of an average human observing the world through their own five senses, processing the sensory information and forming an opinion on what is right, what is wrong and what could work to make a better future for the species as a whole. But it is all just opinion and although many others will be of the same or similar opinion, many more will undoubtedly not, and in this lies the frustration, but also the magnificence, of the human race.

What is known for sure, is that we are all universally connected, everything that ever existed or ever will exist in this Universe came from a bizarre singularity billions of years ago. We cannot change what has happened and what our species has done in the past, but we do have the power to choose where we are going and the direction we take our species from this point on. Overcoming *ridiculous, insignificant* differences, to find peace with one another is what matters more than anything. Doing what we know to be right (not necessarily what we are told), to make positive and unique contributions. Living with integrity, respecting life, learning from our mistakes, striving to be the best creatures we can possibly be, simply by each and every one of us accepting personal responsibility for the future. At the end of time, when the inevitable, cold, dark curtain descends, this will be the only thing that will have mattered, and the only thing that could have saved us.

Epilogue

"If you want a picture of the future, imagine a boot stamping on a human face - forever."

"Who controls the past controls the future. Who controls the present controls the past."

- George Orwell, Nineteen Eighty Four, 1949

The following are two contrasting hypothetical futures. This is a work of fiction. Any characters resembling real-life persons, is purely coincidental.

Hans Rosling's famously called 'age of peak child', the pre-emptive moment when the population stops increasing, did not conveniently occur as predicted. The human population smashed predictions and reached 10 billion back in the mid-21st century; still climbing at an unsustainable growth rate, particularly in Africa and Asia. The overwhelmed world leaders, too cowardly and uncooperative to act sooner, for fear of losing popularity and control, had broken humanity with relentless war, disease, poverty and famine, making day to day life impossible. They were left with no option but to put the future of the human race in the hands of a shadowy oligarchy, who promised to deliver the solution covertly, without the world leaders having to sacrifice their positions, or the richest half of the world having to share their wealth. It sounded too good to be true, but by the time the world leaders had realised the mistake they had made, it was too late, there was no way out of the deal with the devil.

The year is now 820NE (New Era). Earth, governed for over eight centuries by a powerful empire, is home to the world's 2 billion population of cloned human labourers, Homo replicanus, and an elite race of modified immortal humans, Homo superios, rumoured to total only around a thousand worldwide. Although they never reveal their true numbers.

Fiercely loyal and hardworking, the Homo replicanus race, contented and comforted to have employment, labour tirelessly to support their saviours; the elite Alpha race of superhumans. The most honourable and rewarding job is to be a part of the global military, credited with keeping the peace for 800 years following the end of WWIII.

This phoenix civilisation is regrown from the ashes of a forgotten social catastrophe of nuclear proportions. Forgotten, because all of the abominable truths have been removed from the Homo replicanus history books. The supreme leader of the Homo superios believes that the truth of what the human race used to be, is a lethal weapon that simply cannot be allowed to undermine the peace and order sustained for eight hundred years.

Homo replicanus, created sterile, are unable to reproduce on their own, but there is no shortage of facilities to grow them. Any clones that develop flaws are terminated before completion.

Parenthood is a thing of the past, as leaving the Homo replicanus at the mercy of individual parenting was long ago deemed an unnecessary risk. They remain in state facilities until their mandatory education, (conditioned programming), is completed and they are old enough to work. Childhood, tediously long before, as the brain had to finish a lot of its growth after childbirth, has been crushed down to only eight years with genetic tampering. The 'family unit' no longer exists. There is no need for it and individuals are far easier to control than groups.

It took 700 years to achieve, but as promised by the ancestors of the Homo superios, no one starves anymore, (so long as they work for the empire), there are no more wars, and there is very little crime, but the human race paid with its pride, dignity and liberty. It ceased to exist centuries ago, replaced with something false, that has been given historical amnesia and controlled ruthlessly with a police state. If any radical Homo replicanus' publicly vocalise old-era rebellious ideas, such as democracy, family or retirement, they are made an example of, labelled terrorist activists and imprisoned for life, in harsh conditions. Inciting protest and criticising the empire is punishable in the same way. There are large financial rewards for anyone who reports rule breakers. The requirement for actual police is not great, as the Homo replicanus is conditioned in such a way that they enjoy policing themselves and each other. One human trait was left unaltered. The insatiable thirst for more remains in the form of greed. Homo replicanus is ambitious, and unlimited financial rewards are there to entice them into compliance. Competition is encouraged, whilst cooperation is discouraged. Those who work hard enough, and snitch hard enough on their competitors, are misled into believing they have the chance to become Homo superios one day, but it is merely propaganda and false hope to further ensure compliance. The species can earn the right to purchase the material possessions they desire, but they never achieve truly great things and are never allowed to progress; the society is stagnant, fearing change will disrupt the peace. Consequently, technology available to the Homo replicanus has not changed much since the formation of the empire.

The final twist in the sickening scheme: as if Homo replicanus have not suffered enough indignity, the Homo superios, with all its delusions of grandeur, no longer feel Homo replicanus have the right to dwell in the same realm as they do, and so, they are conspiring to lock them away forever, hooked up to an artificial reality purely for entertainment purposes. To fill the labour vacancies, they are planning to manipulate the sub-species further, creating an even more docile, imbecilic and smaller slave labour force to serve them more efficiently.

With nothing better to do and feeling unfulfilled, immortal Homo superios, will sit gawking at their genetically dampened cousins artificially induced suffering. Watching them repeating the entire brutal history of the human race from savagery to civilisation, until the sun burns out and they perish together, as equals once more.

A day in the life of H-utopia.

I would hate to finish on a low note, so I will finish with a journey forward in time, to a reality where everything went right, and the human race is fulfilling its potential in H-utopia. The human race is not perfect, still retaining character flaws, but it has clearly made some great progress and is far wiser than it once was.

Earth date: April 29th 2259. Martian date: Kepler 56th 32AC (After Colonisation).

In Martian basecamp DB-91, Adamek Przodek glanced blankly through blue eyes at the readout on his retina display, brushing his mousey hair out of the way as it flopped down into his eyes. The latest vessel carrying colonists and supplies was due any day, and Adamek could almost taste those bio-ribs! By force of habit, he glanced over at his strontium optical atomic clock, as if to give himself a false hope that he somehow managed to get the time and date wrong, before quickly adjusting his focus back to his retina readout.

"Staring through that won't make them get here any quicker!" Startled by the interruption, Adamek jumped up, tapping his temple with his index finger. His retina display vanished.

"Evita, you made me jump!"
"Serves you right for slacking off. You know, the batch ain't gonna pick itself. We're gonna be relyin' on old-world food a while longer yet, surely you don't expect your pregnant partner to do all the work around here?"

Adamek knew better than to answer Evita's rhetorical question, grabbing his tools and following her through the gravity lock that kept the inside of their pod at Earth's gravity. To avoid their muscles weakening, daily exercise indoors at Earth gravity, as a minimum, was strongly recommended to all colonists. Working out could be as fun or as arduous as the colonists chose. With fully equipped gyms, adjustable gravity up to 5 times that of the Earth, and total immersion virtual environments, that linked with the brain, tricking the neocortex, frontal lobes and hypothalamus into reacting as if really in any simulated environments.

As they walked into their garden, Adamek winced whilst his eyes adjusted to the artificial ultraviolet lights concentrated on the pyramid planters in their garden. The emitted light, and heat, proved less of a problem for his partner, Evita Darwish, with her dark eyes and skin tone. Growing up in Gibraltar, with her Moroccan father and Israeli mother, she was no stranger to ultraviolet rays, and could handle the artificial light and heat somewhat better than her Eastern European boyfriend.

"Can we at least turn these lights down a bit now Evita?"
"Sure thing, two secs...there, how's that?"

"Bit better, thanks."
With the artificial lights dimmed slightly, the distant sun pierced through the dull purplish haze of the terraformed planet's newly acquired atmosphere.

"You know I can't stand this vegetable stuff Evita."
"Apparently it's better for us than our normal food. That's what Professor Huxley at the institute said anyways".

"He's like a hundred and thirty years old, I guess chowing down this brings a sense of nostalgia to him, but for me, it's like eating soil.

Give me a rack of juicy bio-ribs and a vitoshake any day over this muddy stuff". In the true rebellious spirit of a young forty year old, fresh from the academy, Adamek swore under his breath as he rinsed off and bit into a rather sorry looking, misshapen carrot.

"They're nicer if you peel and cook them first Adamek" Evita muttered, rolling her eyes.
"Maybe the colonists 32 years ago could get excited about growing root vegetables on Mars, but personally, I can't wait till they start building the first bio-meat labs here next year".

"Ironic you can't stand the taste of Earth Adamek", Evita smirked. The irony was lost on him, ignorant to the meaning of his name, having not studied Ancient Hebrew at school as Evita had chosen to, alongside Arabic, to honour her father's ancestry, as well as the standard French, Spanish, English and Universal Sign of course.

The sociologists working with the scientists who planned the colonisation of Mars were stubbornly insistent on using pre-industry farming techniques to make the colony as self-sustaining as possible. This took its toll on the pampered 22nd century Earthling volunteers, who were spoilt by the convenient efficiency of bio-meats and supplement shakes on demand.

During his theoretical agriculture training back on Earth, Adamek had struggled to stay awake, daydreaming of joining the heroic adventurers to Alpha Centauri; not of settling down and becoming a Martian farmer. Adamek was not alone in his disdain for farming, the only thing worse than the dull theoretical virtual classes, was the loathsome, backbreaking practical work of farming with primitive hand tools. The teachers never failed to remind any moaning students that the nanobots efficiently supplying oxygen-rich blood to their muscles, and their nutrient-rich diets made it a walk in the park compared with what it would have been like for their poor and hungry ancestors who depended on farming for their survival. Nevertheless, the gruelling practical work saw off many a research participant in the early days of the project. Truth be told, the only reason Adamek stuck it out, was because of Evita.

With the latest colonist and supply ship from Earth delayed by a couple of days, training the colonists to be self-dependent, as a contingency in the event of a technological failure, was already proving the right decision though. Even Adamek could not deny that.

It had taken global cooperation and investment, and 150 Earth years to terraform the Martian surface and atmosphere. It included the planting of billions of seeds from a variety of plant life, followed by the introduction of insect life. But by far the most ambitious parts of the transformation saw the manipulation of the extra-long Martian seasons, with the engineering of gargantuan mirrors in space to reflect more of the sun's energy to Mars, and even more impressive, an artificial satellite two thirds the size of Earth's moon, and hollow at the core, being built in orbit around the red planet, dwarfing its natural moons, Phobos and Deimos. The designers were considerate enough to pre-empt the sentiment of homesick colonists, and consequently, the satellite was built to resemble the Earth's moon as closely as possible. They even went to the effort of detailing some large faux craters. They appropriately named the moon Ares, father of Phobos and Deimos.

Since the main bulk of Earthling intervention was completed in 2199, and the eco-system was left to evolve naturally, thirty two Martian years had passed, (around sixty Earth calendar years). The term 'red planet' began fading from use amongst the younger colonists pretty much immediately, as much of the planet's surface already flourished with patches of blue and green upon their arrival. From some photographs in the more established areas now, it could even be mistaken for the Earth, if not for the light purple sky. These photographs helped when it came to recruiting new volunteers as colonists, including Evita and Adamek who arrived on the latest ship six months ago. They are now included in a total of around a quarter of a billion humans who live across the planet, leaving a further eight and a half billion back on Earth.

Following the revolutionary global investment to redistribute wealth equally around the developing world in the 21st century, Earthlings were able to get their average population growth rate down to a sustainable level, putting an end to suffering, poverty and starvation. With domestic issues resolved, public support for the space colonisation program grew massively, as humanity craved a project; and thanks to proportional representation, everyone had a chance to contribute, making the colonisation of Mars an unprecedented global effort.

At the heart of the Martian civilisation stood an impressive city, including a hospital and university. The city is home to over 2 million people, including some of Earth's top governing planners, doctors, scientists and even some royalty who chose to abdicate their positions of power on Earth, taking the one-way ticket to become part of the Martian colony as equals.

Adamek emerged back outside after taking the last of the batch to the vacuum freezer.

"Adamek, come check this out!" Evita yelled, breaking the eerie silence of the Martian environment, still pretty devoid of noisy animal life - as humans no longer consumed animal meat, livestock was only brought to the planet once vegetation reached a level that required herbivorous species to act as nature's gardeners.

"What is it?" Adamek panted - he still was not quite used to the Martian oxygen, but the planet's reduced gravity, and the nanobots coursing through his arteries made it plenty bearable.
"Look up there!"

Adamek placed his hand against his brow and squinted up. Perched on top of an eighty year old oak, (one of the oldest organisms on Mars), was a tiny squirrel.

"One of last season's kits"?

"Perhaps. It's the first baby one I've seen here".

"Come to think of it, me too".

They gazed at the little squirrel, who was sat inspecting an acorn in its tiny paws.

"For a thousand years, this oak tree could be home to your descendants little guy, keeping them sheltered and fed. You couldn't care what planet you're on eh? So long as you have this tree, and your family, you could live anywhere in the Universe, and it would be home".